The Twelve Months of the Year

The Twelve Months of the Year

DAVID & CHARLES
Newton Abbot   London

Picture Credits

Photographs

Ardea 46 (*below, centre*); J A Bailey/Ardea 11
(*below*); I R Beames/Ardea 17, 27 (*above and
below, left*), 36; Wilco Bergmans 84; Brian
Bevain/Ardea 40; R J C Blewitt/Ardea 49;
G W Th de Bont 29 (*below, right*), 41; Ruth van
Crevel 97 (*above*); W Cuth/Ardea 29 (*below,
left*); KNMI 53, 69, 72, 89; J P Laub/Ardea
19, 33 (*below*); Ake Lindau/Ardea 46 (*below,
left*), 56, 96; J L Mason/Ardea 27 (*centre, 2nd
from left*), 46 (*above*); Coen Postma 33 (*above*),
37, 75, 97 (*below* × 5), 98 (*below*), 114 (*above,
right*), 118; S Roberts/Ardea 27 (*above, right*);
B L Sage/Ardea 48; Peter Schutte 21 (*above and
below, left*), 27 (*below, right*), 44, 47, 51 (*below*),
67 (*below*), 88, 94 (*below*), 99, 104; R T Smith/
Ardea 11 (*above, right*), 29 (*below, 2nd from
left*), 112; Stockcolor 92, 94 (*above*), 98 (*above*);
Paul ter Straeten 10, 18 (*left*), 34, 38, 39, 46
(*below, right*), 50, 51 (*above*), 58, 67 (*above*)
80–81, 82, 83, 86, 106, 107, 113, 114 (*above,
left*); Richard Vaughan/Ardea 18 (*below*);
Rens Veenstra 11 (*above, left*), 59, 114 (*below*);
B Zwart 21 (*below, right*).

Drawings

Diet van Beek 20 (*below*), 37, 39 (*below, left*), 50,
52 (*right*), 77 (*below*), 86; Jan Brandt 59 (*below,
right*), 61 (*above*), 76, 77 (*above*), 88, 96, 99, 109
(*right*); Charles Donker 9, 12, 16, 25 (*above*), 28
(*right*), 60; Bart van Erkel 25 (*below*), 32, 51
(*left and centre*), 53 (*left*), 57 (*right*); Guusje
Kaayk 10 (*right*), 28 (*left*), 39 (*above and centre,
left; above, centre*) 52 (*left*), 58, 59 (*below, left and
centre*), 75, 83, 115 (*below*), 117 (*centre and right*);
Marius Kolvoort 10 (*left*), 13, 17, 18, 34, 35, 39
(*centre, below*), 40, 46, 53 (*centre*), 57 (*left*), 64,
65, 66, 73, 74, 80, 84, 87, 89, 93, 100, 105, 106,
108, 109 (*left*), 114, 115 (*above*), 116, 117 (*left*);
Co Loerakker (*composite picture strips*) 8, 16, 24,
29, 32, 37, 44, 53, 56, 64, 69, 72, 80, 87, 93,
100, 105, 113; Henk Slijper 6–7, 14–15, 22–23,
30–31, 42–43, 54–55, 61 (*below*), 62–63, 68,
70–71, 78–79, 85, 90–91, 102–103, 110–111;
Loek Smulders 94; Pax Steen 20 (*above*);
J Thijsse 101.

British Library Cataloguing in Publication Data

The twelve months of the year.
 1. Seasons – Great Britain
 574.5′43′0941   QH138

 ISBN 0–7153–7918–6
 ISBN 0–7153–7919–4 Pbk

Text © David & Charles Ltd 1980

Editors: Euan K. Dunn (April–December)
and David Black (January–March)

Published by David & Charles (Publishers) Ltd.,
Brunel House, Newton Abbot, Devon

Printed in The Netherlands by
Smeets Offset BV, Weert

Preface

No matter how urban we have become each one of us notices with pleasure some of nature's seasonal changes: the blackbird's early morning courtship song; toadstools pushing up in the woods; the first snowdrop; brightly coloured butterflies; the scent and sound of the harvest; the varied movement of the clouds. As fishermen or golfers, as walking or climbing enthusiasts, as campers, photographers or simply sun-lovers, millions of us are out in the countryside at times. We may not all call ourselves nature-lovers but we enjoy the sun and the wind and the water, and subconsciously appreciate the unrolling of the year.

From the first warm spring days until the attraction wanes with autumn's shortening daylight we tend to spend as much time as possible out of doors. Thereafter we restrict our contacts with nature to the taking of a weekend walk in the park, watching a wildlife documentary on television or reading a book like this. Perhaps this book will help us to appreciate that the winter months are in many ways as beautiful as the summer. Wild geese and ducks fly in from the north to feed on our wet meadows and estuaries. Along our coasts storms whip up the waves and pound the shingle on the beaches – a vivid example of nature's forces in action. In our gardens familiar creatures are surviving in their own different ways and there is unforgettable beauty in woods still and white after a heavy snowfall.

In this book we try to show every month as an individual, each one distinct and discrete, yet part of the whole. For those who look, there is continuing activity outdoors all the year round. The excitement lies not only in the finding of a rare plant, in the sight of a rare bird or even in participating as a spectator in the occasional micro-drama – like, to quote a specific incident, seeing a skylark fleeing from a sparrowhawk into the safety of a barn only to emerge minutes later in a cat's mouth – but in the gradual understanding of the overall pattern. How it all works, how each part fits into the whole and how the observable behaviour of each and every animal, bird, insect and plant can be related to this pattern, is of unending interest.

Following naturally from these observations comes a realisation of how enormously necessary is the immediate and continuing protection of our environment. Although this message is not explicitly stated it underlies the whole book.

January

This is a month of contradictions, of alternating cold and warm spells. It can be freezing, thawing, or mild. The north-easterly winds can bring severe cold, but with south-westerly winds the days can be springlike. Whatever the patterns, January is on average Britain's coldest month of the year. The coldest day of the year is traditionally associated with St Hilary's Day, 14th January. Around this time London and south-east England often have severe cold. But early January is often mild and stormy, a continuation of December weather.

Unless it freezes for the whole month, which is rare, there are always at least a trio of hardy plants in flower. For the first one you don't have to go far: the ordinary grass that we find sticking out from paving stones or sprouting from the kerb or flowerbed, which often at this time carries seed – which birds, at least, take seriously. I have often seen a brace of partridges on a piece of waste ground busily harvesting the 'crop'.

The second one is chickweed (*Stellaria media*). Its small white flowers are almost unnoticeable. It has an unusual feature: if you pick it with its stalk, you find that the stalk is completely smooth, but if you turn it round in your fingers, at one point you will see that a row of quite long hairs runs along it.

Most of the smaller birds would appreciate the name chickweed, as do many cage-bird owners, who use it for feeding as it grows throughout the year and is easy to find. Some birds eat the green parts, others the seed-heads. In my garden both wood pigeons and sparrows eat it.

The third plant I have chosen is the common groundsel. One can see the yellow flowers and seed-heads well into spring. The scientific name of this plant is *Senecio vulgaris*: the specific name *vulgaris* implies 'everyday', a little lowly plant, something to look down on. The first part of the name, the generic name *Senecio*, also tells us something. *Senecio* means 'grey-haired man' and the fluffy seed-heads are a whitish-grey. This also is eaten by birds.

Chickweed, a common annual weed flowering almost all the year, even in January

The list of flowering plants for this month could easily be extended – dandelion, daisy and red dead-nettle come at once to mind. Close to the edge of the dunes, and after the snow has melted, you may find the fresh green leaves of winter purslane, which looks good enough to eat. Actually it is a member of the spinach family, and the leaves do make a nourishing winter vegetable. It is most abundant on our east coast and likes to grow on soil rich in nitrogen.

Another common plant here is the sea buckthorn, which lives 'in symbiosis' with a fungus. The two-way relationship works like this: the fungus fixes atmospheric nitrogen into a form readily assimilated by the buckthorn, and the buckthorn in turn provides the fungus with plant sugars, as well as shelter in an otherwise exposed and inhospitable habitat. The build-up of nitrogen in the soil by fungus and buckthorn encourages the growth of that first plant, the winter purslane.

Look out also for the common garden birds. It is not unusual at this time to see pair-formation among hedge sparrows, wrens and robins. It is worthwhile to keep an eye on the wild ducks in parks and on reservoirs. Good use of eyes and ears soon shows that, whether it is freezing or thawing, outdoor life carries on.

Nearly every January I notice more molehills around; a thaw may bring almost an explosion of earthworks. The tunnels are often worked near the surface and every so often small mounds of earth are thrown up. These 'tumps' give an indication of the direction of the tunnel. Also in winter one finds large molehills which indicate winter nests where several moles may huddle together for warmth. At the entrance of one of these I have found stores of insects and worms which provide food during times of severe frost when tunnelling becomes impossible. But as soon as the temperature rises, the mole is in business again: he may excavate hundreds of metres of burrows and patrol them for worms that drop into his winding maze. The mole's name is a corruption of the Anglo-Saxon word *moldwarp*, which means dirt-thrower (*molde*, dirt, plus *weorpan*, thrower).

At this time hedgehogs are hibernating – in theory, but not all of them are. Every year in January I come across one or two foraging about. They are nearly always small specimens, young ones which probably have not accumulated enough body-fat to last through the winter. Unless these animals are taken in and properly looked after until the spring they are unlikely to survive.

There is a lot of other activity at this time; the blackbird will give a little song even when the weather is cold, and a bit more if the temperature rises; the great tits will give a rasping note, the wood pigeons will coo and on some hollow bough the pied woodpecker will from time to time set to his mechanical drumming, sounding very similar to the more intense drumming he will produce later in the year.

Sprouting in winter

The days get longer, but suddenly a heavy frost chills everything and all that was green shrivels up, turns grey and sooner or later is buried under a fall of snow. These raw days can seem to last forever, but for me the month is full of

Grass   Chickweed   Common groundsel   Purslane

Mole and hedgehog

Jackdaws pair for life

Rook

The jay hoards up supplies for the winter

The nutcracker occasionally arrives in eastern counties from Siberia

Carrion and hooded crows

Magpie

The magnificent heron is seen ever more frequently in town parks or gardens

Black-headed gull

Gulls, especially the two kinds shown here, come inland to feed and are common in town and country alike

On the left are birds of the crow family, which form a striking winter group

Herring gull

A mole in its tunnel. Above: the underside of the head, with the pointed snout. Top right: the forefoot, showing the sensitive hairs

surprises – there is often a mild spell and then you can spot the greenery.

First there are the tough, resistant grasses that sprout at the least opportunity, giving a sense of life to any winter walk. Then there is the lesser celandine of the hedgerows, with its beautifully designed rosette of heart-shaped leaves growing flat against the earth. The heart of the plant will survive frost, protected by the dying outside leaves that are sacrificed as an insulating blanket. This is one of the first spring plants. Its name means 'swallow-herb', the plant which welcomes the swallows back, although here they are never early enough to see either leaves or flowers. In the same hedgerows one can see the blue-green bush foliage of the cow parsley, which will suddenly burst out later in the year, forming banks of creamy-white flowers along our country lanes. Also to be noticed at this time are the fresh green leaves of the corn camomile dotted about on waste ground.

Meanwhile, at the edge of the woodland, the hazel catkins are coming into flower. Known to country children as 'lambs' tails', they are the earliest heralds of spring. The long, delicate golden-yellow pendants are made up of a large number of male flowers composed of several scales that protect the pollen-yielding stamens.

The female catkins are less conspicuous, and they are solitary, small and crimson-coloured; before they open they look like mere swollen buds.

The hazel has a special history. It must have been our commonest tree after the last great Ice Age when the land was still relatively cold. Britain was probably covered with hazel forest until the larger and more dominant oak established itself. Hazel has been extensively used by man: tough, long-living, pliant and fast-growing, it is the ideal tree for coppicing, a practice introduced by the Normans in the eleventh century and continued right until the beginning of this century. Sections of a hazel wood were cut down, at seven-to-fifteen-year intervals. The wood was used for a variety of purposes, from making hurdles used for temporary fences – especially in days before real hedges were widespread – to windbreaks for the garden (try this – it's very effective), hoops for barrels, walking sticks and even water-divining rods! The multi-purpose hazel tree is worth looking for, particularly at the beginning of the year, and again in September when its nuts are ripe.

Suddenly on a warm day . . . the winter aconite opens. Not just like that – first you see the shoot, then the flower bent over in self-

protection, then on the first warm day, at the first possible opportunity, the petals open and the beautiful yellow flower stars the earth. In a cold spell the flower closes up for a few days, reopening when conditions relent. This plant is not a native of Britain. It was introduced about 400 years ago from the mountains of southern Europe and is now a well-established plant of woodland in the south and east. It does well in gardens on fertile soil (not manured). We should not dig up wild ones for the garden – order some of the small black tubers from a bulb specialist.

A builder's yard for birds

Within six to eight weeks most birds will have started building, and to encourage them you can supply a box filled with various kinds of nesting materials. The boxes are discussed in the February chapter, but you can also enjoy providing a good selection of furnishing materials for them. Somebody once took the trouble to take a sparrow's nest apart and found 1,063 pieces of dried grass, 126 pieces of bark, 15 pieces of paper, 10 pieces of cellophane, 13 pieces of fabric, 25 threads of cotton, 28 feathers, some string and an old bandage. Though the sparrow is not fussy about what it uses, other birds have more specific requirements – the chaffinch, for instance, trims the outside of its nest with mosses and lichens, the long-tailed tit incorporates spiders' webs into its delicate structure.

For your birds' builder's yard, all you need is a small box open at one side and divided into four or five compartments. The open side should be covered with wire netting of a mesh just wide enough to allow birds to poke their beaks through. I fill the compartments with a selection of the following: withered leaves (not too dry), a little hay, moss, cotton threads and tufts of wool such as the sheep leavings you find stuck on barbed wire. Hang the box up so that its contents stay dry and in a spot where you can see the comings and goings of different birds, and when it needs refilling. An interesting experiment is to see which colour threads are best liked by the different birds.

January

Lesser celandine in flower, a January joy

Winter aconite – a yellow star on the bare earth

Winter strangers: crossbill, nutcracker and waxwing

From time to time through autumn and into winter we receive an influx of strange visitors. Here I am referring to a curious trio of birds, the crossbill, nutcracker and waxwing. They are not normal winter migrants that reach our shores regularly each autumn, but birds that arrive as an irruption from northern Scandinavia and Russia. These periodic visitors have been coming to western Europe for hundreds of years; our oldest record dates from 1251.

Since Roman times, people have taken special note of unusual birds and their behaviour; often they were seen as a portent of disaster. One curious expression remains in European folklore: 'When the sand grouse arrives, the women get cheap'. Nowadays we look to the science of ecology, rather than to superstitions, for an explanation of anything out of the ordinary in the natural world. We know that invasions of birds such as the crossbill are the result of conditions hundreds of miles to the north and east in the great coniferous forests of Russia and northern Scandinavia. Here, well within the Arctic Circle, the climate is more extreme and freakish than our own: the absence of normal day–night cycles, the sudden occurrence of enormous snowfalls, or of severe frosts, followed by floods of melting ice and a short intense summer, mean that the wildlife must be ready to adapt to all extremes. Also, although the 'taiga' forest is composed of a vast number of trees they are of relatively few types.

Of the conifers, the seeds of spruce, pine and larch serve as the main food supply for many different small mammals and birds. There are good, bad and moderate years; sometimes that seed crop fails. The life of the common crossbill is intimately connected with the spruce tree's annual cycle. The crossbill breeds early in the spring before the spruce sheds its seeds. Then, during a gap of a few months in May and June, while new spruce seeds are forming, the crossbill turns to the seeds of the pine.

It is usually at this time of year that parties of crossbills cross the taiga forests in all directions looking for food. Normally they cover a distance of a couple of hundred miles, well within their normal home range. However, in certain years the birds become excited (rather like those swallows we see chattering on telegraph wires before their autumn migration) and take off in small flocks which gather strength, always flying in the same direction, south and west towards Western Europe. We know for certain that they do not stop even if a good food supply is spotted en route, and a poor seed crop is probably not the main reason for these occasional irruptions. Animal psychologists have established that if the population of any particular animal or bird builds up beyond a certain point within a limited area it causes a restlessness which can sometimes turn into panic. This, connected with a poor or only moderate crop of spruce seeds, is likely to be the impetus that stimulates the birds to gather together and fly off to spread over a large area.

Not all crossbills migrate from their homeland, young birds and females appearing to make up a high proportion of the wanderers. Ornithologists have gathered a lot of valuable material on the numbers, sex-ratio and direction of movement for crossbills. One dedicated observer in Finland travelled over the same route on skis every Sunday in March for eleven years counting the number of crossbills he encountered on his journey. We owe a lot to individuals like him, yet still we do not know for certain all the factors involved in these freak invasions.

Once the crossbill reaches Western Europe it generally has difficulty in obtaining a regular food supply; thousands of the birds perish. But others, the more resourceful, often stay to breed. Our resident crossbills in the Breckland of East Anglia came as invaders from the north in 1909 and stayed. There is another distinct population of these birds living in the pine forests of north-east Scotland. With every new influx of crossbills our population swells and then shrinks again until the next invasion. Whatever the weather, the crossbill is an attractive resident and visitor and should be looked out for, especially in conifer plantations

The nutcracker also feeds on tree seeds, particularly pine, and is very partial to hazel nuts. It is a jay-like, chocolate-brown bird with white drop-like markings. It turns up in England, often in the eastern counties, in autumn and winter as an invader.

In contrast the waxwing is a berry-eater, but is also a resident of northern Russia. The waxwing is a handsome bird, and gets its name from the curious waxy red tips to its secondary feathers. It should be watched for wherever there is a good crop of berries. It often feeds in hedgerows, and is especially fond of the berries of the guelder rose which grows on those solid lumps of land called alder carrs in our eastern fens and marshes.

A 'builders' yard for your local bird

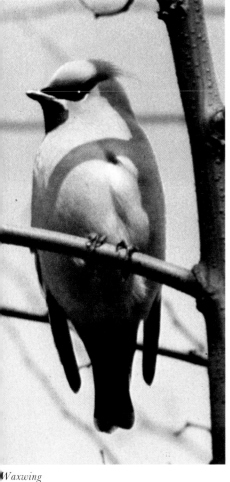

Waxwing

Crossbills

Hibernation

Not all hibernating mammals spend the winter in the same way. Take the hedgehog, which is a true hibernator. During late summer and early autumn it feeds up in preparation for its long winter sleep. Usually by the end of October it has made its winter nest, often in some abandoned wasps' nest in a ditch or bank. It lines the nest with leaves and moss to make it snug, then curls up and goes to sleep. In the meantime all the surplus food it has eaten previously has been efficiently converted into a thick layer of brown fat. This fat produces 30 per cent more energy per gram than normal body-fat, and it needs this to last the winter. Its sleep is no ordinary sleep: the breathing-rate gradually drops to 5–8 per minute (compared to 50 per minute when active) and the demand for oxygen drops to 2 per cent of normal. Sometimes there are gaps of 15 minutes between breaths. At the same time the heartbeat slows down to 20 per minute (compared to the normal 100–150).

The composition of the blood also changes: fewer red blood corpuscles are produced, to prevent clotting. The body-temperature falls to that of its surroundings, though as a safety measure heat is produced when the temperature drops below 2°C. The hedgehog makes heat by contracting its body muscles, just as we do when we shiver. During severe cold a hedgehog sometimes over-compensates, warms up too much, and awakes, often leading to fatal results as it is hard for its body to cope with going back to sleep, and the hedgehog may end up by starving.

Dormice and bats go into a similar type of hibernation. Other mammals like the badger do not sink into a permanent sleep but rather have a less-deep winter rest and can be seen on mild evenings foraging around the woodland floor.

The buds are swelling

A compensation for January's gloom and chill when walking in the woods or over the fields is the varied silhouettes of the trees. Their bare branches allow us to get a better look at many different kinds of birds. Beneath its stark exterior, the tree is coming to life; the buds are always swelling. In damp places the buds of the osier have already burst through, showing their silver-coloured catkins, and in parks and gardens we find the curious flowers of the witch-hazel and the spring cherry (*Prunus subhirtella*), both of which withstand a moderate frost. If during the day the sun warms the trees, and at night the temperature drops well below freezing, the tree bark will alternately expand and contract. Sometimes you can actually hear it swell and tear. Once ripped open by the contrast in temperature it only heals up again when all danger of frost has passed.

A small bird, the tree creeper, takes advantage of these openings in the bark to probe for insects. Winter is the best time to observe this bird, which is so well camouflaged that at other times it is 'lost' amongst the boughs and leaves. It starts investigating a tree at its base, working up the trunk in a spiral path aided by its stiff tail and wide-gripping

Badgers may be seen foraging about near their setts during any mild spell in winter

January

feet. Sometimes even in winter you can hear its shrill little song: 'see, see, see, sissy-pee'.

In the lower shrub layer of the woods, particularly in large parks, you will see a lot of rhododendron shrubs; in severe weather notice how the leaves droop down. This is common among evergreen shrubs, a clever adaptation to catch less wind and so prevent loss of water from the plant.

Clues from the kill

When the ground is bare in winter one sometimes comes across the remains of a bird that has been part-eaten. The carcass often indicates what predators are around: the size of the prey, the type of ground and the season are all clues. Birds the size of doves and pigeons can only be taken by buzzards and the peregrine falcon. Small birds are seized by sparrowhawks and the rarer hobbies and merlins, but kestrels and owls will also take small birds. Sparrow-hawks are mainly woodland birds and hedgerow-hunters, while the merlin and hobby prey over open country. In winter the merlin comes down off the moorland to scour the marshes and coasts for wading birds. The slightly larger hobby is still in Africa, not returning until mid-April at the earliest.

The peregrine falcon like most birds of prey will at this time of the year venture from its normal inaccessible habitat of cliff and mountain. It is a supremely efficient killer, attacking from above; it stoops on its prey from a terrific height, and with outstretched talons kills ducks, wading birds and pigeons. You can tell one of its victims almost immediately, because the peregrine is a finicky eater and generally takes only the chest muscles of its victim; in contrast to the hawks it leaves the wings and chest skeleton intact. Large hawks like our rare goshawk will pull out the large wing-feathers.

The excitement of a bird of prey

Under a grey winter sky, the reed marsh stretches out in all directions. A large bird glides low above the sea of yellow stalks. It is dark brown with a creamy-white head and has a peculiar wobbling flight and slanting wings. These features tell us it is a female marsh-harrier. Backwards and forwards she quarters the reeds; occasionally she slows down, swerves a little and, with her broad tail outspread, hovers briefly at the sighting of some prey. Then she makes a quick dive and disappears for a moment into the reeds. So far she has been unlucky and takes to the wing again to scour another patch of reed bed.

A crow approaches with quick wingbeats and dives aggressively at the harrier, then withdraws, gains height and repeats its attack. The harrier elegantly avoids the crow and continues hunting, apparently unconcerned.

Harrier and crow

But soon the crow is joined by a companion. You can hear their raucous call, the 'krr, krr' that crows use to relieve their feelings. It is fascinating to watch the antics of these birds through the binoculars. As they twist and turn the light catches their wings, illuminating for a brief moment the glossy plumage of the crows or the bright-yellow legs of the harrier which hang down almost limply from the body. After a while the harrier has had enough and with quick wingbeats speeds away; the crows have to give up their teasing.

Just as the crows attacked the harrier, so man continuously persecutes all birds of prey, out of suspicion, fear or unjustified self-protection. In this country we have our fair share of conservation bodies such as the Royal Society for the Protection of Birds. These and other organisations do a great deal to relieve some of the ills of our overcrowded, urban society, the loss of wild places and the general public ignorance of wildlife and its ways. My particular gripe is against gamekeepers, because of the strings of corpses one still sees hanging from their gibbets. 'It was a pleasant thing for everybody when a man could go out and shoot a couple of brace of partridges for his table' (Nicholson, E. M., *Birds in England*, 1926). But this was not, and is not, the norm; shooting estates and the protection of gamebirds led to a mass slaughter of birds of prey. Some may argue that overall these estates serve as refuges for wildlife and preserve wild country; maybe the songbirds benefit, but not the hawks, owls and falcons.

For the time being we are only concerned with the fact that birds of prey are endlessly fascinating, beautiful and skilful, an aspect of our countryside that should not be missed.

The commonest bird of prey is the kestrel; indeed, these birds seem to be multiplying, especially alongside our motorways. I have counted at least a dozen individuals hovering by the roadside on a 200-mile journey. As you speed along you may miss seeing one of them flying up with its kill in its talons, but if you keep your eyes open you will probably see this occasionally.

Another raptor often seen and surprisingly indifferent to man is the buzzard, encountered as a large brown bird sitting motionless on a telegraph pole or flying low over a hillside. The buzzard is a scavenger and can be seen in the company of crows and ravens picking at the carcass of a dead lamb or sheep; our nearest equivalent to the useful vulture of the African savannah. A car can be used to advantage when looking for these larger birds, as it will convert into a mobile 'hide'.

The behaviour of other animals, especially birds, can give clues that a bird of prey is about. In the woods, a general excitement among the tits and smaller birds may mean that an owl has been spotted resting against a tree trunk. This banding together of different species gives them all moral support and usually ends with the owl being chased away. In open countryside lapwings, starlings and crows will suddenly fly upwards en masse when a sparrowhawk, merlin or hobby comes near. This flocking behaviour presents a unified front to the potential killer, who finds it less easy to single out a quarry. Gulls are quite courageous when a predator appears and often resort to a wheeling flight, a kind of merry-go-round behaviour, if a bird of prey is sighted feeding or the ground. Gulls become incensed by this and will bombard any hawk unwary enough to be caught on the ground.

The coldest month?

On average this month is the coldest, but this is hard to believe when thinking of the number of really mild, almost magical Januaries experienced in the early 1970s; January 1979, however, endorsed the statistics.

Our climate, even in at least the first half of January, is dominated by westerly airstreams coming in from the Atlantic. This gives us our typically changeable, often mild, wet and slightly gloomy weather. These large depressions originate far out to sea in the North Atlantic, a few hundred miles off the coast of North America at latitudes between 40 and 45°N. Here dry polar air mixes with a moist tropical airstream, producing a vortex of cloud and air spiralling upwards to a considerable height. Once formed, the clouds are swept east across the Atlantic towards our shores. But by the second half of the month, another giant force may take over: a large anticyclone (high-pressure) area centred over Russia and Central Europe, producing typically cold, still and dry weather.

One disadvantage of being an island is that if the anticyclone is centred over Scandinavia rather than Central Europe, it produces not only cold weather but also a lot of cloud, due to the airstream picking up moisture over the North Sea. Once established, such an anticyclone is difficult to budge and the sky may be monotonously grey with cold temperatures lasting for weeks on end. If the anticyclone is centred further south over mainland Europe, the chances are the days will be brighter though probably even colder.

Mild winters are often due to high-pressure areas being centred over southern Europe and the Mediterranean; then mild south-westerly airstreams may be swept northwards over Britain.

The coldest January months occurred in 1940, 1942, 1945, 1963 and 1979, with average monthly temperatures well below freezing. In contrast, the warmest Januaries occurred in 1921, 1971 and 1975. In 1975 the temperature reached or exceeded 10°C (50°F) on 19 days of the month; this January was one of the mildest on record. Sometimes it is hard to adapt to these changes; balmy springlike days when the grass is sprouting, everything looks green and there are even daisies flowering in the fields and gardens. It's as though our biological clocks are temporarily put out of action, suspending childhood memories of waking up to frosty windowpanes and of cracking ice on frozen puddles on the way to school.

Snow crystals

People often say 'It's too cold to snow', and indeed the colder the air, the less moisture it can hold, so in bitterly cold weather there is little chance of rain or snow. When snow comes the atmospheric pressure drops; you can actually see this happen if you have a barometer. But what is really happening? More often than not an area of high pressure is temporarily ousted by a low-pressure area coming in from the Atlantic. At the boundary of these two air masses, high up in the clouds, the moist air freezes into ice crystals. As these fall they increase in size by taking up moisture and by colliding with each other, producing snowflakes.

These snowflakes differ in form, depending on atmospheric conditions. In very cold temperatures we get flurries of fine dry snow, because there is not enough moisture for the flakes to stick together; the snow is blown about in different directions by the wind, sometimes almost like a fine white mist. At temperatures around freezing point, we get the typical clumping-together of ice or snow crystals into snowflakes, sometimes as big as 1cm ($\frac{1}{2}$in) across. This is good snow for snowballs, and it is also worth taking a closer look at these snowflakes under the magnifying glass: they are most beautiful, forming innumerable patterns all on a hexagonal theme, some needle pointed stars, others branching into a multitude of forms. During a slight thaw they change; the contours become more rounded, although the shape remains six-sided.

A sacred tree

During January the leaves at last drop down from the oak. Britain has two native oaks, which at first look similar. The pedunculate oak, however, carries its acorns on little stalks or peduncles, whereas on the sessile oak the acorns are 'seated' directly on the main twigs. Another difference is in the leaves; those of the pedunculate oak have little or no stalk and are usually highly indented, whereas the leaf of the sessile oak is less indented and has a definite stalk. There are other minor differences but these are the main ones. As a general rule the pedunculate oak is found on rich clay or alluvial soils, especially around London and in the south generally, whereas the sessile oak prefers a light, shallow, acid soil with good drainage, mainly in the north and west of Britain.

The oak was the sacred tree of the Druids, possibly because it was the tree that most often harboured the mistletoe, another sacred plant. It is believed that large oak trees were the sites where sacrifices were made to Odin, Thor, Frigga and other Norse gods. After the Druids had been and gone, the oak remained an important tree. The oak's fruit, the acorn, served as food for people as well as for pigs and cattle. One possible derivation of the word 'corn' is that it superseded the acorn as the chief source of food in temperate countries. Forests of deciduous trees once stretched uninterrupted as a vast belt across the northern hemisphere, and acorns must have been far too abundant to be ignored, even though today we do not find them palatable.

Nature and farming

It isn't unusual to come across people who are biologists by training or naturalists by inclination and know a lot about one particular group of animals and plants, yet nothing about a related subject. Ornithologists, herpetologists and entomologists can become almost entombed in their particular interest. Specialisation probably originates at school, with those tight compartments for history, geography, biology etc; yet all these subjects overlap. Too often nature-lovers show no interest in domestic animals and agricultural crops. Yet it is ridiculous when an expert in wild grasses can't tell the difference between wheat and rye.

In Britain there are over twenty breeds of cattle and a lot of crossbreeds from continental stock. There is of course a general trend towards standardisation and many of our less common types like the Blue Albion are becoming rarer as indeed are some of the old-timers. For milk and meat production, some of these old breeds are not efficient enough for today's mass-production farming and could soon disappear. But not only are they of historical interest; they could also serve as a useful gene pool (as blood-stock) should any widespread epidemics affect the breeds now most popular. One organisation concerned with the issue is the Rare Breeds Survival Trust, based in Wiltshire.

The buzzard's purposeful beak

Snow crystals seen under a magnifying glass

February

February was one of the new months added to the Roman calendar by the second King of Rome, Numa Pompilius, one of those Romans who have given us the basis of the calendar we know today. The word February is derived from the Latin *februa*, a means of purification, the theme of a ceremony held in ancient Rome at this time of year.

The month is often cold and dark, but it usually starts off stormy, continuing the unsettled weather at the end of January. By the second week of this month the weather generally becomes calmer and typically there follow long, quiet, dry, moderately cold spells. Folklore relating to this month stresses the idea that a mild February is an ill omen, with bad weather sure to follow:

A farmer would sooner see his dam on a bier
Than a fine Februeer.

(Here dam refers to wife or lady.)
Another proverb many country people still believe is:

As many fogs in February
So many frosts in May.

Similar weather prophecies are connected with Candlemas Day, 2 February. All told it seems better to have a cold February and get the winter over than have those chilly late springs which seem to go on forever.

The bird table

One pleasure of a cold spell is to watch the activity at the bird table. The raucous starlings are not welcomed by many people, as their sheer numbers mean that all food is polished off in moments. But it is worth taking a closer look at these birds. After their autumn moult, their chest and stomach feathers have light edges, giving them a completely new look. This flecked winter coat doesn't last all that long; as the lighter edges of the feathers wear away the flecks get smaller, until by the end of the month the starlings become resplendent once again in their sleek spring costume. These changes vary

The starling in autumn, winter and spring plumage

from one individual to the next.

It is also worth looking at their beaks. Around December time, the beak is colourless as a result of wear and tear and low hormone activity. By February it starts colouring up again, turning yellow gradually from the base up to the tip.

At the bird table the starlings push and shove each other around. Some are more aggressive than the rest but generally it is a free-for-all whenever there is food around. One starling may apparently let his neighbour take some food, but it is no use humanising this as kindness; the bird is merely concentrating on other food rather than on his companion's.

My particular starlings roost nearby in trees or buildings, but every winter afternoon I see huge flocks of hundreds, even thousands, of them pass overhead on their way to a communal roost in town. At this time of year it is not unusual to find dead starlings lying on the pavement or in the gutter. One might mentally accuse the local council of having laid poison in the interests of public health, but nine times out of ten, death has resulted from natural causes, from cold or simply overcrowding – the effects of excess numbers in a confined space. Large winter roosts may contain hundreds of thousands of starlings.

Underneath my bird table I often see a single hedge sparrow discreetly picking up the crumbs or a wren forced to modify its insect diet during these hard times. Another visitor is the long-tailed field mouse, easily distinguished from the house mouse by its russet-coloured coat, large ears and white underparts. It is normally nocturnal but is very adaptable and can change its habits wherever there is a ready source of food. This animal is a frequent occupant of houses and garden sheds during the winter months. Mine store their food in small piles behind books in the living room. I don't actually mind finding the odd dog biscuit hidden away, but I do object when they chew up my clothes to make their nests. Another black mark against this endearing little creature is its liking for peas and beans. I have lost many a crop to these rodents by sowing too early in the year. This is just a warning if you ever wondered why your early vegetables got off to a poor start.

Freshwater life

A trip to the reed beds can also be rewarding now, not only to watch the yellow and brown reeds sway and rustle in the wind; in

In cold weather a lot more birds than usual will arrive in gardens where food is growing or provided

Chaffinch

Tits are often seen in groups; their acrobatics at bird tables are a delight to watch

Great tit

Robin

Blue tit

Collared dove

In cold weather birds fluff out their feathers to increase their insulation

Wren

Snowdrops

Wood pigeon

Blackbird

Song thrush

Hedge sparrow

A male smooth newt begins to move about in a pond

shallow pools life is beginning to stir, and you may see the odd water beetle careering about or the slow paddling of water scorpion. Even newts can become active at this time, though it is April before the females lay their eggs on the water plants.

The robin and his territory

The robin seems such a dear, tame, cheery little bird, with its big eyes and red breast. We like the way it follows us round the garden, always just behind us ready to pick up any insect turned over by the spade. Robins and human sentiment go hand in hand – aided by Christmas-card artists.

Appearances are deceptive, however; the robin is an aggressive bird, and if you happen to be another robin is downright nasty. Its high-pitched 'tic, tic' is not uttered to please us but to demonstrate in no uncertain way its presence and its territory.

The sweetness of bird song in all cases serves some function in nature. 'Sound signals' would be a better term than song, even if its use would be pedantic. Amongst our garden birds the robin is one of the marathon songsters. Its spring song starts as early as December and continues without a halt until early June! The autumn song, which is thinner and less rich, normally starts in August although it can get feeble during the dark days at the end of November.

December is the time robins pair up, although this has nothing to do with courtship, which occurs just before nesting in March. All

the tradition around St Valentine's day on 14 February, the day when all wild birds were thought to find their respective mates, has been dispelled, like so much colourful country folklore.

The most important use of song to the robin is to advertise itself. It is strongly territorial, a point that cannot be over-emphasised, and will defend its territory with all its might.

When an intruder appears it sings louder and faster; the angry staccato is often enough to frighten off the visitor, though probably not if this is an inexperienced juvenile of the previous season, or another male displaced from his own territory and keen to gain a new one. In this case the robin uses its red breast almost like war paint, exposing as much as possible of it and striking odd postures, puffing itself up and jerking its head up and down. The normal 'tic, tic, tsit' call changes to a high-pitched squeal as it lunges at the visitor. Boundary disputes often end with a fight – a quick flurry of wings, a few pecks and it's all over; usually the intruder retreats. The female's behaviour is just as pugnacious; with many other garden birds, the males will fight males, and females fight females, but both male and female robins attack neighbours of either sex. If you want to see this high drama, get up early, around dawn, when most garden birds are at peak activity.

Though so much a tame garden bird in England the robin is much shyer on the continent, where it lives in forests and woodland areas. Its place as a tame bird is taken by the redstart in lowland countries and by the black redstart in upland areas like Switzerland.

Who killed cock robin? Not the sparrow with his bow and arrow, but sheer hunger. A severe winter can kill off up to 60 per cent of

Wood mouse

February *1. White-fronted geese   2. Bean geese   3. Pink-footed goose   4. Barnacle geese*

robins. A large proportion of these are males, as the females tend to migrate. During hard weather the normal diet of insects and berries can be usefully supplemented by scraps from the bird table. Lumps of fat put out at this time are sure to encourage them.

The wren

As the days lengthen other birds become active around the garden. One of these, another favourite, is the tiny wren which plays a rather different game from that of the robin, though both birds are loners in their different ways. The wren is one of our smallest birds, measuring less than 10cm (4in) from beak to tail; it can live in and around a large garden for years without being noticed. Instead of announcing itself like the robin, it survives by retreating from view, by being well camouflaged and skulking in the ivy or between branches. When disturbed, or when its territory is invaded, it sings a high-pitched 'tic, tic, tic' to ward off intruders.

Tree trunks

In February there still isn't a leaf on the trees and hedges; it is worth paying attention to the trunks. Tree trunks serve as a habitat for a host of other plants, mosses, lichens and bryophytes. On an overgrown trunk you can often make out dark lines running down. These are caused by the condensation of fog and mist, forming minute streams of water which run to the base of the tree. This flow of water leaves a deposit of soil and sand at the base.

Winter fungi

When one thinks of toadstools, one automatically thinks of autumn and walking through the woods. It can therefore be a surprise to come across a bunch of toadstools sprouting from a tree trunk, perhaps in the garden, in the middle of winter. One of these is called velvet shanks, named after the lower part of the stem which is dark-coloured and of a velvet texture. The cap is slimy and yellow-brown, and the gills are a creamy-buff colour. During the rest of the year the velvet shanks plant exists inside the wood of the trunk as a mass of branching threads called the mycelium, the main body of the fungus. Many other fungi stop forming toadstools as the temperature drops, but this one comes into flower in winter, pushing out the fruiting bodies or toadstools. The cap contains millions of minute spores which are carried by the wind and so dispersed to infect other rotten timber.

Velvet shanks (flammulina velutipes)

Another real winter toadstool is the winter polypore, a tough leathery toadstool, at first dark brown but later having a rather bleached look. *Polyporus brumalis* grows on stumps of deciduous trees, sometimes on partially buried fallen branches so that it looks as if it is growing in soil.

Winter polypore (polyporus brumalis)

Flocking by finches

Other birds gave up their territories months ago, after the last breeding season, and until their spring courtship starts they live peacefully side by side. Starlings form groups and finches form loose flocks as they scour the countryside for food. Take a closer look at any small finch flock and with binoculars you can usually see three or four types feeding together, perhaps chaffinches, goldfinches and greenfinches. Why do they group together? The habit must have some survival value connected with their feeding habits. Finches are seed-eaters; when their food plants are available, often there are pockets of abundance, and sharing brings no hardship. The flock strips the patch of seeding thistles, or whatever, and moves on.

In a group there are more eyes on the alert to look for food; for a single bird to find enough seeds at this time of year would take too long. Another obvious advantage in flocking behaviour is the safety brought by numbers; birds of prey find it more difficult to single out a victim. Flocking is strongest early in the

mornings. By ten o'clock the birds of different species tend to separate to preen and rest, and then the bands re-form in the afternoon until they roost. To watch finches scour the fields and wayside patches is interesting; suddenly a deserted landscape becomes alive with twittering birds – another reason to try to get up early, although at this time of the year it isn't the easiest thing to do.

Rarer birds

Robins, wrens and finches are familiar garden birds. Shrikes are not common in this country, but are definitely worth looking out for. In winter the great grey shrike visits England from northern Scandinavia. It favours scrubby heathland and sunny spots at the edge of woods.

Shrikes come midway in behaviour between the smaller insect-eating birds, like the flycatcher, and our larger birds of prey. A shrike can wait for hours at its lookout above a patch of heath, then suddenly it pounces on a mouse or small bird. In their winter feeding-grounds, shrikes claim mobile hunting territories; at this time of year food is thin on the ground and any other shrikes that fancy the same spot are soon put to flight.

The species that nests in Britain is the smaller red-backed shrike, also known as the butcher bird from its habit – shared by other shrikes – of impaling its prey, mainly small birds and insects, on thorns surrounding the nest. It frequents dense thickets of gorse and hawthorn and only breeds with any frequency in our southern and eastern counties.

Bird photography

Today it is hard to imagine how early photographers managed in the field with their bulky and cumbersome plate cameras, heavy-duty tripods, and long exposures. And yet it was just such pioneers as Richard and Cherry Kearton who laid the foundations of modern bird photography, setting remarkably high standards in the process. Usually they worked

A thrush, feathers fluffed out to keep warm, is grateful to find fallen apples

at the nest, adopting elaborate disguises to appease the birds. Once they hid inside the mounted skin of a cow, and at other times they tried to look like sheep or trees. It must have been almost disappointing to find that a rectangular canvas hide does just as well!

In later years, three developments revolutionised the art. The first was the introduction of the electronic flash in the 1930s This dispensed with the need for sunny days, made nocturnal birds accessible, and allowed birds in rapid motion to be 'frozen'. Then the advent of the 35mm, single-lens-reflex camera, with its ease of handling and opportunity to see exactly what the lens sees, was a major innovation. Thirdly the telephoto lens, which enabled birds to be stalked and filmed undisturbed from a distance. To this end the car also has been a boon, providing a ready mobile hide which birds seem to take for granted almost as much as we do.

Given the widespread availability and popularity of such equipment, it becomes important as never before to respect birds as subjects, whether waders feeding quietly on a mudflat, or a blackbird tending its brood. The cardinal rule is to disturb them as little as possible, especially if close contact is sought with a hide. Certain rare birds can be photographed only under licence from the Nature Conservancy, and it is the individual's responsibility to remain within the law.

Nest boxes

If you want birds to build in nest boxes in the garden it is time to make or buy the boxes and set them up. The first recorded nest boxes were clay flasks used in the late Middle Ages in Holland, and wooden flasks in Silesia. For the hapless birds, mostly sparrows and starlings, that took to them, they turned out to be tender traps, for the occupants were promptly captured for the pot. Charles Waterton, a nineteenth-century Yorkshire squire, is credited as being the first naturalist to erect boxes purely for the birds' benefit, and his example has been followed widely ever since. The utilitarian motive of the Dutch was not, however, entirely forgotten and Baron von Berlepsch in Germany was the first to use boxes on a large scale to attract insectivorous birds, hopefully to control outbreaks of injurious forest insects. If this was wishful thinking on the Baron's part, at least it showed that boxes are enormously attractive to birds, and ornithologists were excited to discover not long after that entire woodland populations of birds like the great tit could be wooed into nest boxes if enough were provided.

The nineteenth-century box was made of wood, with a round entrance hole, and was designed to attract titmice, nuthatches, redstarts and pied flycatchers. Attempts to disguise boxes to look like logs were soon found to be superfluous; planed wood does

Male great grey shrike on the nest; a rare and interesting visitor

nicely. Nevertheless, there are important specifications. The wood must be strong, seasoned and preferably treated if it is to last any length of time and not warp; the box should not be much bigger in cross-sectional area than the nest it is to contain. The entrance hole should be high enough up the front (or side) for the actual nest to be below the searching paw of a cat. For the same reason, resist the temptation to provide handy perches for the occupants – predators can stand on them too. The roof or lid should be sloping, overlapping the sides to throw off rain, and be firmly attached, the box having an openable front. Or a hinged roof and fixed front can be used instead.

Again, the box must be sited with predators (including children!) and weather in mind. Attach it securely about 3m (10ft) up a tree, post or wall, turned to face away from the hottest sun. Make sure that the birds have an open approach, free from a ladderwork of branches. Ideally the box should be put up in the autumn or winter to give local birds plenty of time to prospect it, but even a box put up as late as May can be snapped up within hours.

Many design variations have been adopted to suit different sorts of birds. If you wish to attract tits, but not sparrows or starlings, take a little care in drilling the entrance hole. One

that is 3cm ($1\frac{3}{16}$in) or a little less (but not more) in diameter will admit blue tits and great tits, but will generally exclude these others, if not always tree sparrows. A tin plate with a hole cut to the same diameter and placed over the entrance hole will further deter gnawing squirrels or chiselling woodpeckers. Removal of half the front panel converts the box into a canopied ledge suitable for spotted flycatchers, robins and others. By increasing the dimensions, kestrels, jackdaws, stock doves and even ducks can be attracted. Tawny owls have been encouraged to nest successfully in long, coffin-shaped boxes attached to an upward-sloping branch.

February

Materials other than wood have been used with varying degrees of success. A potter friend of mine tried flask-shaped 'boxes' of fired clay but the birds didn't seem to like them much, perhaps because they get damp. More successfully, amalgams of cement and sawdust have been used to mould cup-shaped boxes for swallows and house martins. This same amalgam has the advantage of being squirrel- and woodpecker-proof, and has been used in the construction of a cylindrical box which hangs by a wire from a strut attached to the tree trunk. Weasels, nimble as they are, have difficulty entering such a box. Sometimes, however, they will leap across from the tree trunk to the roof, and as a final deterrent a smooth plastic cone overlying the roof will give them nothing to grip on to when they do.

Feeding the birds

Rule number one is to feed birds only when they need it. In normal winter weather they can look after themselves by foraging beyond the garden in parks and woods. Also it is worth remembering that the food we give is never as good for them as their natural diet; spring feeding of stodgy food like white bread can be especially dangerous to young birds.

After all these warnings, if you have a garden it is a favour to the birds and to yourself to install a bird table to be used in hard weather. First make sure it is cat-proof and that it has some sort of roof, or a sudden snow shower will quickly cover the food you put out. Variety is what counts, and you can combine a lot of different ingredients by making a 'bird-table pudding': mix kitchen scraps, uncooked oats, grated cheese, tiny scraps of bacon rind, currants, etc, in a bowl, bind them together with warmed fat, let it set, then turn it out onto the bird table. By the main table string up some peanuts, or buy a small wire nut-dispenser from your local pet shop. This will attract blue tits and great tits well into the spring. Don't forget the finches, those attractive little birds that bring the garden to life with their quick movements and wing-

Alder buds – and rheumatism!

fluttering. Later in the year you can grow sunflowers and thistles to go to seed and attract the greenfinch and goldfinch. Both birds are regular visitors, even nesters, in towns, especially where there are waste plots with a surplus of seed-bearing plants.

Lastly provide some water; birds can be really short of this in icy weather, suffering from thirst even more than from cold or hunger – and remember to replace it when it freezes. Birds need not only to drink but also to take the occasional bath. A well-equipped table can attract many different species.

After the dog, the sheep

According to FAO (Food and Agricultural Organisation) statistics, about a thousand million sheep inhabit the earth, with Australia and the Soviet Union having the largest numbers. Wool is still an important world commodity despite the 1960s boom in synthetic fibres. For warmth and durability wool is hard to beat; even astronauts choose wool for comfort in the confines of their spacecraft. The domestication of the sheep started well after the dog, around 5000 BC, probably in the Middle East. It was, however, much later, in the Bronze Age, around 1900 BC, that sheep were first reared for wool in Britain. Since then, although it has had its ups and down, wool has played an important role in our economy. Today there are some 30 million sheep roaming our pastures and upland areas with between 30 and 40 distinct breeds.

The many different breeds we have are adapted to the varied terrain, climate, soil and vegetation of our islands. Broadly speaking our breeds can be divided into two main groups, long-woolled and short-woolled, found in our upland and lowland areas respectively. But it isn't as simple as that, because there is a lot of crossbreeding and sheep-farming in many respects is more of an art than an industry.

Lambing starts in the lowlands as early as January and by February is at its peak. In the lowlands, one classic way of management, now largely disappeared, is called 'folding': the flock is confined within movable hurdles over an arable crop like roots or kale, the hurdles and sheep being moved forwards over the field. In this way ewes and lambs receive fresh food, leaving the ground soiled behind them. Apart from pedigree flocks this method has largely disappeared because of the high labour costs

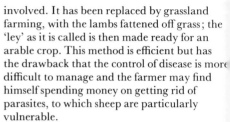
Long-woolled and short-woolled sheep

involved. It has been replaced by grassland farming, with the lambs fattened off grass; the 'ley' as it is called is then made ready for an arable crop. This method is efficient but has the drawback that the control of disease is more difficult to manage and the farmer may find himself spending money on getting rid of parasites, to which sheep are particularly vulnerable.

Alder buds and rheumatism

The alder, a close relation of the birch, is often overlooked, perhaps because it grows in damp places, mainly away from gardens, such as along riverbanks and the edge of marshes. But it is an interesting tree. At this time of year it is quietly in flower, with small waving catkins – the male flowers – and small clusters of reddish-purple scales – the female flowers. Its stalked buds are most distinctive, making the tree easy to identify before the catkins appear. It was these buds that provided an old cure for rheumatism. At the cold, damp times of year, countrywomen would collect the buds just before they opened, dry them carefully and make a tea, which was drunk first thing in the morning; it was firmly believed to be effective.

Whether it was so or not, it would destroy our alders if people restarted a fashion for drinking alder-bud tea. An alternative and equally effective remedy is sometimes suggested. For this you need 50g (2oz) of madder (*Rubia tinctorium*), which you can get from a chemist's or herbalist's shop. The other ingredient is expensive – brandy, and a litre of it! Stand the madder leaves in the brandy for at least forty-eight hours, preferably in a warm, light place – a windowsill is ideal. Then strain the liquid and pour it into a clean bottle. Take a teaspoonful of this every morning, on an empty stomach, and maybe it will relieve the rheumatic pains. If you feel cautious about trying home-made remedies, use half the quantities suggested at first.

Bulbs and corms

February is the month to look out for small bulb flowers popping out of the ground. In January we had the aconite, at the beginning of this month the snowdrop – and later the crocuses start appearing in our gardens. Bulb suppliers even offer February-flowering daffodils.

The true snowdrop, *Galanthus nivalis*, is

It is better now to have a thick fall of snow than a series of raw frosts which stunt the growth of all new shoots. Only conifers and evergreen shrubs suffer from a heavy snowfall: the branches become weighed down and some may eventually crack and break off. The chestnut tree resists the cold, its buds beautifully protected with a sticky resin that does not freeze. As the sun warms the ground the snow melts and we see the snowdrops push up. These 'fair maids of February' as they are often called are locally abundant in woods and copses although not truly native to Britain.

Between the frosts look around in the garden and along the hedgerow for the latest unfurling of leaves. Ground elder comes into leaf now: this notorious garden weed was introduced into Britain in the Middle Ages as a pot-herb and a cure against gout; one way to combat its spread is to eat it! The leaves have a spicy taste and should be boiled for a short time like spinach. Another plant to be found is the charming little ground ivy. Its leaves are pleasantly aromatic and are still gathered by people in the country as a remedy against coughs and colds. It was used before hops were introduced to bitter or 'tun' the ale.

Jack Frost(s)

The ice and frost encountered in the month of February come in various forms. Hoar frost is really just frozen dew forming a thick, white icy sediment on flat surfaces like lawns and cars, and on roofs. It forms most often at night or early in the morning, especially after a cloudless night when heat is rapidly lost to the atmosphere, and moist air close to the ground is quickly cooled and frozen.

Another wintry phenomenon is rime, which in simple terms is frozen fog. Rime takes the form of rough white ice crystals, which often build up on the windward side of projecting objects like tree branches to give an almost fairyland effect – especially if the early-morning sun comes out. Glazed frost is less common in Britain, though hard winters bring it. It is really rain which freezes on contact with cold ground and other surfaces, producing a heavy icy film. Tree branches and telegraph wires can even crack from it. 'Black ice' is just a glazed frost occurring on roads, especially dangerous because it is invisible.

'Black frost' is quite the opposite, a severe frost occurring when there is *little* moisture in the air, so there is little white deposit to see.

Snowdrops, first flowers of spring in many gardens and impervious to February's worst weather

probably not a native of Britain, and plants growing wild in damp woodland areas have multiplied from garden escapees or from bulbs put in by some public benefactor. The bigger, rather later-flowering 'snowflake' (*Leucojum vernum*), which many of us have in our gardens, is not of course a snowdrop at all: welcome as it is, it lacks the dainty charm of the real thing for most of us. The genuine snowdrops,

amazingly impervious to snow, frost and storm, vary greatly in shape and markings.

Among the infinite variety of crocuses available to the gardener, the little blue 'tommies', *Crocus tomasinianus*, are the earliest for most of us, opening at a gleam of sunshine. Planted under shrubs which do not make too dense a shade, they will spread freely, by seeding and by corm division.

Crocuses

March

Weatherwise, March has many sides but the patterns tend to repeat themselves from one year to the next. The month often divides into three. It may start off stormy and unsettled, with cold biting winds that make the temperature feel lower than it really is. Miraculously the middle of March can be calm, bringing a sweet feel that spring is here, with warmish dry days even though the nights are raw and cold. This is often the driest period of the whole year, especially in our southern and eastern counties. By the end of the month the weather reverses, with strong south-westerly winds returning storms and gales to the West Country, and the winds then veering to north-west and north to bring sleet and snow showers to upland areas like the Pennines and parts of Scotland.

March may well come in like a lion – and it often goes out like one.

On those sunny days when we cautiously stroll around the garden it may be chilly at head height, but on the ground the crocuses are fully opened and each in turn is visited by bumblebees. These busy insects are only active when the temperature rises to around 10°C (50°F) and indeed it may be at least 5°C (41°F) warmer at ground level. In sheltered spots against south-facing walls the day temperature may rise to well over 20°C (68°F).

It can be frustrating to find an anthill just where you are starting to picnic, but it is better to move somewhere else and leave the ants well alone, because this species in particular plays an important role in the forest ecosystem. When most active during the summer, a fair-sized colony can consume up to 100,000 insects a day, many being harmful defoliators of trees. The virtues of the wood ant are easily extolled, but more interestingly on the continent, in such countries as Germany and Switzerland, a successful campaign by conservationists and foresters to protect the wood ant has been running for some years. The methods employed include physical protection of the nests by reinforced wire enclosures, and the artificial rearing of new colonies, which are then carefully positioned in forests which lack

them. This has been combined with an educational campaign to tell children how useful these insects are, so that instead of going 'ant bashing' they can help in protecting them.

On bright days look out for the large bumblebees already mentioned, flying low over the ground in search of a suitable hole in which to make their nest; they often choose the abandoned underground home of a wood mouse or bank vole. There are also solitary wasps out at this time, resting on sunny walls cleaning themselves before the busy season. Look out for ladybirds, too.

Flowers already out

The sloe or blackthorn will suddenly burst into flower – its pure white starry blossoms contrasting with its dark and jagged branches. This shrub is more common in the south and east and often forms impenetrable thickets near sea cliffs. The blackish branches and of course the dark soil absorb the maximum amount of heat. Notice how on this shrub, as on other early ones such as forsythia, the buds near the ground open first, benefiting from the radiating warmth.

By the roadside, especially on clay soil, the coltsfoot is in flower. After the neat yellow flowers have faded it hangs its head low as though finished for the season, but really it is just protecting its developing seeds from any bad weather. On a dry bright morning the little seedhead stands up again, opens and allows its fluffy seeds to be dispersed in small batches by the wind. The coltsfoot has its uses; it is one of the main ingredients of herbal tobacco still sold in the old type of herb shops. Its main medicinal use is as a cure for coughs, for which an infusion of both flowers and leaves is made. The ancient Greeks used to smoke the dry leaves through a reed as a cure for asthma. Even the seeds have their uses: being woollier than those of the dandelion, they were used by some country people for stuffing mattresses. Few of us now have the time to try out old herbal remedies but at least the coltsfoot is common enough to experiment with.

Many other wild flowers are beginning to open, including the daisy. Although its main flowering period is April, it blooms intermittently from February onwards.

Some of our prettiest wild flowers are found in the hedgerows and the woods. Here primroses come into flower in clusters, their crinkly rosette of leaves lying flat against a sunny green bank, each stalk bearing a perfect sulphur-coloured sweet-scented flower. Fertilisation of the primrose is a complicated affair with two distinct flower types, pin-eyed and thrum-eyed, depending on the position of the sexual parts. Cross-fertilisation between the two types is necessary to produce viable seed. The primrose is pollinated by insects including bees, but moths must play their part as the flowers are open all night as well as during the day. Often growing with primroses are the wild violets, their flowers peering from beneath heart-shaped leaves. The sweet violet is often given away by its scent, a heady perfume; the dog violet is unscented and smaller. In contrast to the 'shy' violet, the woods may be carpeted with wood anemones with their graceful nodding white flowers and yellow anthers. These take advantage of the light in March before the tree foliage overhead blocks out most of it.

In odd corners a strange-looking plant begins to unfurl, the wild arum or lords-and-ladies. It sends up its bright green sheath often marked with black spots. Later on in the year this plant is even more conspicuous with clusters of orange berries born on its central 'stem', the spadix.

'Spring Poppy Day'

People with their noses to the ground know how one month or season merges imperceptibly into the next. At this time of year nature plays strange tricks, stop-go tactics. One can feel desperate when all development comes to a halt although the calendar races on. Some plants will stand still in a chilly spell, their development arrested until the weather improves. Others push on regardless – for

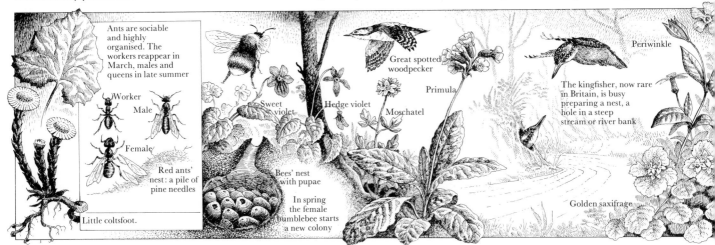

Ants are sociable and highly organised. The workers reappear in March, males and queens in late summer

Worker

Male

Female

Red ants' nest: a pile of pine needles

Little coltsfoot.

Bees' nest with pupae

In spring the female bumblebee starts a new colony

Sweet violet

Hedge violet

Moschatel

Great spotted woodpecker

Primula

The kingfisher, now rare in Britain, is busy preparing a nest, a hole in a steep stream or river bank

Periwinkle

Golden saxifrage

Red dead-nettle

plant which flowers from February until well into October. One can see it at its best now, before other plants smother it with lusher vegetation. The flower is more purple than red and has a rather pungent smell when the leaves are crushed. Like so many of our common plants it was used for medicine years ago, before doctors' prescriptions. The leaves were thought to be very effective in stopping blood clotting.

The red dead-nettle is one of several 'dead-nettles' in the family Labiatae, identified by their unusually square stems, opposite leaves, and flowers with two-lipped petals growing out from the axils of the leaves.

Toads in the pond

In a mild spell, with temperatures above 12°C (53°F), when a shower of rain falls in the afternoon or evening – this is the time to look out for toads. They have been sleeping all winter and at the first sign of spring they emerge from their underground retreats with one intention in mind, to head for water in which to breed. These spring migrations take place at night with the toads always heading for the pond in which they were born. Often they have to cross roads and here the casualties are great; it is sickening to find their squashed corpses littering a country road.

At this time of year the sexes are easily recognised: the female is fat and swollen with eggs while the male has a thin almost hungry look. He also has smoother, more lustrous skin. Note the fingers of the forelegs, which have dark patches of horny skin used to clasp the female when mating. If a male encounters a female en route to the pond, he grasps her there and then and gets carried along.

Once in the pond, as soon as they meet some water-weed the females start laying their eggs, in double rows in a gelatinous cord of spawn; this may be entwined around the weeds and can reach 4·6m (15ft) in length. As the eggs emerge from the female, the male clasps her tight and fertilises them with sperm, making

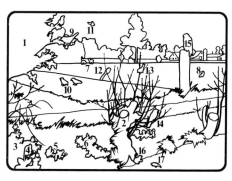

March *1. Sloe   2. Ash tree stump   3. Wood anemone   4. Primula auricula   5. Wood sorrel 6. Lesser celandine   7. Roe deer on winter rye 8. Hare   9. Chiff-chaff   10. Carrion crows 11. Magpie   12. Long-tailed tit   13. Willow tit 14. Redwing   15. Buzzard   16. Frog   17. Great crested newt*

pumping movements with his body. Frogs and toads often breed in the same pond but the toad prefers the deeper parts with plenty of weed.

Apart from the common toad we have another, the natterjack, which is now quite rare. It used to be widely distributed on sandy heathland in the south and all along our coasts where there are damp dune slacks. Now it has lost its specialised habitat. The natterjack only survives in any numbers along the coasts of East Anglia, Lancashire and Cumbria. It is an attractive amphibian, smaller than the common toad, with a yellow stripe down its back; it likes to dig, and then lays its eggs in shallow pools which dry up before the tadpoles can fully develop.

The natterjack toad is protected by law under the 1975 Conservation of Wild Creatures and Wild Plants Act, so this species and its spawn should be left well alone; it has enough problems to deal with, including encroachment on to its habitat by holiday camps!

Sticklebacks

Once I kept nine sticklebacks in my aquarium, two females and seven males. Knowing that these small fish built nests, I knew my 'tiddlers' would give a lot of interest, but of course things worked out differently from what I expected. Within a day, one of the males had driven all the other fish into hiding amongst the weeds. He made most of the tank his territory and to advertise it he displayed his full nuptial dress – bright red underparts and a beautiful blue and green sheen on his sides. The red colour served as a warning to his fellows to keep well away. Scientists call this a sign stimulus, the red breast of the robin being another example.

Nowadays many ponds and streams are so badly polluted that even the hardy stickleback is not that common. Also many of us prefer not to catch and keep wild creatures. Some excellent television films show intimate details

instance during a particularly cold, long-drawn-out spring I suddenly noticed specks of grey-green vegetation on a bare part of the garden, and found these were young poppy seedlings brave enough to sprout. In my diary I wrote 'Spring Poppy Day' which sounds like a national holiday but to me just marked one of the landmarks of spring.

The lesser celandine needs only a little warm sun for its glossy yellow flowers to open. Since this plant first appeared in January it has been gathering strength and growing fast, by means of runners which now and again send down tiny bulb-like growths called bulbils. The celandine has sensitive flowers: they close up before rain, never open before nine o'clock in the morning, even on bright days, and by five in the evening are shut up tight for the night.

Towards the end of the flowering period the plant can look sad; the flowers often fade white, then the whole plant shrivels up, only the bunch of tubers underneath the ground surviving.

Along sheltered hedgerow banks one also finds the red dead-nettle, an attractive little

The growth of the common frog, from spawn to tadpole to adult. For a picture of the warty-skinned toad, see the April chapter

March

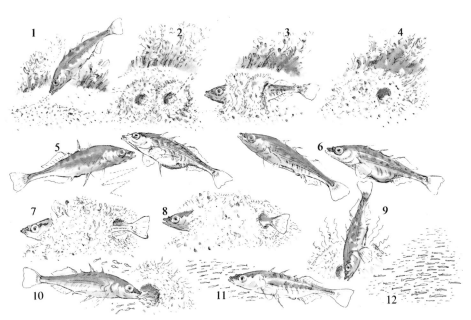

1   *The male stickleback makes a small pile of sand or mud particles*

2   *On this he puts two circles of plant particles, sticking them together with a secretion*

3   *The stickleback creeps through the rings (see dotted line on picture 2) and lifts them up vertically so that they rest on top of each other. Thus he forms the beginning of his tunnel*

4   *The tunnel is finished and well hidden with fragments of plant material*

5   *The male approaches the egg-laden female. He swims his zigzag dance (see dotted line) and shoots backwards and forwards repeatedly, then also swims up and down vertically*

6   *After the change of dance ritual, the female follows the male*

7   *She is lured into the tunnel, the safe place for her to deposit her eggs*

8   *The male fertilises the eggs*

9   *He fans a fresh stream of water over the eggs*

10   *He marshals his straying youngsters back to the safety of the nest*

11   *Already less colourful than he was, he stays on guard with the young*

12   *The young swim their own way. Next year they too will be breeding*

chaff' sounds. I have heard it start with 'chiff-chaff-chaff, chiff-chaff-chaff' and end with 'chaff-chiff-chiff'. Between these two sounds are sometimes a few low muttered notes which come as light relief.

Birds can produce arresting sounds in more ways than by opening their beaks and singing. Take our great and lesser spotted woodpeckers, handsome black, white and red birds. At this time of the year the woods may suddenly resound as they drum on a hollow branch with their strong beaks. They do have a voice, but find 'drumming' a more efficient way of advertising themselves over a large area. The snipe also drums, but this time the sound is produced by the play of wind over tail feathers. You may be fortunate enough to see a pair of snipe circle over the marshes; suddenly one will dive down obliquely, producing the drumming sound, then rise up again, calling 'yuk-yuk-yuk until it regains its former level.

Courtship display

Of course song and sounds may make up only

Willow warbler

Chiff-chaff

part of an elaborate courtship display. You only have to walk through your local park to see ducks performing. Male mallards have had their glossy green heads and chestnut breasts since late autumn. A group may settle on the water and with their heads held high call a thin piping 'iiiie'. Suddenly three ducks will fly fast over the treetops, two males eagerly pursuing a female who tries to avoid their advances by deliberately braking in mid-air. More often than not the female is forced down to water, where the males display the black and white feathers of their rumps before mating with her in quick succession.

The coot is another water bird to look out for. At this time of the year it is particularly aggressive and two males may be seen scurrying over the water towards each other, their necks straining forward, their feathers puffed up to make themselves look as frightening as possible to their opponent.

Closer to home, the resident house sparrows will be more active than usual. The male impresses the female by hopping round and

of animal life, though watching a film cannot be anything like as good as seeing the real thing. For a child any encounter with an animal is special, even necessary. You can learn more about aggression, affection, dominance etc, by your own observations than by reading a host of books or watching endless films.

The two species present in Britain are the three-spined stickleback (*Gasterosteus aculeatus*) and the smaller nine-spined stickleback (*Pungitius pungitius*); this fish likes brackish water with plenty of weeds and, unlike its relative, builds its nest clear of the bottom in dense vegetation.

Calls and songs

A winter walk can be a silent, almost religious experience. Suddenly the stillness is interrupted by a robin or a wren angrily proclaiming its winter territory. Then once again everything lapses into almost perfect silence.

As the days lengthen through February and

March other birds start to call, familiar old favourites like the thrush who will one mild day sing loud and clear from the top of a tree its repeated phrases 'marietje, marietje, marietje'. In woods and gardens, bands of blue tits give their excitable trill calls, 'tsee-tseee-tsu-tsuhuhu'. You can also make out the great tit by its louder and more rasping call, with many variations on a sawing rhythm of 'tietsju-tietsju-tietsju'.

These resident birds are joined in March by the first influx of spring migrants which add their own refined and varied music. One of my favourites is the willow warbler, an inconspicuous greenish-yellow bird which overwinters in Africa. Once recognised, its song is not easily forgotten; it consists of a rippling warble, short, sweet and sometimes plaintive, which gathers strength only to end softly with a delicate 'soeiete-soeiete'. The chiff-chaff looks very like the willow warbler and lives in similar habitats; perhaps it prefers trees to bushes but anyway it is hardly distinguishable from its close relative. The real difference is the song, made up of various combinations of 'chiff-

round chirping loudly, wings drooping down
and tail raised high.

A splendid courtship display combining
sound, colour and graceful movement is shown
by the great crested grebe. This beautiful water
bird served as a model of behaviour for
Sir Julian Huxley, who described it fully in his
famous monograph in 1914. You don't have to
be a specialist to appreciate the grebe's
performance. It is quite a common water bird
on lakes and large ponds, ven within our city
boundaries.

Some early butterflies

It is an exciting time for the entomologist, who
like his insects is now coming out of winter
retreat. Many insects overwinter in the pupal or
egg stage but some manage to survive as adults.
Among these are the ladybirds and lacewings.
Both are beneficial to man as they consume
enormous numbers of garden aphids. The most
spectacular 'early risers' are the butterflies:
some of our most handsome ones overwinter as
adults, and most of these belong to one

Red admiral butterfly

Small tortoiseshell   *Brimstone*

butterfly tribe, the *Vanessids*. These include
the red admiral, peacock, small tortoiseshell
and comma. The odd one out is the sulphur-
yellow brimstone, which belongs with the
cabbage whites in the family Pieridae.

These butterflies may choose a number of
different sites in which to hibernate: the red
admiral likes hollow trees, the comma exposed
branches or a pile of dead leaves, and the small
tortoiseshell gives itself away in spring by
fluttering frantically against a dusty window
pane – garden sheds appear to be a favourite
winter retreat for this species. The brimstone
retreats deep into an evergreen bush.

The colours of butterflies may please us but
have a variety of functions – as means of
identification between species, as camouflage
or even as a warning signal to predators. The
butterflies mentioned all owe their colours to
pigments manufactured from waste products of
their body metabolism. The yellow pigment of
the brimstone is called xanthopteryn, while the
red and brown pigments of the *Vanessids* are
called ommochromes.

Coots may now be in aggressive mood

Pollard willows

March

Flowering willows

The willows deserve a section away from the other flowering trees. Of our nineteen native species, many come into flower at this time. The most obvious is the pussy willow (*Salix caprea*), which grows as a thick bush 1·8–4·5m (6–15ft) high in mature hedgerows and woods. As with poplars, the male and female flowers are borne on different trees; the showier golden-yellow catkins are the male flowers, one of the most familiar signs of spring. The female catkins are silky and a silver colour. The common sallow (*Salix cinera*) grows in damper situations; one can see it forming dense bushes alongside railway tracks. The catkins of both trees provide the church with 'palm' for Palm Sunday.

Two other willows are worth looking out for. The purple willow (*Salix purpurea*) grows as a tall bush 1·8–3m (6–10ft) high near fresh water. It has beautiful neat male catkins, their scales tipped with purple. In contrast, the creeping willow is quite tiny, a compact little shrub of 15–31cm (6–12in), and grows in the dampish slacks behind sand dunes. Its fat catkins are a greenish-yellow colour.

Willows are pollinated by insects and for the entomologist provide an oasis of activity. Queen bumblebees are the most frequent visitors. Apart from the common familiar 'bumblebee', confusingly called the buff-tailed bumblebee (*Bombus terrestris*), three others are commonly seen buzzing around:

1. *Bombus jonellus* (colour sequence: yellow-black-yellow-yellow-black-white)
2. *Bombus pratorum* (colour sequence: black-yellow-black-yellow-black-orange)
3. *Bombus agrorum* (yellow/brown thorax with narrow alternating bands of yellow/brown and black on the abdomen)

The willows provide these queens with a rich early supply of pollen and nectar, on which they form their new colonies. In their company one finds another group of bees, the solitary bees called *Andrena*. These look quite like honeybees but have rougher hairs and a more flattened abdomen, and are particularly common in our southern counties, especially on light, sandy soils, where they dig their burrows.

Willows may also at times be swarming with flies, rather elegant little creatures with dark spots to their wings. These are of a type called *Sepsis*, a member of a small family of flies which appear to have an unnecessarily complicated courtship – the males have a special clasping organ and display to the females, who lure them on with an aphrodisiac odour. Though the adult flies are attractive, the larvae have less elegant habits, feeding on dung and carrion especially in a semi-liquid state.

Another common fly is the yellow dung fly (*Scatophaga stercoraria*). From March onwards you can see groups of golden-yellow hairy males sitting on cow pats waiting for the females, which are much more soberly clad. When you walk by they angrily buzz off, only to resume

Buff-tail bumblebee

Honeybee

'Carder bee' (bombus agrorum)

Bumblebee (bombus praetorum)

their positions immediately you have passed. The life of these flies revolves around a cow pat; they mate on it and lay their eggs in it, their larvae feed on it and pupate beneath it. The adult flies are carnivorous and a fresh cow pat provides a constant supply of food – in the form of other flies that are attracted to the dung to feed or lay their eggs. As a footnote, these flies have the nasty habit of being cannibalistic when food is scarce.

An ancient British tree

It is easy enough to drive along a country lane glancing at the hedgerow trees, dark branches against a dull grey sky, finding nothing in particular to catch the eye – but this apparent monotony is deceptive; you only have to get out and stretch your legs to see something fresh. We have already mentioned the hazel and alder. It is worth having a second look at the alder, a generally dark tree but at this time of year wearing its lightest costume of long

White willow

dangling red catkins, the male flowers which shed a mass of yellow pollen. The female catkins are quite different, round and looking like miniature pine cones.

During the Atlantic Period, approximately 4,000 years ago when Britain was isolated from continental Europe, the weather was mild and very wet and the alder was much commoner than it is today, flourishing on lower ground. Alders have two main requirements: plenty of water and a fertile soil; remember this and it is not difficult to find an alder tree. They grow alongside streams and rivers, often to the exclusion of other trees, and where the river has worn away the bank you may see the thin red roots of the alder swaying in the current. Other habitats for alders are the upland areas of Wales and north-west Scotland, where dwarf trees hug the hillsides, watered by mountain streams. But their last real stronghold is undoubtedly the Norfolk Broads, where alder carrs form thick bushy islands, a real jungle of trees, bushes and flowering plants.

Poplars and willows are closely related, the obvious difference in March being the catkins: those of the poplars are long and dangling while the willows' are more rounded and erect. We only have three kinds of native poplar trees, the aspen, the grey poplar and the black poplar, and we should be proud of them because they are becoming rare, ousted by more vigorous and commercially viable hybrid varieties.

Both the aspen and the grey poplar have catkins like little tassels 7–10cm (3–4in) long. Those of the black poplar are dark red and if one is fortunate enough to come across this tree

The growth of a fish, here a pike

Larva; on its first day it lives on its egg's yolk-sac

After a few days it is more developed and swims freely

At around four months old

The pike is one of the first fish to mate, doing so in March even though the water temperature is still low

Some birds have already paired. The female long-eared owl is even sitting on her eggs. The male brings food for her

Courting

Diverting an enemy

The peewit is the noisiest bird in the fields when alarmed and will make mock attacks on potential enemies

The peewit has laid her eggs too, any taken by a predator will be replaced

is an impressive sight. Unfortunately it is something of a rarity. A recent survey found only one site where male and female trees grew close enough to set seed. One reason for this is unfair sexual discrimination by humans. In East Anglia, where the black poplar was once quite common, mainly male trees were planted; the female tree produces large quantities of fluffy seeds in early summer, which upset East Anglian strawberry growers as the fluff sticks to the ripe fruit, making it unfit for market.

It is sad to see the decline of this impressive tree when the country is being covered with plantations of Canadian and Black Italian poplars; these look pleasant enough in their trimline avenues, but they lack the stature of the black 'giants' that used to dot the floodplains of our eastern counties.

Night music

One of the most haunting sounds of early spring is an owl calling across the chilly night sky. You don't have to live in the country to hear it – when resident in the 'big city' I used to see and hear tawny owls each spring. They seemed oblivious to people, noise and traffic. Often a pair would settle on a chimney pot or roof to perform their double act. The male's call is a hollow whistle made up of three or four short sounds: 'oe . . . oe . . . oe . . .' followed by

Tawny owl   *Barn owl*

a more continuous 'oe-oe-oe-oe-oe'. I used to mimic this call using cupped hands. It took a while to perfect, but it must have sounded authentic, because the owls would swivel their heads and look down at me in a curious way before flying off to an adjacent roof. The female's call is quite different, 'tu-wiet, ti-wiet', alternating with the male's to make the generalised owl-sound of 'to-wiet, tu-woe'.

A much more secretive bird of the north and Scotland is the long-eared owl. In remote woodland you can hear its groaning 'oew . . . oew . . . oew . . .'. It may not sound very loud but on a still night its plaintive notes can be heard over half a mile away.

For such a small bird, the little owl, less than 23cm (9in) tall, has a strong and varied repertoire, which goes something like this: a loud ringing 'kwiew, kwiew, kwiew', a quieter 'pioe, pioe, pioe' and sometimes a frantic 'kwif-kwif-kwif'. I once found the related scops owl in a bird trap in France. I picked it up quite gently but it scolded me with a sound like an electric typewriter! The little owl is the most diurnal of our owls and can be seen calling from gateposts and dry-stone walls in the afternoon and early evenings.

As to the barn owl, the nearest description I can give of its call is an eerie blood-curdling screech, but it also hisses, snorts and barks.

You could say an 'owl is an owl is an owl' because the name is very similar in most European languages: in German *eule*, Dutch *uil*, Danish *ugle* and Swedish *ugla*. In Latin the name is *ulula* derived from the verb *ulare*, to howl.

More weather

One often has the wrong impression about the usual weather for a particular time of year. December is the darkest month, yet some Decembers are mild. On the other hand one always has great expectations for March; you notice the increased strength of the sun, then

feel let down by days of strong cold winds. Wintry conditions can stretch into March – this happened especially in 1947, 1963 and 1979. But we can count ourselves lucky compared with the long, hard Napoleonic winters of 1775–1850, which lasted well into spring.

While the sun is getting stronger, the barometer may register little change from the preceding month. The same anticyclone that brought hard frosts in February may give a mild dry period in March. This can be pleasant but the farmer may suffer; a prolonged drought at this time can lead to erosion, with loss of valuable topsoil.

Extremes in temperatures are common now. The earth can be warmed up by the sun, then a cloudless night will bring ground frost. Dark earth absorbs a lot of heat and radiates little, but sand, usually of a light colour, warms up very quickly; the reason is that sand crystals have a low specific heat and a low conductivity. Here only the top level is affected and a few centimetres down you will find it is cold and wet.

Late falls of snow can be dazzling white, the strong light of March being reflected from it. The upper layer will melt and then freeze again during the night. In this sort of weather notice the long icicles forming along your gutters, formed by the alternate melting and freezing of snow.

April

'March borrows its last three days from April' is an old saying, indicating that the weather of one month may slip into the other virtually unnoticed. But if the weather should deceive us in that way, the very name 'April' comes from the Latin word for 'opening' and the first day of April is given a traditional opening in many European countries. The origins of All Fools' Day are obscure:

The first April, some do say,
Is set apart for All Fools' Day:
But why the people call it so,
Nor I, nor they themselves do know.

Several interesting explanations have been offered for the strange custom of involving a victim in a harmless practical joke. The most plausible suggestion is that 1 April was the final day of the eight-day festivities which marked the New Year when it used to begin on 25 March. A clue to the mood of 1 April comes from a condescending quote of 1766: 'It became a day of extraordinary mirth and festivity, especially among the lower sort, who are apt to pervert and to make bad use of Institutions, which at first might be very laudable in themselves.' Another writer saw the fault in Noah for sending a dove out of the ark before the flood waters had subsided on the first day of the month: 'Anybody who was liable to forget the incident was punished by being sent on a fruitless errand similar to the ineffectual message upon which the bird was sent by the patriarch.'

Whatever the origins, sending an unsuspecting victim on a fool's errand has long been the challenge of the day. In the north of England, the April Fool is a 'gowk' (from the old Norse word for simpleton), and in Scotland the date is Huntigowk Day. In Cheshire the fool is a 'gawby', and elsewhere in the north he is an April noddy, so called from the tropical tern of the same name which earned a reputation among early mariners for being particularly stupid. One nicety widely observed is that a truce is called at noon: the joke is then on anyone who fails to observe it.

Budding kingcup

April Fools' Day past and gone –
You're the fool for thinking on.

This rule may have tested the skill of the practical joker in setting a time-limit on his attempts to outwit his fellows, or it may simply have served to safeguard the gullible from excessive leg-pulling. Whatever else, it let everyone at last get on with the proper business of the day, and every schoolmaster has thanked it for saving the day from total disruption.

The blossoming of Spring

In most years April is the first month we really see the blossoming of spring. Primroses only now begin to flower in any number, as do lesser celandines, wood anemones and some of the early violets. In shady places it is the time to look out for the delicate wood sorrel. Much less likely to be overlooked is the striking marsh marigold or kingcup, making a brilliant show of gold in marshy meadows, ditches and damp woods. The masses of golden-yellow, buttercup-like flowers cluster on robust stems standing up to 46cm (18in) high. The flowers are unusual in lacking petals: a close look shows that they have from 5 to 8 sepals that merely resemble petals. Their buds were once gathered as a substitute for capers, the buds of a Mediterranean flower used for pickling and in sauce. By now the first dandelions are adding another splash of colour to roadside verges, along with the small white flowers of the chickweed or common mouse-ear and the different sorts of dead-nettle.

In the garden, the crocuses are often the target of a strange form of vandalism. The house sparrows descend on them and tear the petals to pieces, much to the consternation of householders, for most of whom these are the first colourful flowers of the year, the only ones in the garden as yet. There has so far been no satisfactory explanation for this behaviour and it would repay careful study. Yellow crocuses sometimes seem to fare worse than purple ones and perhaps the sparrows have a taste for the saffron in their stigmas. But it is hard to see that they actually eat anything – more often it just looks like wanton destruction. It would be more excusable if they were using petals to decorate their nests, as some of the bowerbirds of New Guinea do, but this seems highly unlikely. In some places house sparrows antagonise gardeners further in April by stripping the stems of plants like the hop, and making off with beakfuls of fibres which they weave into their untidy nests.

For many people, the most conspicuous and

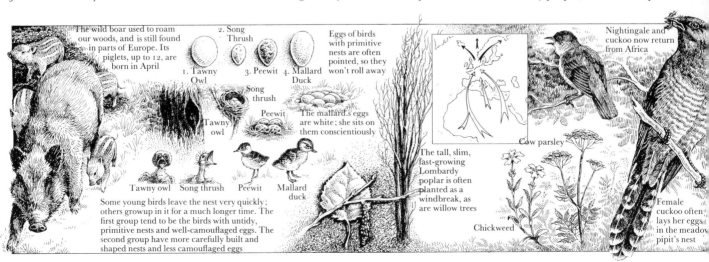

The wild boar used to roam our woods, and is still found in parts of Europe. Its piglets, up to 12, are born in April

2. Song Thrush

1. Tawny Owl

3. Peewit

4. Mallard Duck

Eggs of birds with primitive nests are often pointed, so they won't roll away

Song thrush

Tawny owl

Peewit

The mallard's eggs are white; she sits on them conscientiously

Tawny owl   Song thrush   Peewit   Mallard duck

Some young birds leave the nest very quickly; others grow up in it for a much longer time. The first group tend to be the birds with untidy, primitive nests and well-camouflaged eggs. The second group have more carefully built and shaped nests and less camouflaged eggs

The tall, slim, fast-growing Lombardy poplar is often planted as a windbreak, as are willow trees

Cow parsley

Chickweed

Nightingale and cuckoo now return from Africa

Female cuckoo now lays her eggs in the meadow pipit's nest

welcome feature of April is the bud-burst on trees, and for those prepared to take the trouble, or even blessed with a good memory, it is interesting to compare the timing of this from year to year. The first common tree to come into leaf is the horse chestnut, sporting its fat sticky buds in March, and leafing in early April. The timing of leafing in any year depends very much on temperature, so that trees in the south of England can be well ahead of their counterparts in the north. Altitude or aspect also affect temperature, so a rise in height of only 30·5m (100ft), or a north-facing slope, may retard leafing by several days.

In many cases, leaves look very different when they first emerge from later on in the summer. Beech leaves, for instance, are succulent and a translucent light green at the outset, but as summer progresses they get opaque and tough – almost leathery by the time autumn comes round. This change in texture is due to the build-up of tannins, chemical compounds which represent the tree's natural insecticide, a protection in particular against defoliating caterpillars. As the tannin levels increase, the leaves become more indigestible and unappetising, so that caterpillars find it more difficult to grow properly on them. The same is true of oak leaves, and there is even some evidence that late-nesting tits, which feed their nestlings on multitudes of oak-leaf-eating caterpillars, may in turn suffer from the tannin loads in the caterpillars and have a harder time raising their young than tits which nested earlier in the season when there was less tannin in the food chain. New leaves of some oaks, in common with sycamores and poplars, are reddish-brown in colour, and only later turn typically green.

If we compare the leaf-burst of poplars with other roadside trees, such as horse chestnuts, beeches or limes, we find one striking difference. Nearly all the individuals in a row of poplars come into leaf at the same time, whereas individuals of these other species show great variation; a particular chestnut might leaf ten days before another not far off, and the difference will be maintained year after year. The explanation lies in the way the different trees reproduce themselves. Poplars are nearly always propagated from cuttings; a branch planted in the ground sends out roots and a new tree develops. A hundred cuttings will produce a hundred trees identical to the one from which they came, with the same leafing time. Chestnuts, beeches and limes, by contrast, grow from seeds which have a 'father' and 'mother', each with its own ancestral line. As such, they show the same range of variation we would expect in children, with early and late developers among the offspring.

Birds burst into activity

If April is wet, and earthworms are abundant on the surface of the ground, the bulk of the

Lime flower (enlarged)

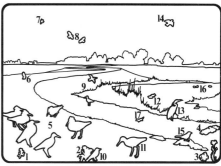

April *1. Daisy 2. Dandelion 3. Cuckoo flower 4. Kingcup 5. Ruff and reeve (female) 6. Short-eared owl 7. Snipe in courting flight 8. Peewits 9. Black-tailed godwit 10. Meadow pipit 11. Redshank 12. Shoveler duck 13. Grey heron 14. Skylark 15. Blue-headed wagtail 16. Coots 17. Weasel*

blackbird and thrush population gets nesting under way. Dry spells may slow them down but since they potentially have one of the longest breeding seasons of any European bird – March to July – they can usually ride out one bad month in the hope of better breeding conditions in the next. If by midsummer the ground is dry and earthworms scarce, they stop breeding early, but if the soil remains moist they carry on longer. A wet April also helps their nest-building, since both blackbirds and song thrushes line their nests with mud. The thrush uses a smooth layer of it, sometimes mixed with fibres of rotten wood, moistened with saliva. If mud is not locally abundant she may use dung instead. This internal plastering enables us to distinguish at a glance a thrush's nest from a blackbird's, in which the mud is

Song thrush and young

April

Common mouse-ear or chickweed – for a recipe see page 37

usually sandwiched between an outer shell of grasses, moss and rootlets, and an inner cup of dry grasses for the eggs.

Just as the prevailing weather influences the behaviour and the nesting timetable of blackbirds, so it affects the arrival time of our summer migrants. In many years, late March will already have seen the first landfalls of chiff-chaffs, wheatears and sand martins, and in favourable years a few blackcaps, tree pipits and willow warblers may have joined them. Swallows arrive around mid-April, and house martins and swifts about two weeks later. Nightjars, which look a bit like swifts but are actually more closely related to owls, also arrive in late April to early May. Country folk used to believe the nightjar used its great gaping mouth to milk goats which then went

blind, and called it 'goatsucker' for its pains. The belief is unfounded, however, and the nightjar's bill is actually a beautifully adapted insect trap.

Along with swallows, eagerly anticipated April arrivals include the nightingale and the cuckoo. Most children used to learn a variation of the verse:

> *The cuckoo comes in April, he sings his song in May*
> *In the middle of June he changes his tune, in July he flies away.*

It is really only the male cuckoo that everyone knows so well, because only he makes that famous call. The female's reply, a series of bubbling notes, is not nearly so well known. Observant people used to associate the arrival

of these celebrated migrants with plants that flowered around the same time. Thus cow parsley is sometimes called nightingale herb in Holland, while in England the lady's smock also goes by the name of cuckoo flower. April likewise sees the flowering of that bizarre plant the cuckoo-pint, perhaps better known as lords-and-ladies. The tiny male and female flowers cluster in dense whorls on a fleshy spike, enclosed by a cowl-like sheath – hence the local name parson-in-the-pulpit. Flies are attracted into the sheath by the smell of decomposing manure exuded by the flowers, and are trapped inside by downward-pointing hairs till they have carried out pollination, escaping dusted with pollen only when the sheath withers. Cuckoo-pint is common in hedgerows and copses where it is often more conspicuous once the central spike is covered in bright orange-red highly poisonous berries.

One last phenomenon which popular nature-lore has associated by name with the arrival of cuckoos is 'cuckoo-spit', those blobs of white froth found on the leaves and stems of many plants and trees in the spring. This is the work of little bugs called froghoppers or, more aptly, spittlebugs. By expelling air through a sticky secretion on their abdomens the sluggish young (nymphs) make a lather for protection against desiccation and, perhaps, against enemies as well.

Amphibians and reptiles

Late in March or early in April, frogs, toads and newts make their annual pilgrimage to water in order to spawn. This is something they cannot avoid doing for, despite all their adaptations to life on land, amphibians have not yet evolved an egg or larva that can live out of water. Frogs and toads emerge from hibernation and set out to find a particular pond or ditch, probably the one they were born in, and every year that one and no other is the unswerving goal, even if it is a mile away from their winter lair. Exactly how they find it is something of a mystery. Travelling by day and night, sometimes for up to ten days, the toad ignores other apparently suitable ponds along the way till it has found the right one. The natterjack, a toad, now rare in Britain, seems less fussy in its choice of ponds, so usually travels shorter distances to spawn.

Common frog

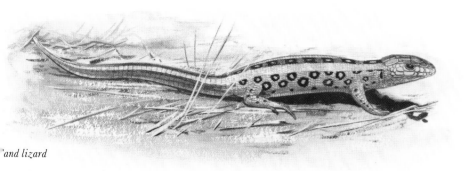

Sand lizard

Any one pond can be a mecca for hundreds of toads and frogs in the spring, and when they arrive the frantic business begins of securing a mate against all the competition. Each female finds herself beset by hordes of eager suitors, and is often seen with several males clinging to her for dear life; nor is the description in a sense exaggerated, for on the ability of a male to hold tight and ultimately fertilise the female's eggs depends the continuity of his own family line. For the females, egg-laying is a momentous task, whether it be the newt's 200–300 single eggs, or the toad's string of up to 7,000. The males may sire more than one batch of eggs by seeking a second female after they have fertilised the eggs of the first.

The males, whether frogs or toads, help to attract females by croaking in the evening. You can get a male toad to utter his high-pitched croak by gently pressing him on the back, a response that can be explained in the following way. Male toads in the mood for mating have the inclination to clasp on to each and every other toad that passes, regardless of sex; so many mistakes are made and males often find themselves mounted by other males. The victim of mistaken identity can then point out the other's error with a croak. In May and June you can elicit the same response from croaking edible frogs, if you are lucky enough to find one.

Birds have long enjoyed the benefits of protection in this country, but amphibians and reptiles have, till recently, been poor relations. This does not mean that their numbers have kept up; their population levels would long ago have given justifiable cause for concern. It speaks for the relative attractiveness of different animals. If rats ever became rare it would be hard to mobilise public opinion in their favour, and toads are scarcely better off. In actual fact, our amphibians and reptiles have been under siege from a host of different pressures for many years. Unlike birds, they cannot fly away at a moment's notice when danger threatens, and if their ancestral pond should be rendered uninhabitable or drained, it may be a long way to the next suitable one, assuming one could be found at all.

Loss and change of habitat have, indeed, been the main problems for these animals, as for so many others. In many places, like East

Edible frog

Natterjack toad

Crested newt

Anglia, serious declines in populations of the common frog date from the 1940s with the widespread reclamation of wetlands in the wartime 'dig-for-victory' campaign launched to boost agricultural production at home. The intensification of agriculture has continued up to the present day, with far-reaching effects on wildlife of all kinds. For amphibians, changes like the massive shift to cereal-growing in the low-lying (and once marshy) eastern counties have taken their toll. Farmyard ponds have also become largely a thing of the past, and farmland itself is poorly endowed nowadays with tracts of water. Field ponds have always been specially favoured breeding sites of the common toad which prefers to spawn in deeper water than the natterjack and frog; it has suffered seriously from their gradual disappearance.

In the 1950s and 1960s, the decline may have been aggravated, at least locally, by the widespread introduction of insecticides like DDT and Dieldrin, frogs proving more susceptible than toads. Though the use of these highly toxic chemicals is now banned, many persist in the environment. Other ponds became heavily enriched with fertilisers and sewage effluents, and some of the algal blooms that resulted were detrimental to toads especially. In the post-war years, herbicides also became an increasingly important weapon in the farmer's arsenal, though their effects on amphibious populations are little known. In some cases their application may even have helped frogs in ponds, by allowing edible algae to flourish at the expense of large plants.

But there are other hazards. Hundreds of frogs and toads en route to their breeding grounds are annually run over by motor vehicles. I read of one public-minded citizen who devoted hours of his time in March and April to helping toads to safety over a busy stretch of road near the pond on which all of them were converging. Most local toad populations do not, however, enjoy the assistance of such Good Samaritans. The cumulative effect of all these pressures has had drastic effects on some traditional frog and toad strongholds. In some parts of the Fens, for example, declines of 99 per cent in the numbers of the common frog have been recorded since the 1940s.

Caring for endangered species
Against this gloomy picture, however, there have been a number of notable improvements in the last decade. Since the late 1960s, when conservation became a household word, various steps – voluntary and legislative – have been taken to stem the decline of our amphibians and reptiles. Creation of special nature reserves has helped to safeguard key breeding sites for the rarer species, but perhaps the greatest, and yet most unsung, revolution has been the provision by the public of garden ponds. These have become increasingly

April

Common toad

important refuges for spawning frogs, as well as smooth newts. A choice garden pond, even quite a small one, can to the owner's delight attract hundreds of breeding smooth newts in the spring. So some common frogs and smooth newts have staged a successful retreat from their beleaguered traditional countryside haunts, finding sanctuary in the growing popularity of suburban garden ponds.

Farmers, too, are reconsidering the advantages of ponds in the wake of the alarming drought of 1976 which posed such a serious threat to livestock. In one small parish I know, two extensive new ponds were excavated in the aftermath of the drought, and although one has since been stocked with rainbow trout (not a friend of tadpoles), both may turn out to be ports in a storm for dispossessed toads and frogs.

If the 1976 drought was an ill wind that might blow our amphibians some good, it dealt a serious blow to the status of the smooth snake and sand lizard, our two rarest reptiles. They are restricted to dry woodlands, heaths and dunes, now mostly accorded Reserve status, in the southern counties, especially Hampshire and Dorset. Both like to live in areas of mature heather (ling), a lot of which was destroyed by uncontrollable heath fires in that tinder-dry summer. Many animals died outright, others fell prey to predators in the more exposed habitat that followed the fires, and yet others must have been forced into less suitable habitats where they could not thrive. As a result, several of the locally important reptile populations suffered badly.

Even if conditions for heath regeneration are good for some years we cannot expect the reptiles to stage a rapid recovery. Frogs, with their immense reproductive powers, were quick to exploit the new opportunities afforded by suburban ponds, but reptiles, like birds, lay quite small clutches of eggs, and cannot make good heavy losses quickly. The sand lizard lays up to 12 eggs at a time, the smooth snake 9 or 10. Their preferred mature heather habitat is also a slow developer, and will take many years to restore itself. Ironically, smooth snakes once fed chiefly on sand lizards, so it is hard to protect one without contributing to the demise of the other.

New laws have been passed to safeguard these endangered reptiles, as well as the natterjack toad. All three receive protection under the Wild Creatures and Wild Plants Act of 1975, making it an offence even to touch or disturb one, far less kill one, except under licence. Our other scarce lowland amphibian, the crested newt, may also be added to this protected list. In the meantime this, our most handsome newt, is being kept under close surveillance, with research proceeding on its status and distribution. Equivalent measures are also being taken in other European countries where amphibians and reptiles face similar pressures.

For the time being, our most familiar amphibian, the common frog, seems to be holding its own, and for the foreseeable future children should be able to continue that favourite time-honoured pastime of bringing a jar with a *little* bit of frogspawn into the house

or classroom to watch it develop into miniature frogs. As long as the practice never gets out of proportion it is a small price to pay for the respect and interest it gives one for living things.

Unlike toads, which don't break their winter hibernation till late March at the earliest, the frog emerges in February, at least in years when conditions are not extremely cold. Spawning occurs from March to April, and because there is little weed in ponds at this time of year, the familiar clumps of eggs are relatively easy to spot. The female sheds her eggs, up to 3,000 of them, for the male – clasped to her in a limpet-like embrace – to fertilise. At first the eggs sink to the bottom of the pond, but as their protective coat of jelly swells they float to the surface as frogspawn, there to remain buoyant till the tiny gill-breathing larvae, the tadpoles, hatch out at the end of May.

A female toad may lay twice as many eggs as a common frog, extruding them in a long string 2–3m (7–10ft) long so that they become entangled on a water plant. The eggs themselves, black in colour, and the surrounding coat of jelly, are both smaller than those of the frog, and so are harder to find, for all their superior numbers. Natterjacks, like frogs, like to spawn in shallow water, even puddles. They also tolerate brackish water and sometimes breed in dune slacks near the sea. The egg chain, containing up to 4,000 eggs, is somewhat smaller than the common toad's, as befits the natterjack's smaller body size, but the male's rattling croak is much the louder call of the two.

Britain's other amphibious species, not so far mentioned, are the edible frog, marsh frog and palmate newt, a mountain species. Both frogs are natives of western and central Europe and were introduced to Britain, where they live without any special protection in restricted areas in the south-east of England. The edible frog is about the same size as the common frog, but has a greenish back with black spots and a pale green-golden stripe down the backbone. The marsh frog is half as big again, usually dark brown and capable of swallowing not only common frogs but also small mice and nestlings. Both edible and marsh frogs have a later breeding season than our native frog, spawning between mid-May and early June. Then the male edible frog's croak proves to be the loudest of them all, amplified as it is by balloon-like sacs flanking the mouth. For all its imposing size the marsh frog, by comparison, has a puny voice.

Insect activity

When the soil and leaf litter warm up, lots of insects are busy on the surface of the ground. Predatory wolf spiders swarm over grassy meadows, and shieldbugs, so-called from the resemblance of their broad, flattened bodies to

36

Male newt in mating dress

Amphibians differ from reptiles in having no scales, in depositing their eggs in the water, and in their young hatching as larvae. In April they emerge from the mud after hibernation

Small newt

Young newt

Toad tadpole

Toad

Common frog

Toad with string of eggs

Kestrel, which nowadays occasionally breeds in towns

The nightjar, more nearly related to the owls than to the swallow family

The pipistrelle bat (*actual size*), can sometimes be seen flying around street lamps after the moths and other insects attracted by the light

eraldic shields, emerge from hibernation. ne of the commonest, the pied shieldbug *hirus bicolor*, attractively mottled black and ream, feeds on the fruit of white dead-nettle, ut most other species are leaf-green in colour. hey are sometimes called stinkbugs for their istinctive smell, which however is not npleasant.

There are many more Lepidoptera, utterflies and moths, to be seen now, pecially on sunny days. One of the andsomer moths is the orange underwing *rephos parthenias*, which may be found flying igh on the leeside of birch trees. Butterflies ke the small tortoiseshell, peacock and comma ppear as if by magic from hibernation, though w as early as the dazzling yellow papery-inged brimstone.

Among spring insects, we should also ention the diminutive brown groundhoppers he Tetrigidae), similar to grasshoppers but istinguished by the backward extension of a ood', the pronotum (insect equivalent of the reastbone'), which reaches the tip of the odomen. Also unlike grasshoppers they have audible chirp and, as their name suggests, e adapted to more open areas, where they n move unhindered by dense ground cover.

andelions

uring the month of April, on grass verges verywhere, we find the bright yellow andelion shining up. Within a few weeks, the ower heads will give way to fluffy white balls seeds, the 'dandelion clocks': children are ill told that the number of puffs it takes to low away all the seed will give the hour of ay. Without children's help the dandelion is ell enough served by the wind for dispersing e buoyant seeds like parachutes. The success this means of dispersal is evident in the ormous range and adaptability of the plant, hich numbers more than a hundred species in ritain.

Not surprisingly, people have long sought to nd uses for so profuse a weed. The dried root

serves as a chicory substitute, the flower heads for making wine and beer, while the leaves are an interesting, if slightly bitter, addition to a salad. The Belgians and French, in particular, consider dandelion leaves a delicacy, calling the plant 'dent de lion', literally lion's tooth, probably in reference to the saw-edged leaves. They used to seek leaves which had become a bit blanched growing in molehills, and nowadays the cultivators also market blanched leaves. In Britain we have to find soft and tender leaves for ourselves, making sure to avoid plants too near roadsides.

Dandelions – too long despised as 'weeds'

To make a salad, pick a few fresh leaves and, after washing them carefully, dress them with a mixture of 1 dessertspoon of vinegar and 3 of olive oil, a little salt and a finely chopped shallot. Small squares of bread, deep-fried in hot oil and then sprinkled with a little garlic, serve to decorate and improve the salad. The resulting dish is packed with minerals and vitamins.

The finely chopped young leaves of other spring plants like stinging nettles, plantain and chickweed, added to soup or eaten with bread, are likewise recommended for the constitution. More specifically, eating four dandelion leaves a day is supposed to relieve the most persistent constipation, while the milky juice in the root used to be prescribed for liver complaints.

Mashed chickweed!

Even after a severe winter one can find the ubiquitous chickweed (*Stellaria media*) sprouting in parks and gardens. This plant was introduced under the month of January, but I didn't mention then that it makes a nutritious vegetable, occasionally useful at this time of the year when the choice of greens and salad is limited. You can either eat it raw as a salad or

cooked – either way you need a good few handfuls of the stuff, which should be carefully washed and sorted to see it doesn't contain bits of less edible plants and to remove the stringy stems. I prefer it raw with a light oil and vinegar dressing; alternatively it can be boiled in a little water for a short time, then seasoned with salt and pepper, and also a little grated nutmeg if you like it.

Chickweed may not be the most attractive-looking vegetable but it is full of vitamins and is worth persevering with, even though your children may screw up their noses and say 'ugh' in unison. You can always disguise it by mashing it up very fine. The first time I tried it was when visiting friends who had recently moved to the country; it lay limp and straggly in the colander and we all laughed at the 'back-to-nature' movement, but by the end of the week it was accepted quite readily.

Chickweed is also a sensitive barometer if you root a piece in a pot and put it on your window-ledge. When the small white flowers stay open the weather will be fine, and as soon as the flowers close you can expect rain.

Woodland flowers

Like the first summer migrants to arrive, the woodland flowers of April have a special charm and magic, and we welcome them like long-lost friends. Arranged at right angles like the four faces of a clock tower, with a fifth pointed skywards, the green flower heads of the moschatel have earned it the vernacular name of 'town-hall clock'. In damp weather, the flowers give off a subtle, musky smell. The leaves resemble those of the wood anemone, whose carpets of nodding white flowers are to the woodland floor in spring what primroses are to the hedge banks and stream sides. The wood anemone has been described as emerging from the ground like an eastern slave in obeisance, for as the stem stretches itself upright the flower head remains humbly bowed, as if in homage. Less dramatically, country folk called it 'granny's cap' for the same reason! This drooping habit returns on damp days and at night, to protect the pollen, but on fine days the flowers turn skywards, casting caution – and pollen – to the wind. Equally delicate is the wood sorrel, a cousin of the geranium, with its characteristic trefoil leaves and solitary white flowers, finely veined with mauve. It too is highly sensitive to changes in temperature and humidity and can thereby protect itself against the sudden changes of weather that April inflicts. If the day gets too cold or wet, or simply if dusk is approaching, the flower droops and the clover-like leaflets fold up. Town-dwellers can see these responses in common garden flowers like the crocus and winter aconite.

Many of these spring flowers also have different ways of propagating themselves,

Wood sorrel

perhaps because the fickle spring weather may not guarantee fertilisation by insects. Moschatel flowers, for example, should produce berries but they rarely do in Britain, and the plant spreads mainly by an extensive system of underground stems. Wood sorrel and violets are very pretty to look at, but their flowers are little more than that – they rarely or never set seed, as if they had evolved for the

special pleasure of bees and human beholders. Instead, other flowers, inconspicuous, petal-le[ss] and scentless, quietly go about the task of bearing seed later in the year.

A very different looking April flower is Solomon's seal, a member of the lily family. The small bell-shaped flowers, white tipped with green, droop in small clusters along the angled stem. It gets its name from the belief

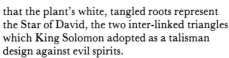

The orange-underwing moth is perfectly camouflaged on a tree trunk when its upper wings are folded over the lower

Moschatel

Dandelions – as a superb design motif! Their roots can be used as a chicory substitute in coffee, the leaves for salad, the flowers for wine or beer

that the plant's white, tangled roots represent the Star of David, the two inter-linked triangles which King Solomon adopted as a talisman design against evil spirits.

There are three common primulas in England. While the greatly beloved sulphur-yellow primrose is a flower of the shade, often hugging steep, sheltered banks, the cowslip, now sadly depleted by modern farming

Shieldbug now emerging from hibernation

Phlox is shooting in our gardens

methods, is most often seen in open fields. The third primula, the oxlip, is found only in dampish woods in south-east England, where it largely replaces the primrose. Like the cowslip, it has a head or 'umbel' of yellow flowers growing out of a strong main stem, distinguishing it from the primrose whose flowers are each borne on an individual, slender stem.

The closely related white, yellow and purple primulas we cultivate in our gardens originated not on the moist woodland floor but mostly on the Alpine mountain ranges of the Old World. One of the loveliest, the least primrose (*Primula minima*), with its rose-pink flowers nestling in small rosettes of leaves, grows on alpine turf, rock ledges and crevices, often at the edge of melting snow, up to 3,000m (10,000ft) in the European Alps. In the marshes of Japan grows the *P. japonica* of our bog gardens, while southern China provides the originals of the indoor pot plants found in thousands of British households. Most spectacular of all, the 1m- (3ft-)high *P. imperialis* is found in the central highlands of Java. Few of us would trade any of these for the unassuming beauty of the primrose, but all the primulas have attributes that endear them to gardeners: some have a very long flowering period, February to May in mild springs; many will multiply readily and rapidly by means of spreading rhizomes.

For many of these perennials, the leaves have an important role to play in building food reserves for the following year, and so they tend to persist for several weeks after the flowers have died, quietly manufacturing sugars in the sunlight of lengthening days. The feather leaves of the wood anemone, the corrugated ones of the primrose, the heart-shaped leaves of

Flowering currant glows deep pink against an April sky – but it is unpopular indoors because of its 'catty' smell

April

the lesser celandine, all work in this way to
ensure the continuing vigour of the plant.
Some, like the wood anemone, store the
products of photosynthesis in an underground
rhizome; others, like the daffodil and bluebell,
in a bulb. A clump of primroses or primulas has
a great mass of roots which 'pull' the leaves a
little deeper into the ground after the flowering
period is over. The incipient buds of next year's
generation of flowers are already present in the
axils of the upper leaves, there to lie safe and
dormant in the depths of the plant till the
following spring. Serious damage to the leaves
before they have had a chance to build up
reserves can, therefore, do more harm to the
plant in the long run than picking the flowers.

In the garden, cultivated daffodils have
larger flowers than their dainty wild cousins
which grow in damp meadows and woods in
England and Wales. Unfortunately wild
daffodils are becoming increasingly rare, not
only because of drainage but because

Sclerotinia tuberosa, *the fungus that grows on the
rhizome of wood anemones*

thoughtless people persist in digging them up
for their gardens. This is inexcusable, especial
as daffodils are so easy to cultivate, and
moreover there are plenty of other flowers to
grace the garden at this time of year without
plundering hedgerows and meadows. To thos
already mentioned, we may add grape
hyacinths, bergenias and scillas, whose azure,
star-shaped flowers grow in the wild on sea
cliffs as spring squill. And already other garde
favourites like the phloxes and delphiniums
may have started sprouting to let us anticipat
future pleasures.

Night frost

On calm, cloudless nights, all the warmth the
earth's surface absorbed during the day can
escape freely by radiation and April frosts can
then be expected. An air frost occurs when the
air temperature is at or below 0°C (32°F). If
the air is saturated with moisture, the air frost
may then be accompanied by hoar frost,
though this is not so common this late in the
year. Like dew, it deposits itself first on surfac
near the ground where cold air has settled, an
the nature of the ground will then determine
how severely it is affected. Anything that
hinders conduction of heat, like the thick mat
of grass on an old lawn, dead vegetation or le
litter, will tend to register the lowest
temperatures on clear nights in spring and
early summer. This was known to the Roman
who exploited the fact in making 'dew ponds'
to trap condensation from the atmosphere.

It is air frost that offers the greatest threat t
plant tissue, while hoar frost may even, in
certain circumstances, provide some protecti
against air frost. Thickly encrusted over the
glass of a cold frame, for example, hoar frost
may prevent heat loss by radiation from insid
and thereby add an extra skin, worth 2°C (35
more than the glass alone could provide.
Moreover, because it settles first on the groun
hoar frost may not extend to foliage a few feet
above where the temperature may remain
above freezing point, a phenomenon fruit
growers have had cause to thank in spring. T
tall trees in old-style orchards were particular
well protected in this way, and only suffered
damage from severe night frosts, but the low,
bush-like trees used in modern orchards are
much more vulnerable.

The vegetable grower may be less lucky tha
the fruit grower. To quote a specific instance,
in 1974 a disastrously late night frost on 1 Jun
wiped out about half of England's potato crop
Long after the event, such frosts leave in their
wake a tell-tale aftermath of brown wilted
leaves and stems. The physical layout of some
places, called frost hollows, makes them
especially prone to frosts. Usually these consis
of low-lying ground with no natural outlet, in
which dense cold air drains from higher up.
One well-known hollow in England is at

Primroses, becoming scarce in some of their old haunts

Clouds with sharp outlines often develop in the cold, relatively dry air of April

Rickmansworth, Hertfordshire, where a natural valley is dammed by a railway embankment. In 1935 the air temperature here fell to −8·3°C (17°F) as late as 17 May.

April showers

Apart from April Fool's Day, the word that everyone associates with April is 'showers', and most of us could more readily describe typical April weather than any other: 'April weather, rain and sunshine together'. If the farmer has been blessed with a dry March for ploughing and sowing, he will dare to hope for the spring rains April usually brings to germinate his seeds.

When April blows his horn,
Tis good for both hay and corn.

The 'horn' is a reference to thunder and the squally showers we associate with this month.

They are frequently heavy, since in spring there is conflict between polar airstreams, still at their coldest after winter, and sun-warmed air rising from the land, ideal conditions for generating towering cumulo-nimbus clouds, periodically disgorging sharp downpours, pelting hailstones or even snow. The sea temperature, though lowest at this time of year, is also relatively warm compared with these Arctic winds, and contributes to the upward air currents and unstable atmospheric conditions that concoct showers.

Spectacular rainbows may form as the sun, gaining in height and intensity with each passing day, breaks through and shines on departing showers. These are less a feature of high summer, at least in the middle hours of the day when the sun is overhead, since rainbows cannot be seen when the sun's altitude is higher than approximately 53°. The refracted light then passes above the head of an

observer on the ground and is invisible to him. Even on days when storm clouds and rainbows are absent, April generally excels as the month of dramatic cloud formations, especially those cauliflower clouds with edges so sharp they look as if they have been cut out.

It would be misleading, however, to think of April as usually a rainy month. Records collected at Kew Observatory from 1916 to 1950 show that the average rainfall in April was 4·6cm (1·8in), which made it the fourth driest month of the year, equal with May. Perhaps it is only the ferocity and coldness of the showers that tend to make us anticipate April weather with a little trepidation. It is this fickle, almost treacherous, element which is remembered in a number of European shafts of wisdom, such as 'Sweet April sometimes wears a white hat', a forewarning of snow, and 'April does as he pleases'. Interestingly, April is given a male gender in most such sayings!

May

May is traditionally the Merry Month and for many May Day, 1 May, marks the beginning of summer. May supports a rich cast of pagan rituals symbolising earth, fire, water, life, death and resurrection, and to this extent is a microcosm of the entire yearly cycle.

Above all, however, May excels in birdsong, flowers and foliage. Appropriately, therefore, May Day celebrations originated with the ancient Roman festival dedicated to Flora, the goddess of flowers and fruit, though this itself was rooted in much older pagan rites. Even if the original meaning had become obscured, homage to Flora continued to be the essence of later May Day festivities in Britain which reached their height during the Middle Ages. Then young men and women arose soon after midnight and, amidst the clamour of cows' horns and drums, stole off to the woods where they broke off branches of trees and decorated them with flowers. During the celebrations which followed, a May Queen was crowned as the reincarnation of Flora, and a Lord of the May was also chosen. Spring was represented by a spritely man who danced inside a cage structure bedecked with greenery. Jack-in-the-Green, as he was often called, along with the decorated Maypole, reflected the strong pagan elements enshrined in May Day pageantry. Religious bodies periodically tried – once successfully – to purge them but they had a strange primordial appeal, perhaps containing not a little rejection of authority and convention which survives to this day. Jack-in-the-Green held a specially strong fascination, and oddly enough was championed by chimney sweeps, who regaled him on May Day, their annual holiday.

On the Old Calendar, May Day fell eleven days later than it does now with the result that 'may', the flower of the hawthorn, was probably much more prolific in those days. This lends credence to the theory that it is hawthorn flower and not, as popularly believed, the month itself which is referred to in the well-known saying:

Ne'er cast a clout
Till May be out.

Silver birch trunk, beautiful all year round

Whatever its origins, it remains a useful reminder: don't be deceived into thinking that cold days are over yet, for despite celebrations to the contrary, summer doesn't officially start till June, and May can be a variable month! Perhaps because the British have a habit of expecting the worst and then making a virtue out of it, a cold May has traditionally been considered better both for people and harvest. 'A cold May and a windy, a full barn will find ye.' More sinisterly, 'A hot May makes a fat churchyard'.

One of the best-known verses around Maytime, and the subject of much disagreement, is:

If the oak is out before the ash,
Then you'll only get a splash.
But if the ash beats the oak,
Then you can expect a soak.

The retort is 'If the ash before the oak, We shall have a summer of dust and smoke!' Clearly no

female birch flower

birch

male catkin

Greater celandine

Lily of the valley

Solomon's seal

Garlic mustard or Jack-by-the-hedge

In late May the roe deer usually drops two young which remain hidden while she goes off to feed

Reptiles reappear around May after hibernation. In Britain snakes are fairly uncommon, mostly found on sandy heaths. They mate in May and June

Smooth snake

Grass snake, an expert swimmer

Slow worm or blind worm, not a true snake but a legless lizard

Common lizard, which in summer gives birth to 5–10 babies

Adder (or viper), our only poisonous reptile

Sand lizard

one should plan summer holidays on the basis of this piece of tree lore. In my experience, oak always leafs before ash. A more reliable, but short-term, prediction uses the observation that the leaves of certain trees, notably poplar, lime, sycamore and lilac, tend to turn over and show their paler undersides when humidity is high, and this is often a portent of rain.

Leaf litter

By May most of the catkin-bearing trees have shed their pollen and come into leaf, in that order, but a few like birch (by which we mostly mean the silver birch and in the Scottish Highlands often the downy birch) flower and leaf at the same time. It has been suggested that the reason most trees bear catkins before leaves is that the wind has unimpeded access to the pollen to disperse it, and perhaps the birch, with its very small leaves, is the exception that proves the rule. The male catkins which dangled like grey lambs' tails from the bare twigs in winter, start to shed masses of golden pollen in April. Birches are monoecious – they bear the male and female flowers on the same tree, the latter standing erect in small tufts at the base of the male catkins. While the pendulous catkins, dangling in the wind, are adapted for releasing pollen, the smaller female flowers with their sticky protruding stigmas are made for intercepting it. After the catkins have outlived their usefulness they fall off, while the short female spikes, now fertilised, begin to form fruit, swelling and gradually turning down, as the male catkins did earlier. This change in the female structures takes place in May, the developing fruits keeling over a little more each day till, by the end of the month, they hang completely.

Apart from the spent birch catkins, the woodland floor is enriched by the fall of a great variety of other litter from the canopy. Beech trees produce a threefold rain, first the russet scales of the sprouting buds, then the supporting leaves, and finally the globose male flowers, now devoid of their pale yellow pollen.

For all the leaf litter yielded by beech trees, relatively little grows on it, partly because of the dense, light-excluding canopy of foliage above, and partly because, unlike oak for example, the leaves do not break down so readily to form a nutritious mould. Lords-and-ladies (cuckoo-pint), wild arum lily, wild strawberry, wood anemone and the helleborines may be found flowering in the beechwoods in May but we must wait till summer to see two of their most characteristic flowers – the yellow birdsnest and the birdsnest orchid.

Leaf litter is also a vital commodity to the large wood ants which get really active in May, often attracting our attention as they rustle industriously about, carrying leaves and twigs to incorporate into their nests. Much of the nest is below ground but typically there is a

superstructure up to 1m (3ft) high, resembling a neatly swept pile of pine needles and other such debris. The pine forests of Scotland are a specially good place to look for them. Just as the Australian mallee fowl has discovered that a mound of vegetation will provide enough free heat as it decomposes to hatch its eggs, so the lowly wood ant has learned that a small compost heap over its nest provides welcome insulation. One German researcher sprayed the top of a nest blue; after a little while the coloured litter had disappeared but strangely enough it was on the top again shortly after: the ants turn over their compost heap for maximum efficiency, just as we do in the garden.

Our quiet animals

Elsewhere in the wood, the large mammals are also quietly busy in May attending to their own underground 'nests'. Earlier in the year, foxes clean out several dens or 'earths' before deciding on the one for bearing their three to six cubs mostly in late March or April. The young emerge from the earth at $3\frac{1}{2}$ weeks of age onwards; so if you can match their parents for stealth and keep downwind you might be rewarded with charming scenes of the cubs at play on a summer's day. By May, too, badgers are regularly coaxing their cubs to the surface, and again if you hide up a tree near the sett early in the evening, and wait quietly and patiently, you may be lucky enough to see the whole family at play.

Unlike badgers, who only reduce their activity in winter, hedgehogs have a proper winter hibernation which they break in March or April. By May many females are pregnant but they will not drop their litter of four to seven young till June. Many young of the previous year are apparently killed on the roads in May, perhaps in the course of seeking territories and mates. Hedgehogs used to regard motor vehicles as being like any other potential hazard and curl up at their approach: not surprisingly this proved a not very effective strategy, and with the enormous increase of road traffic in recent decades hedgehog behaviour has progressively changed towards running across roads instead. Not that we should imagine hedgehogs looked at their sadly squashed comrades and decided to abandon curling up in favour of a quick dash; a few must always have been in the habit of running across roads; they survived better than 'curlers' and passed on the superior strategy to their offspring, so that it gradually spread in the population. A nice example of natural selection.

If a spiny coat is no protection against car wheels, nor is it any problem for foxes and badgers, the hedgehog's natural enemies. Foxes are said to kill hedgehogs by manoeuvring them into water, where they are forced to uncurl in order to swim, and the fox then attacks the head. Badgers, which are

May *1. Hawthorn in flower 2. Oak and hornbeam wood 3. Hazel 4. Guelder rose 5. Swallowtail butterfly, now rare in Britain 6. Fly orchid 7. Woodruff 8. Early purple orchid 9. Greater stitchwort 10. Stinging nettle 11. Soldier orchid 12. Yellow archangel 13. Lords-and-ladies 14. Garden or oak dormouse 15. Badger 16. Little owl 17. Honey buzzard, sometimes seen in southern England*

immensely strong and versatile animals, somehow find a gap in the spines and aim for the unprotected belly. We know very little about how often hedgehogs succumb to these predators, but their absence in the woods around my home in Oxfordshire is attributed by some to the high density of badgers. Man himself used to fancy a bit of hedgehog meat; gipsies of old would encase the spiny exterior in mud and bake the whole in the embers of a wood fire. Capable of producing litters of up to seven, hedgehogs can probably make good their various losses, and may even live to the ripe old age of six. They can be fairly intrepid predators too, occasionally tackling and usually killing adders, to whose venom they are immune.

With a bit of initiative, we can often track down a family of foxes or badgers; a much harder task is to find the newly born young of our common deer species, the red, roe and fallow. The smallest of these, the roe, starts calving in late April, normally producing twins. The red and fallow hinds generally bear a single calf in late May or June. Newly born deer are vulnerable creatures and, unlike badgers and foxes, cannot be secreted underground. For the hind (mother) to let her weak-kneed calf (or fawn) try to follow her around all day would be to invite predators; nor can she spend all day lying alongside it. All deer solve this dilemma in much the same way, the hind striking a compromise, leaving her calf hidden in the undergrowth for the first few days, feeding it two or three times a day, and not allowing it to follow. The calf, then, receives little mothering at the outset, but as soon as she allows it to follow her, she is most attentive, and suckles it every hour or more. In the slack part of the day when the hind relaxes her own feeding, she may spend up to an hour licking the calf's head and ears, which seems bliss to both of them. The calf is not weaned till at least the following February, so it is not completely deprived of milk till after the winter: a significant factor, for in the Scottish Highlands about four out of ten red-deer calves die in winter.

Deer calves, including the roe, are dappled at birth, good camouflage in the bracken and undergrowth where they lie, but lose their spots as the weeks go by, so that by August they resemble their mothers.

Wild bees

May is a month of endeavour for the serious-looking queen bumblebees. When they emerge from their overwinter hibernation, they quickly seek their first meal. In April there were willow flowers and primroses to visit; in May the choice is much wider, with the proliferation of dead-nettles, ground ivy and so on. The sight of a bumblebee flying purposefully, heavily laden with pollen baskets, is a sure sign that she is building a nest somewhere. Usually the site is underneath a clump of dead grass or leaf litter, down a deserted mousehole, in a rock crevice, or even in a nesting box provided for birds. First the queen collects dried grass, moss and the like, and fashions it into a light ball in the nest cavity. Then she flies off to collect some pollen and nectar to make into a small plate of 'bee-bread'. This she places in the centre of the nest, and then lays up to a dozen eggs on top of it, surrounding them with a protective wall and cap of wax produced by special glands on her abdomen. She also builds a thinner-walled pot near the nest entrance to sustain her and her brood in bad weather.

Then the queen sits on the brood cell to warm the eggs, which hatch after about five days. Thereafter she opens the cell to replenish it with food for the larvae which pupate within a fortnight and emerge soon after as sterile female bees, which serve as the first generation of workers, foraging for food and enlarging the nest. This enables the queen's next batch of eggs to yield bigger and healthier workers and, at its peak, the nest may contain up to 150 bees. Late in the summer, some of the eggs develop into new queens and drones which eventually fly and mate. The drones die afterwards and the newly fertilised queens hibernate over winter prior to starting nests of their own. As for their natal colony none of the occupants survives the winter, and the little society disintegrates.

In May also a lot of other wild bees emerge. There are six species of cuckoo bees, each of which resembles the bumblebee species it parasitises. Having located a suitable nest of the right species, the cuckoo bee enters, survives the initial onslaught of the workers, and starts to lay her own eggs, which are then reared by the resident workers. Meanwhile the cuckoo ensures the downfall of the host queen by killing her and eating any eggs she has laid, and using the food stores for her own progeny of new queen cuckoo bees and drones.

Mining bees, of which there are more than sixty species in the British Isles, are similar in appearance to honeybees but solitary, smaller, and less furry. Each female makes her own nest burrow, up to 60cm (24in) deep, digging with her forelegs and scattering the soil around the entrance hole. Three to six chambers lead off the main shaft, and each is provisioned with a ball of bee-bread on which an egg is laid. The female plays no further part, and returns to the surface to die.

Other solitary bees are the leaf-cutters of the genus *Megachile*, which construct cells from pieces of leaf, often from rose bushes, neatly snipped out with scissor-like jaws. The wool-carder bee leads a similar existence, upholstering holes in trees with down stripped from the stems of such plants as mullein and campion. The mason bee, represented in Britain by *Osmia rufa*, as its name suggests, builds a nest of earth and saliva in crevices and roofs. Like the leaf-cutters, *Osmia* has a pollen brush on the underside of the abdomen. The mining bees, by contrast, carry pollen on the hairs of their hind legs, while the small *Prosopsis* bees are almost hairless and have to store both nectar and pollen in their crops.

Along with wild bees, a notable May spectacle is the swarms of metallic shining moths with antennae (feelers) which may exceed the body length six-fold. These are the males of the sub-family Adelinae commonly called 'longhorns'. Their caterpillars lead a strange life, starting as 'miners' inside leaves, but later they abandon their mines, biting off leaf fragments to make a flat portable case, which they then inhabit on the ground amongst the leaf litter. Longhorn moths bear a strong superficial resemblance to the 'silver horn' caddis flies, so we must be careful to distinguish between them.

With the sudden explosion of flowers in May, we can expect to find a lot more insects. Cow parsley is always worth a look though it may not, at first, appear very promising, especially compared with the late Umbelliferae like hogweed and angelica which are literally crawling with the most beautiful insects. Not

that these are any more attractive to insects; it is simply that, relatively early in the year, there are fewer around to exploit cow parsley. Nevertheless, if we start to follow the visits of insects a little more systematically by catching and counting, it appears that quite a number still find their way to the plant. Not only the species with short tongues which are completely dependent on such shallow flowers, but also honeybees and a few digger bees. Most of the visitors, however, belong to that much maligned Order, the Diptera – two-winged flies or true flies. There are already a lot of hoverflies (Syrphidae), including the drone fly, better known by its larva, the so-called 'rat-tailed maggot'. The drone fly is a dull blackish insect with a few amber markings, much less boldly patterned than the black and yellow, wasp-like pattern of typical hoverflies. The warm weather also coaxes out the fast-flying bluebottles (*Calliphora*) and the greenbottles (*Lucilia*), collectively known as blowflies. *Lucilia* does not often come indoors, although it may show an interest in discarded meat scraps in the dustbin. Among bluebottles, it is usually only the females that come indoors, the males preferring flowers. In May too, a smaller cousin of the March fly, with no common name but officially called *Dilophus febrilis*, emerges, sometimes in massive swarms. The larvae live

Hoverfly

Ground ivy   *Cow parsley*   *Hogweed*   *White dead-nettle*

Even the conifers show that summer is coming. On Scots pines the young shoots first appear as long pale candles, but by now the difference between old and new shoots is less obvious

'Cockchafers seldom abound oftener than once in three or four years; when they swarm, they deface the trees and hedges. Whole woods of oak are stripped bare by them.' He also observed that a young house sparrow was fed almost wholly on chafers by its parents.

In ponds and streams, insignificant-looking nymphs now emerge to moult twice into resplendent mayflies. Many are snapped up by fish and birds before their final moult, when they are called 'duns', but if they survive to be free-flying insects, they may live for up to four days – not one, as is often believed.

Not so elegant in their habits are the bristly flies (Empidae), which number over 300 species. In late May, our attention may be drawn to a dancing swarm of them. Closer inspection may show that one has another insect dangling from it, which turns out to be a corpse, usually some sort of fly; a male bristly fly will have presented it to a female before mating, and now she is in the process of sucking it dry with her long horny proboscis.

Breeding patterns

In the wild, the lifespan of animals is often much shorter than it is in captivity. For example, robins in aviaries have lived for 11 years, blackbirds for 20, and herring gulls for 44. Lifespans like these may occasionally be achieved in the wild, but on average a free-flying robin cannot expect to live more than a year, a blackbird not more than 2½ years, and a herring gull not more than 20. Very few of these birds survive to become senile, simply because existence in the wild is such a hazardous business that a moment's lapse of attention can be fatal. An aviary, by comparison, is a haven of warmth, security and reliable food supply.

The highest death rates recorded in the wild run at around 50–60 per cent for small birds (the so-called passerines), while the mortality of their fledglings is much higher; in great tits, for instance, as many as 80 per cent of the young produced fail to reach breeding age, a mere one year after they are born. Not that this is any argument for transferring wild birds to aviaries! The most remarkable thing about wild bird populations is that for all the pressures on them, they remain surprisingly buoyant and fairly stable from year to year, partly because high mortality in some years eases competition for food and other resources, so enhancing the survival and reproduction of the remainder. Yearly production of young can keep pace with the death rate, and losses are made good. Each species has evolved its own solution to the equation of deaths and births. Thus small, short-lived birds like sparrows breed like proverbial rabbits, while large, long-lived ones like albatrosses produce a dignified trickle of offspring. Others, which have failed to balance the equation along the way, have dwindled to extinction.

in all kinds of rotting plant material, and give rise to the first adult generation in May. If the wind swings to the north, as it often does at this time of year, *Dilophus* may succumb in large numbers, literally falling out of the sky. By May, many birds like blackbirds and song thrushes will already have made one nesting attempt, and either fledged the brood or failed. Either way, they leave behind discarded nests which are one other interesting place to look for insects. Although a bit gruesome, any nests with dead young in them can be particularly rewarding for the entomologist, especially those interested in carrion-eating beetles!

Elsewhere, late spring flowering now reaches its peak. In shady woods, dense carpets of bluebells (wild hyacinths in Scotland) give off an intoxicating fragrance. It is still the season for Solomon's seal, which started flowering in April, the closely related lily of the valley, garlic mustard (smelling like garlic), and the greater celandine with its poisonous deep-orange juice. Cow parsley begins to brighten verges and motorway embankments, while in damp fields buttercups start to appear in numbers. The bulbous buttercup (kingcup), with down-turned petals when the flowers are fully open, appeared first in March, but is now joined by the creeping buttercup and the tall and graceful meadow buttercup. In muddy ditches, we find the celery-leaved buttercup in May, later the lesser spearwort, and locally the rarer greater spearwort.

In the garden, if you dig up a spent crocus you will find that a new bulb has formed on top of the old one. This raises an interesting

problem: if the capping process was to repeat itself year after year, without any adjustment in depth, the crocus would soon grow itself right out of the ground. Fortunately the roots pull the bulb and its new growth deeper into the ground, thus restoring the *status quo*.

Many colourful and dramatic insects now join the bands of butterflies and bees already abroad since April. The first of the bold red and brown cinnabar moths emerge to seek ragwort leaves on which to deposit their yellow eggs. The equally vivid ladybirds are also increasingly on the wing, while on willows and alders, small metallic *Agelastica* beetles appear after their winter hibernation to mate; by the end of the month larvae may infest the leaves, munching them down to skeletons. In the evening, a ponderous cockchafer or maybug may rudely interrupt us by blundering into the lighted windows. With its formidable size, up to 35mm (1·4in) long, and buzzing flight it is a rather intimidating insect. However, it is quite harmless to us, though not to trees and crops, to which it does untold damage by eating foliage and flowers. A single maybug makes a respectable snack and rooks and little owls, among others, are especially partial to them, the rook also relishing the juicy chafer grubs, which live underground in plant roots. Little owls are sometimes seen standing vigilant on top of a telegraph pole, periodically sallying forth to snatch a maybug from the air. The emphasis must be on 'periodically', for maybugs are nowhere near as common as they used to be. In his *Natural History of Selborne*, first published in 1789, Gilbert White recorded that

May

Solitary breeders

In general life is much more hazardous for a sparrow or great tit than for an albatross or herring gull, and this is the basis of their different survival strategies. The great tit, one of our most familiar woodland and garden birds, has yielded a great deal of information on how populations change, not least because it readily occupies nest-boxes, rather than natural tree-holes, which makes it relatively easy to study. Every year, about half the adult tits die, but during the breeding season large clutches of 8–12 eggs defray the losses. The young are raised on caterpillars, which are only really abundant for about three weeks. After that they dwindle rapidly, but even so a few great tits manage to fit in a second brood. By contrast the herring gull, of which only 5 per cent die each year, never has more than one clutch (unless the first is lost early in the season and it can quickly be replaced), and then of no more than 3 eggs. So the number of eggs in a clutch varies from species to species, as does the number of clutches (and broods) they raise each year. Usually the number of eggs laid corresponds with the greatest number of young the parents can expect to raise, so birds are trying as hard as they can, without over-stretching themselves which would be as wasteful as not trying hard enough.

Reproduction is therefore a vital endeavour for birds, and it taxes all their skill and guile to make it successful. Having invested a great deal of time and energy in producing a clutch, every care must be taken to protect it from predators, and once the eggs hatch, the safe fledging of the young becomes the next hurdle. Most small birds cannot hope to fend off a determined predator like a fox or weasel, so their first line of defence is effective concealment. This is not easy, considering the number of times the parents must visit, and so advertise, the nest site, especially when feeding a demanding brood of young. The nests of many small birds are built of materials – grasses, moss, lichens – that blend subtly with their surroundings. Often the location of the nest in dense undergrowth or high in the fork of a tree, lends added protection. Birds like dunnocks, bullfinches, and long-tailed tits often nest in the middle of a thorn bush or bramble thicket, while auks and gulls may perch their nests on inaccessible cliff ledges. In the tropics, some birds even nest alongside a colony of wasps, which evidently regard them more kindly than their predators. For the same reason, sandwich terns nest among pugnacious black-headed gulls – you can see one, with the black cap coming lower down its face than the tern's – sitting right at the back of the group of birds in the photograph.

Woodland birds have to contend with a host of wily mammalian predators, so much so that blackbirds, for instance, may raise only one brood successfully from several nesting attempts each season. The young in the nest

Sandwich tern colony

call noisily to spur their parents to even greater efforts at feeding them, and this inevitably attracts enemies. Not that their parents need much encouragement, for every day in the nest survived is like a battle won, and the sooner the fledglings leave it the better. Young blackbirds flee the nest, therefore, before they can fly properly, to seek the comparative safety of the surrounding undergrowth. This makes good sense in a wood, but not always in the city where the cover is less, and fledglings may suddenly find themselves stranded on a street pavement in full view of every cat in the neighbourhood.

Many other woodland birds have abandoned nesting in the open to find safety in tree holes. Even certain ducks have foresaken ground-nesting in favour of hollow trees. In some natural woodlands, however, and to a much greater extent in modern 'managed' woods, there are not enough suitable holes to go round, which often leads to intense competition both within and between species. In Britain and Europe, woodpeckers, tits, flycatchers, redstarts and starlings commonly nest in holes. The woodpecker has the advantage of being able to chisel out his own, but even this does not guarantee ownership, with so many other birds, especially opportunist hole-nesters like starlings and jackdaws, poised to dispossess him if they can.

Once a species has taken to holes, it has no need of carefully camouflaged eggs, and can abandon all those cryptic squiggles on the shells. Thus while the rook, even in its lofty tree-top, retains heavily blotched, bluish-green eggs, those of the hole-nesters, like woodpeckers, owls, swifts, martins and the black redstart, are plain white. Burrow nesters like storm petrel, manx shearwater and puffin likewise have white eggs. Other hole-nesters, however, lay eggs that are white with small red spots (eg tits, nuthatch) or pale blue (eg wheatear, redstart, pied flycatcher, starling), perhaps suggesting that they abandoned nesting in the open more recently in their evolutionary history.

Hole-nesting has not given these species immunity from predation, for in many ways a hole may be as easy for a predator to spot as a nest in a thorn bush, and if it can only find a way in, it can do very well. We know very little about predation on nests in natural holes, but in one population of tits studied in nest-boxes, up to half the boxes in some years were plundered by weasels, which easily climb the trees and enter the hole. Other nests succumb to grey squirrels, which enlarge the entrance hole to get at the contents, while the great spotted woodpecker sometimes does the same to get at other birds' eggs. When the eggs hatch, the woodpeckers switch to drilling holes lower down at the level of the nest, or even, when the young are large, grab them out of the nest-hole itself. Presumably the young tits reach up on hearing the arrival of what they assume to be a parent with food, and fall easy prey to the lurking woodpecker. Adult tits

ey herons on nest in colony

but again, the strength in numbers may go some way towards compensating for this. A recent idea is that colony members, whether land- or seabirds, may benefit one another by revealing the positions of localised food patches scattered in the hinterland of their colony. For example, by studying the flight path taken by a bird returning with food, others might follow suit and discover the source for themselves. The idea was developed by Peter Ward after observing roosting colonies of quelea, a small African finch, in which some individuals left the roost first thing in the morning, while others waited to follow their more 'purposeful' neighbours. He suggested that the watchful lingerers had been unsuccessful in their previous day's foraging, and were waiting to follow successful birds.

All this seems the more likely when we realise how far such birds may have to travel to find food. Gannets may journey 150km (93 miles) or more to track down mobile and elusive fish shoals. Sandwich terns, too, may travel far afield to fish; this was demonstrated rather nicely by finding fish tags from salmon smolts and silvering parr brought back by these terns to a breeding colony in Scotland. One tag was found on a nest only 48 hours after the smolt had been tagged on a river 67km (42 miles) away!

The nest territory of colonial birds, though devoid of food, still serves many useful functions. Once the male has staked out his patch and established ownership of it, he has a valuable asset – a place to build a nest – to offer a female. This he may display from his territory, or at least keep returning to it, as proof of possession. Chaos is avoided by neighbours gradually coming to respect each other's boundaries so that each pair can conduct its mating and nesting activities in peace. Until this mutual respect develops, there are numerous encroachments, whether by herons to steal nest material or terns and gulls simply to try and annexe their neighbours' sites. After all, some nest-sites are better than others – they may be better drained or better sheltered, or if on a cliff ledge may offer a superior escape route.

For all their fighting and bickering, however, bird colonies are remarkably sociable gatherings, and this in itself may be important. Some believe that the tempo of a colony is contagious, so that most of the birds synchronise their breeding behaviour and lay at the same time. Whether this is true, or whether individuals at the same readiness for breeding nest together, is not clear, but either way it is an advantage, for although synchronised egg-laying means that lots of birds are vulnerable to predators at the same time, equally it means that none is more exposed than the rest. In short, if you are one among a thousand, you, your eggs or your chicks are less likely to be found and eaten by a fox than if you were only one in ten.

metimes frighten off the predator or at least all it just long enough to escape.

Such birds as these rely greatly, therefore, on solitary, secretive approach to breeding – litary because the nest is usually sited in the iddle of a large territory; secretive because erything possible is done to conceal its hereabouts.

olonial breeders

ther species take a different line, breeding in ge, crowded colonies, with each bird metimes separated by only a bill's length om neighbouring nest territories. So it is with e sandwich tern which stakes out a circular rritory, not much wider than its body length, revolving on the nest with beak itstretched, thereby just separating it from e birds doing likewise all around it. There is tle attempt at concealment, and not rprisingly when one hears the clamour of a e colony of grey herons or rooks, or an island lony of gannets, gulls, terns, cormorants,

shags or auks. Sandwich terns splatter white droppings everywhere which, almost paradoxically, may help to camouflage the colony, consisting as it does of white birds and pale eggs.

What are the advantages and disadvantages of the colonial system of nesting? Firstly, the siting of the colony, in the tree tops, on a remote island, cliff face or sandy spit, offers some protection, so predators are not openly invited. Secondly, the colony members co-operate in a variety of ways to their mutual gain, not least in driving off would-be predators. Terns, for instance, will mob a human intruder, swooping at his head with shrill, menacing cries, and not infrequently drawing blood. So compact are their colonies that a single careless intrusion at incubation time could wreak havoc; many eggs would be broken underfoot, while gulls might exploit the general confusion to steal others. Clearly the individual territories no longer provide food, as they do for woodland or open-country birds,

May

Budding beech

Season of new growth

The promise of May fulfils itself: the trees are in leaf and the forest starts to close over the wood anemones and primroses. These die, disintegrate and virtually disappear in the rank growth of new herbage, like the dog's mercury that carpets so many shady woods, except in north Scotland and Ireland. Being poisonous, dog's mercury enjoys a perennial immunity from disturbance on the woodland floor, from early spring till autumn. At first sight it is a uniform sward of green, but closer inspection shows that there are separate male and female plants, which usually grow in large patches entirely of one sex, the male's yellow-green stamens conspicuous as protruding spikes while the female flowers nestle hidden in the upper leaves.

In the woodlands, nothing is more beautiful at this time of year than the tender new beech leaves. The slender, pointed buds are wrapped in numerous scales which now float downwards as the leaves burst forth. At first, these are pale green, edged with silky-white hairs, and nearly transparent against the light. As the days pass they remain pale beneath, but gradually develop a darker green sheen on top. Also, the fine hairs are lost, though long ones are retained on the larger veins.

The versatile stinging nettle

Stinging nettles are plants with a variety of uses. Dried nettle leaves make a refreshing tea, and in olden days, before the advent of cotton, the fibres of nettle stems were woven into cloth for making sheets and tablespreads. In the kitchen the nettle can be cooked to taste rather like spinach, but choose only the tender young leaves – the older ones are too coarse. Wash the leaves in cold water, boil them rapidly in as little water as possible, and serve like spinach. The addition of a little grated cheese and onion in the roux used to thicken the nettle leaves improves the taste. Another use for a handful of tender, pale green leaves, left to soak in water for five minutes to remove the sting, is as a last-minute flavouring for soup, just like dill or chervil. It is also said that hair washed in the water the nettles were boiled in becomes healthy and lustrous, while a solution made from mature nettles makes an effective, and environmentally sound, insecticide for use on all kinds of bugs and some caterpillars.

To make such a solution, put a bundle of nettles, stems and all, in a bucket of water and

leave for 24 hours in a cool place, after which the water feels tingly to the hands and can be sprayed on any plants affected or threatened by bugs. If you let the nettles stand in the wat for several days, they begin to rot and smell, but this may make a more potent brew agains insects. Also the solution is said to strengthen the leaves of the plants and make them more resistant to attack. If you make a strong soluti of this sort, it should be sieved carefully and then diluted 1 part to 5 parts water before spraying.

Evergreens grow too

In the obvious profusion of flowers and deciduous foliage, it is easy to overlook the more subtle changes taking place in evergreen conifers. Many exotic varieties of conifer are now a familiar part of the landscape, especial in new plantations. People often use the term 'fir' trees loosely, to cover a multitude of conifers, but usually they mean sitka spruce o Norway spruce. The sitka is the fast-growing species most widely cultivated by the Forestr Commission in upland Britain since its introduction from Alaska in 1831. The bark i dark purplish-grey with coarse small scales, and the needles bright green. The Norway spruce, the original Christmas tree, is also grown extensively for timber in the highlands and can be distinguished from sitka by its coppery-brown bark and papery scales – at least in younger trees – and its darker foliage. Both have cylindrical cones, but the Norway are about twice as long as the sitka's—12–15(versus 5–8cm ($4\frac{3}{4}$–6in versus 2–3in).

Turning to the pines, the most widely grov species nowadays is the Corsican, which thri on the lowland sandy areas and shallow peat of Eastern and Midland England. The leaves are long, slender, and in bundles of two, whil the cones are short and squat. More familiar south-east England is the Monterey pine, wit its more expansive sideways growth, leaves three to a bundle, and cones similar to the Corsican. The lodgepole pine is another exot introduction, this time to the high peatlands, but the traditional and truly native highland conifer is the Scots pine, with its scaly, crocodile bark and shaggy foliage.

The whole year's growth in spruces and pines takes place between May and July by t expansion of the existing buds. The one at th very top of the tree sends forth a straight new candle-like shoot, and a number of side shoo of about the same length. Thus a new whorl cluster of branches is formed annually, and b counting the whorls, we can estimate the age many such conifers; some pines, however, gr two or even three whorls in a season. Either way, the result is the symmetrical spire shape we know so well.

The conifers bear inconspicuous catkin-lik flowers and the two sexes, though separate, a

ots pine cone

Norway spruce

Norway spruce cone

Corsican pine

ually to be found on the same tree. In May
e male flowers appear in small clusters near
e tips of the branches, shedding clouds of
lphur-yellow pollen, while the female flowers
e bud structures varying in colour from
een and blue to white or crimson. The
llen scales of some conifers are 'winged' with
ired air sacs, effectively balloons, which help
em disperse. Even without wind they may be
oyant enough to get airborne in warm, rising
. At the time of pollination, the incipient
male 'cones' stand erect at the ends of the
anches, and the alighting pollen grains sift
wn through their scales towards the ovules at
e base. These in turn secrete a drop of resin
ich, having once trapped the falling grains,
aws them deeper as it dries. Eventually the
llen grain grows a tube, down which a sperm
l ultimately passes to fertilise the egg.
In the spruces, hemlocks and others,
llination and fertilisation follow within a few
eks, but in pines fertilisation is delayed till
: spring of the following year, and only then
es the cone start growing. Spruce cones are
wn and downward pointing by autumn.
ch cone scale carries two small, papery-
nged seeds which are windborne to the forest
or, there to germinate the following spring.
e cones have a longer, two-year
velopment; after fertilisation it takes till the
lowing year for them to become compact,
en and downturned, and it is the year after
ore they become typically grey and woody
d start to shed their seeds.

ricultural poisons

e last fifteen years have seen intensive
earch and debate on the use and misuse of
ricultural poisons. Undoubtedly species like
peregrine falcon, sparrowhawk and barn
l are very vulnerable to this class of toxins
ich we call biocides.
It is now known how this poisoning works its
y into the animal world. The lower
anisms absorb only the smallest quantities

but these in turn are passed on to, and
concentrated in, the higher organisms which
prey on them, and so as we ascend the food
chain increasing concentrations of the poison
are accumulated, till we have arrived at the top
carnivores, including birds of prey and owls.
These poisons, mostly chlorinated
hydrocarbons, only break down slowly in the
body and are a very present danger before they
do so. Even if the poison is not instantly deadly
it still accumulates in fat, liver, and brain tissue
until, at a time of stress, the dose proves lethal.
Often this happens in a period of food shortage
when the animal is forced to mobilise food
stored in the body, and thus suddenly releases
poison contained in the liver or fat. A serious
side effect, even if the birds don't die, is that
their eggshells may become so thin that they

break under the slightest pressure. This has
been a major source of breeding failure in
peregrine falcons and other birds of prey.

Measurements of the effects of these toxins
have been made in many countries affected,
and as a result of the campaign which followed
them, the use of substances like DDT, Dieldrin
and Aldrin is now forbidden or strictly
regulated in Britain, America, and several
European countries. These corrective measures
do appear to be helping, and the populations of
different birds of prey have recovered
significantly – especially the sparrowhawks
where Britain is concerned. Also it has been
demonstrated that positive response to such
threats can help, and this provides an
enormous incentive to persevere on other
environmental battlefronts.

May

Limestone country

In May when all the terrestrial plants and animals are looking their best, it is hard to believe that the countryside around my home in Oxfordshire was once part of a great coral sea – in fact, part of a raised tropical fringing reef that has been traced for 80km (50 miles) down into Wiltshire. There are plenty of tell-tale signs, however, between the rows of sprouting spring barley; there the soil is littered with beautifully preserved specimens of the oyster *Gryphala* (the 'Devil's Toenail'), so complete you can see just where the muscles attached to open and close them. Also, every now and again, I unearth a lump of brain coral in the garden. There too, the profusion of live snails is a sure sign of a chalky or limestoney soil, since snails need lime to build their shells. The particular type of limestone here was laid down in the Jurassic period which started almost 200 million years ago and lasted for almost 60 million years. It was a time when much of Asia, Europe and Britain was invaded by warm seas, while the remaining land comprised forests of conifers, cycads and ferns, swampy plains, lakes and rivers. As the myriads of marine organisms flourished and died, their lime shells accumulated on the sea bed, became overlain with sediments, and ultimately compressed into limestone. In this country, Jurassic limestone was thus laid down in a great belt 65 to 160km (40 to 100 miles) wide, stretching from Dorset to Yorkshire. Subsequent upheavals threw this into great folds, like the Cotswold Hills. Further south, the even gentler contours of the Downs indicate a predominance of the softer, more recent Cretaceous limestone we call chalk. The oldest limestone of all dates from the Carboniferous period (about 250–350 million years ago), when again much of Britain was inundated by clear shallow seas. These are the crystalline rocks of north and west England, Wales, central Scotland and Ireland, much harder and less pure'than chalk, and weathering reluctantly to form steep cliffs and outcrops of bare rock.

Limestone soils support highly characteristic faunas, both living and fossil. Cliffs of Carboniferous limestone can be packed with fossils, including the curious pentagonal forms of the coral *Lithostrotion*, and *Productus* shells, while the Jurassic cliffs of Lyme Bay in Dorset are famous for spirally coiled ammonites. Even if extinct, most of these have descendants alive today, some less obvious than others. The sharp, cigar-shaped fossils we call belemnites, for example, belonged to ancestors of squid and cuttlefish, while the segmental trilobites were forerunners of lobsters, crayfish, and shrimps.

Today, plants are the most characteristic life forms of the ancient coral reefs and shell banks. The beech tree flourishes on calcium soils, riding high on chalk downs and Jurassic limestone ridges, while ash replaces it on Carboniferous limestone. Rugged limestone

Fossil-bearing carboniferous limestone

regions support some of Britain's rarest flowers, such as the Cheddar pink which grows on the rock ledges of the Cheddar Gorge in Somerset, spiked speedwell, rock pepperwort and round-headed garlic in the Avon Gorge, Jacob's ladder on the steep cliffs of Malham Cove in Yorkshire. The chalk downs are an orchid stronghold, including some of our rarest and most beautiful varieties.

In modern times, radical changes in land use, especially by farmers, have benefited some wild plants and creatures, and brought heavy pressure to bear on others. The limestone uplands of the north and west still support large areas of sheep pasture, mostly sheep's fescue, meadow oat, crested hair grass, quaking grass and blue moor grass, along with numerous representatives of the pea family. On the South Downs, sheep grazing has largely given way to arable farming, but in undisturbed areas, scrub like juniper has gained from the disappearance of sheep, as also from the demise of rabbits hit by myxomatosis. Rank growth, however, doesn't suit yellow meadow ants, whose oval ant-hills are nowhere near as common a feature of downland as they used to be. The best-known downland insects, however, are butterflies, and some like the chalkhill blue, adonis blue and silver-spotted skipper are almost confined to this habitat. Perhaps the most exclusive bird species is the stone curlew which, as a ground nester, is fast disappearing from traditional grassland haunts with the spread of cereal growing and mechanisation.

Horsetail – scourer and plant spray

The horsetail family belongs to a very primitive and once abundant group of plants which were gradually displaced; there are now only 23 species left in the world, 11 of which occur in Britain. Leafless and flowerless, horsetails are of relatively simple construction, with an erect, tubular, conspicuously jointed stem, and a whorl of toothed sheaths arising from each joint. Their mode of reproduction by spores is equally primitive and a feature they have in common with their ancient relatives the ferns.

Horsetails used to be known as pewterwort

because of their value as pot scourers. The most effective species was *Equisetum hyemale*, a stiff, robust plant found in damp places in North America and Europe but very rare in Britain. Most supplies were therefore imported from Holland and they became known as 'Dutch rush'. Dairymaids used them for polishing their pails, archers for smoothing the shafts of arrows, and jewellers and comb-makers for putting a fine finish on their craftwork. They can scour because they absorb large quantities of silica from the soil and redeposit it as tiny crystals on the stems and sheaths, imparting to them a fine abrasive surface. To this day they are still sold occasionally on stalls in Austria and eastern Europe. The common horsetail *Equisetum arvense* found in Britain is not a bad substitute and does a good job of cleaning plates and pans at a picnic. You could also add the young shoots to a salad.

Horsetails were used as a healing herb in medieval times, for they have a strong staunching effect on bleeding, both internal and external. In old gardening circles, they were also held to be an effective remedy for the powdery mildew that attacks roses.

When looking for horsetails you will tangle with blackberry plants, and then it is worth picking some nice tender leaves, taking them home and drying them in an airy place to make a wholesome and refreshing tea – an ideal beverage for the winter months ahead.

Jellyfish

When they lie on the beach after a couple of days of easterly wind, jellyfish look dirty and slimy, but floating in the sea they are both graceful and colourful. Jellyfish are 'cavity animals' (coelenterates), a primitive level of organisation. They are composed mainly of water, 95 per cent or more. They have a swimming bell (cap or umbrella) fringed with tentacles, and a mouth tube (stalk, tail), around which four oral arms are attached. We have to be wary of certain species, for the tentacles bear an enormous number of miniscule stings (nettle threads) which can produce an alergic reaction (white blisters) and a burning sensation when they come into

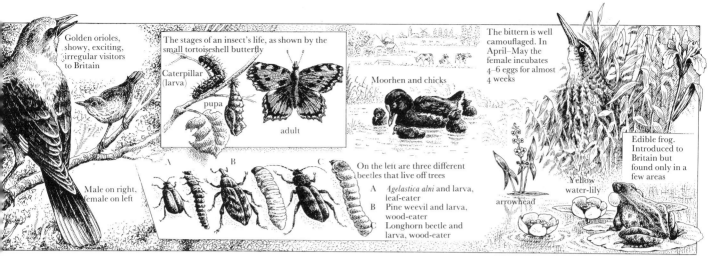

Golden orioles, showy, exciting, irregular visitors to Britain

Male on right, female on left

The stages of an insect's life, as shown by the small tortoiseshell butterfly

Caterpillar (larva)

pupa

adult

Moorhen and chicks

On the left are three different beetles that live off trees

A *Agelastica alni* and larva, leaf-eater
B Pine weevil and larva, wood-eater
C Longhorn beetle and larva, wood-eater

The bittern is well camouflaged. In April–May the female incubates 4–6 eggs for almost 4 weeks

Edible frog. Introduced to Britain but found only in a few areas

Yellow water-lily

arrowhead

ntact with the bare skin. On repeated or lid contact with certain large species, mild isoning reactions and even muscular aralysis can occur. Not all species, however, e dangerous.

The moon jellyfish *Aurelia*, our commonest ecies, doesn't sting. It can be identified by its most colourless (milky or pale pink) nbrella, and the four purplish, ring-like productive organs in the centre. A jellyfish vasion generally involves only one species, nd if it should be *Aurelia*, then there is no ed to refrain from swimming. You do have to careful with the blue *Cyanea lamarcki*, nspicuous for its great bunch of tentacles ound the mouth as well as the umbrella. The mpass jellyfish, *Chrysaora hyoscella*, cognisable by brown streaks radiating from e centre of the umbrella and brown patches the edge, is also best avoided. The jellyfish *izostoma octopus* is quite uncommon and not ngerous. It is spherical in shape with a very m, whitish umbrella, edged with purple.

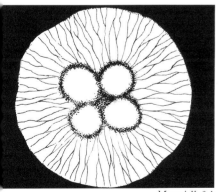

Moon jellyfish

eese

ancient Egypt, goose breeding flourished for ousands of years, as the tombs of the araohs testify. Geese were then divided into ven breeds, one of which looks so identical to e wild Nilotic goose that one presumes the mestication of the goose must have started ere. Most of the geese kept nowadays,

Domestic goose

however, are descended from the greylag goose, also domesticated very early on but in Asia. In olden times goose flight-feathers were used for writing, which made the birds indispensable to society for a long time. They had other uses too, and still have: tame geese can be plucked two or three times a year, yielding in total about 500g (18oz) of down ideal for stuffing quilts.

Winter's last stand

April, as we saw, was the fourth driest month of the year according to Kew records, with an average monthly rainfall of 4·6cm (1·8in), and it may seem surprising that May is no drier. This is partly because even in late spring Britain is still susceptible to a major low-pressure system centred around Iceland which can suddenly turn arctic weather southwards. Such an airstream brought snowstorms, widespread frost and black ice to Britain at the beginning of May 1979, bringing fresh chaos to the roads after an already harsh winter and spring – and disrupting the start of the cricket season! Temperatures rose to a mere 8°C (46°F), about 11°C below the May average, and well below the record 28°C (82°F) of May Day 1976 which heralded the scorching summer of that year. The highest temperature

A thick cloud belt heralds the approach of a depression. Even in May, these can be generated from the Arctic

ever recorded in May, however, since records started in 1868 was 32·8°C (91°F) in 1944. Perhaps a similar heatwave led to the following doleful pronouncement from a Hampshire village on 9 May 1654:

'There happened a sudaine and lamentable fier in ye parish of Worting which being carried on by ye wind and exceeding heat, and drought of the weather burnt all that was combustible, and melted even the church bells.'

June

June is a queenly and radiant month – if not always 'flaming' – and not without feminine associations. It was the fourth month in the old Latin Calendar, and is said to have been named in honour of Juno, wife of Jupiter. Midsummer's Day, the nativity of St John the Baptist, falls on the 24th of the month, and St John's Eve used to be marked by a chain of bonfires blazing across the country from west to east in a symbolic boosting of the power of the sun which, of course, begins to ebb in strength after this date. But the best-known midsummer ritual is the somewhat bizarre Druid ceremony at Stonehenge; even if its real and more macabre significance has been lost in the mists of antiquity, it serves to remind us that the Summer Solstice itself falls on 21 June.

Freshwater life

It is a month of intense activity for plants and animals of all kinds, as they concentrate on creating and nurturing the next generation, and nowhere is life more teeming at this time than in freshwater ponds. By the pond's edge the native iris, yellow flag, plays host to bumblebees and hoverflies, while in the water itself the tadpoles of frog, toad and newt are growing fast. And so they must, for theirs is a precarious existence. A variety of predators, vertebrate and invertebrate, can make short work of a pond of tadpoles, and the tadpoles themselves are not averse to preying on one another.

At the water's edge

By June, freshwater ponds and canals support a rich variety of flying insects. If we sit quietly, we may detect a number of dull brown insects, about 1·5cm ($\frac{1}{2}$in) long, with heavily veined wings folded roof-like over the back at rest. In May these would have been *Sialis lutaria* but in June they are joined by a close relative, *S. fulginosa*. Both species are alder flies (Neuroptera); they live for only about three weeks, but in that time they mate and lay batches of several hundred brown, oblong eggs

Yellow flag

on plants and stones near the water. After 10–14 days the larvae hatch and live under stones, later in mud on the pond bottom, where they prey on small aquatic animals. They are quite mobile, walking on three pairs of sturdy, thoracic legs. Many fall prey to bass and trout, but if they survive the larval stage, which can take two years, they leave the water and pupate in the soil.

Looking rather like brownish moths, but with fine hairs clothing the wings instead of scales, the caddis flies (Trichoptera) also live at the water's edge, either sitting motionless with their large wings folded alongside the body and long feelers extended in front, or in the evening rising in dancing swarms. The larvae of most species make a tube-like movable house from silk impregnated with sand grains and fragments of leaves and shells; different species can often be recognised by the particular

materials they use and the design features they incorporate. This protects and camouflages their soft body and gills as they creep about, dragging their case along with them. They are largely vegetarians, although in flowing water others weave silken nets in which they lie motionless, waiting to enmesh passing prey. In earlier times the name 'caddis' would have been more obviously apt than it is now, being an old word for a pedlar who wandered the countryside with his clothes decorated with samples of his wares.

If there is a lot of floating vegetation, such as water lilies, you may spot a small, attractive bronzy-green leaf beetle (*Donacia*) running about on top of it. The adult is not a thorough-going water beetle, and yet its larva is properly aquatic, living on submerged roots and shoots. As with the amphibians, it has taken a great deal of artful design in their life history to adapt all these insects for a larval existence in the water and an adult one out of it. Some aquatic insects have special regions of the body where a rich supply of breathing tubes called 'tracheae' is covered by only a thin protective wall so that oxygen can diffuse from the water into the body. Such areas may cover the whole body, as in the larvae of chironomid midges, or be concentrated in feathery gills, as in alder-fly larvae which have seven long pairs of them flanking the abdomen. Caddis-fly larvae have a similar system, but the gills are reduced, to suit existence inside a narrow tube. Other larvae do without gills and instead come to the surface to take in air. Some do this through small holes called spiracles, commonly drawn out into a tube or siphon, with various waxy or greasy substances making them watertight when submerged. *Donacia* larvae have just such a pair of hollow tubes at the end of their abdomen with which they puncture and tap the air cavities inside water plants.

Pollen exchange

Elsewhere, the profusion of flowers approaches its peak, with some of the most evocative

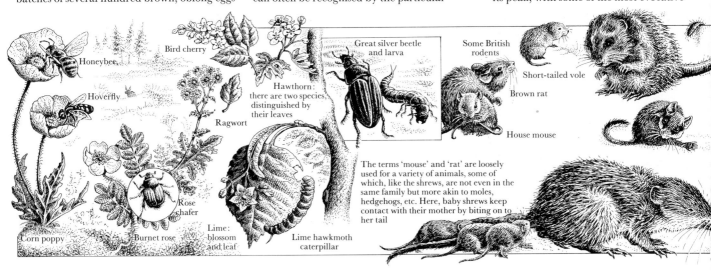

Honeybee

Bird cherry

Hoverfly

Ragwort

Rose chafer

Corn poppy

Burnet rose

Lime: blossom and leaf

Lime hawkmoth caterpillar

Hawthorn: there are two species, distinguished by their leaves

Great silver beetle and larva

Some British rodents

Short-tailed vole

Brown rat

House mouse

The terms 'mouse' and 'rat' are loosely used for a variety of animals, some of which, like the shrews, are not even in the same family but more akin to moles, hedgehogs, etc. Here, baby shrews keep contact with their mother by biting on to her tail

Bumblebees on bird's-foot trefoil (enlarged)

rn poppy

sociations of summer among them – the neysuckle, charlock, comfrey, oxe-eye daisy id first corn poppies. It is a bonanza for bees hich are now working flat out. Bumblebees e busy from early morning until late evening, it honeybees are apparently lazier, sallying rth later in the morning on their quest for llen and nectar and retiring earlier. riginally flowers must have been fertilised by ndborne pollen, but when insects came to cognise pollen as food, plants must have been ick – in evolutionary terms – to exploit their tential as pollinating agents; pollen grains came sticky, and some plants also secrete eet fluids – nectar – as an added attraction. time, the shape and colours of many flowers came adapted to the needs of their chief llinators.

Some of the most highly specialised 'bee-wers' are the orchids, fumitories and apdragon' flowers of the thyme family abiatae), the latter including some of our most familiar summer plants like self-heal, yellow archangel, dead-nettle, hemp-nettle, ground ivy and bugle. In these the two or four pollen-bearing stamens are concealed below the upper lid, but are hinged below to a flap which obstructs the route to the nectar at the base of the calyx. The robust bumblebee can press against this flap and force its tongue into the calyx, bringing down the stamens as it does so and smearing its back with pollen. This operates in the youngest flowers, called the 'male' phase, since the forked stigma projects horizontally for easy entry into the flower. In older flowers (those in the 'female' phase), however, the stigma hangs down fully exposed at the entrance; so if a pollen-coated bee now arrives, it will inevitably fertilise the stigma as it pushes past.

A similar pollination sequence occurs in the peaflower family (Papilionaceae) which includes whin, gorse, broom, clovers, trefoils and vetches. These also have highly distinctive flowers of five petals, a broad and often erect upper one known as the 'standard', two narrower side ones known as 'wings' and two central lower ones, the 'keel', enfolding the ten bundled stamens and stigma.

There are flowers – like the corn poppy, wild roses, peonies, etc – that offer their visitors no nectar but superabundant pollen instead. Some are dependent on pollen-eating beetles which become coated with the sticky pollen as they feed. Poppies are also visited by bumblebees which walk around amongst the stamens, collecting the dense blue-black pollen and periodically flying up to comb it down on to the shins of their hind legs. Once it is finished the bee will almost certainly visit another poppy for more, just as another bumblebee will visit one bird's-foot trefoil after another. Clearly this specialisation is of great value to the flowers involved, for it would be of no help to a poppy to impart its precious pollen to a bee and then to see it rubbed off on a nearby trefoil. For their part, the insects – whether bees, hawkmoths or 'high grade' flies – must gain from the ready recognition and rapid exploitation of the selected flower. With familiarity they will learn, for example, the best posture to adopt, and how far and in which direction to insert the proboscis, thereby increasing their foraging efficiency.

Some trees, too, such as the lime, are great nectar producers, though the earliest varieties don't flower till late June, and the common lime not till early July. The foliage is often shiny with honeydew from masses of aphids which infest the tree, and their secretions rain down, along with nectar, turning black with sooty mould anything they strike below.

Wild aphids milk the sap, the lime hawkmoth caterpillar munches the leaves. Like the pond larvae, it is a time of frantic eating and growing for the young stages of many moths and butterflies. Caterpillars of the cinnabar moth start hatching on the newly flowering ragwort, swarming over the leaves and stripping them bare. The larvae of the Lasiocampid moths likewise live gregariously in their early stages, sometimes covering hawthorn, bird cherry and other rosaceous fruit trees with their silken 'tents' which present an effective barrier against the probing beaks of would-be bird predators.

June

Rose month

June is the rose month. First to flower is often the low-growing burnet rose, whose creamy-white petals are sometimes eaten by the brilliant green rose chafer. The burnet spreads by suckers, forming large patches, especially in coastal sand-dune areas. Sweetbriar usually betrays its presence by its fragrant scent – hence its other name of apple-scented rose – given off by brownish glands on the underside of the leaves. In England the commonest species, however, is the dog rose, with its delicate shell-pink flowers and long overhanging branches. In Scotland it is largely replaced by the downy rose, generally a low shrub with deep-pink flowers. Last to bloom is the field rose with cream-coloured flowers gracing woods and shady places in July and August.

Looking for shells

Beaches, mudflats and gravel banks support a great variety of the so-called bivalve molluscs made up of two shells hinged together. The best-known bivalve on the beach is the common cockle (*Cardium edule*) with its rounded shell and prominent radiating ribs. Concentric ridges help to identify the attractively striped venus shell, *Venus striatula*. Cockles are good to eat, and in certain parts of the country managing and harvesting cockle beds is still a thriving industry. Another sand-dweller, as numerous as *Cardium* in some places, is the cut trough shell *Spisula subtruncata*, a robust triangular shell with lengthwise striations. Somewhat shallower and broader is its close relative *S. solida*, the thick trough shell, which grows to 3·8–5cm (1½–2 in) across. Both *Spisulas* have thick solid shells, in contrast to the rarer rayed trough shell *Mactra corallina*, similar in shape but housed in a thin glossy shell of yellowish-white colour.

Occasionally we find one of the bores or 'piddocks', like the small white *Barnea candida*, or the oval piddock *Zirfaea crispata* which shows a conspicuous groove traversing the shell. Like other rock-boring bivalves, these get protection

Burnet rose

by tunnelling into soft stone with their tooth-edged shell valves. The superficially similar but in fact unrelated *Petricola pholadiformis* is an American species in origin, probably introduced with imported oyster stock about 1890 and now well established round our shores.

All the bivalves so far described are 'suspension feeders', living buried in their chosen substratum, filtering out suspended plankton and detritus from the current of water drawn in through their siphons. Others are 'deposit feeders', using much longer and more flexible siphons to vacuum-clean organic deposits lying on the sea bed. The most beautiful of these is the banded or purple-toothed wedge shell *Donax vittatus*, yellow, brown and purple specimens of which may be found in shallow sandy bays. Less handsome, but prolific, is the Baltic tellin *Macoma baltica*, often found on estuary mudflats and replaced

on sandy shores by the thin tellin, *Tellina tenui* our commonest deposit feeder.

Most of these bivalves are shore dwellers, b after a storm we may find species from deeper seas cast up above the tideline. They may include the common gaper *Mya arenaria*, one c our largest bivalve molluscs, some 15cm (6in) across when full-grown. Its close relative, the smaller and aptly named blunt gaper *Mya truncata*, may also be found. Both live in the sea-bed, *Arenaria* buried up to 20cm (8in) deep, the top of its siphons just flush with the surface of the sand.

Razor shells are unmistakable. They use their flexible foot for astonishingly rapid movement through the sand, being matched only by moles for mining their way out of sigh in the blink of an eye. There are three commc species, the small slightly bowed *Ensis ensis*, th medium-sized *E. arcuata* and the larger *E. siliqua*, about 18cm (7in) long.

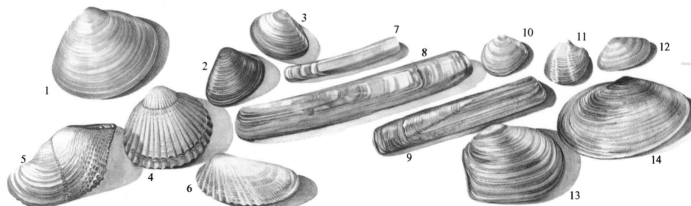

1. Mactra corallina   *2.* Spisula solida   *3.* Spisula subtruncata   *4.* Cardium edule   *5.* Zirfaea crispata   *6.* Petricola pholadiformis   *7.* Ensis ensis
8. Ensis siliqua   *9.* Ensis arcuata   *10.* Macoma baltica   *11.* Venus striatula   *12.* Donax vittatus   *13.* Mya truncata   *14.* Mya arenaria

Black-tailed godwit, a specialised feeder wading well out into the water on its long legs (see page 61)

Butterflies and moths

Many people are inclined to say of hot summers and butterflies that neither are as common as they used to be. There may be some truth in this, but the fact remains that most of us cannot resist seeing our childhood through a golden haze and concluding that things were better then than they are now. While some of our butterflies are indeed declining, others are holding their own or even on the increase. 'Clean' farming methods, with their arsenal of selective herbicides and insecticides, have been detrimental, but even there we can find some compensations.

Two of our best-known Nymphalid butterflies, the red admiral and painted lady, are migrants to these shores anyway, which helps to explain why their presence here is so erratic. Of the resident Nymphalids, the fritillaries seem to be scarcer, but the small tortoiseshell and peacock, whose caterpillars feed on nettles, are doing well. The white admiral, till recently less common in many of its known haunts in the south, has made a remarkable recovery and many people became acquainted with it for the first time in the outstanding butterfly– and drought – summer of 1976.

The economically important butterflies, the potential pests, are the so-called 'cabbage whites'. The small white is perhaps the most destructive, its pale green caterpillar destroying cabbages and other cruciferous crops, while the large white, with its yellow and black caterpillar, is almost as bad. The green-veined white is less of a menace, preferring cruciferous weeds to cultivated brassicas. Its attractive relative the orange tip (only the male has coloured wingtips) does likewise, choosing for its eggs and caterpillars the food plants jack-by-the-hedge (garlic mustard) and cuckoo flower. Also included in this group is the dazzling yellow brimstone, whose caterpillars are found on buckthorn in June and July. As all gardeners know, there is no shortage of food for the cabbage whites which may swarm over brassicas in June. In farmland, with the decline in mixed farming, there is now less acreage of kale, a brassica fodder crop for livestock, and this has eliminated one food crop for whites. On the other hand, oil-seed rape is an increasingly widespread cash crop and highly attractive to cabbage whites. All things considered these butterflies are doing well, and will probably continue to thrive as long as we grow brassica crops.

In woodland areas, some new local colonies of the delicate wood white have been discovered in recent years, while the speckled wood (one of the Satyridae or 'browns'), once localised in some regions, is now more widespread. It is really a species of the forest edge, flying jerkily for short distances in sunny glades, clearings and forest rides. Another brown, somewhat aberrantly coloured, is the

Orange tip on jack-by-the-hedge

Large white (top) *and small white*

Grayling

June

marbled white; it too showed a capacity for rapid recovery in the summer of 1976.

The largest of the 'browns' is the grayling, with a wingspan of 5cm (2in) or more. It lives on dry grassland, usually chalk downs or sandy heaths, mostly near the sea. It has a most elegant sequence of courtship movements, whose climax is reached when the male bows and clasps the female's antennae in his forewings, imparting scent to her from a band of special, brush-like scales near his 'eye-spots'. These spots, which we can readily track down in the more widespread meadow-brown butterfly, are at a glance rather good eye-mimics, and may distract a would-be predator, such as a bird, just long enough for the butterfly to escape, at worst perhaps with a damaged wing.

One of our woodland butterflies which has undoubtedly become very scarce is the white-letter hairstreak (Lycaenidae), named from the white W-shape on the underside of its brown hind wings. Its numbers have probably suffered a decline as dramatic as that of its main food plant, the elm, which was decimated by disease in the 1970s. The adult is said seldom to fly far from the tree on which it was raised, and if so this cannot have helped the species to outflank the rapid spread of Dutch elm disease.

The hairstreaks, of which there are five British species, are woodland relations of the exquisite 'blue' butterflies. The large blue, whose life history is described in the 'August' chapter, is now extremely rare in this country, and is the only insect to receive protection under the Conservation of Wild Creatures and Wild Plants Act, but in June we can see plenty of its smaller cousins, the common, holly and chalkhill blues. Not all of them in fact are blue, females of some species being predominantly dark brown. The caterpillar of the common blue feeds largely on bird's-foot trefoil, the chalkhill on vetches, and the holly, predictably, on holly, ivy and buckthorn. This blue seems to have a seven- to nine-year population cycle, so that periods of scarcity alternate with great abundance. In other words, we shouldn't necessarily view any decline in the holly blue with undue alarm, for it may only be temporary.

Apart from hairstreaks and blues, the Lycaenid butterflies also include the dazzling coppers. Our only common one nowadays is the small copper, easily identified by its metallic orange wings, and habit of flying late into the autumn. Essentially an open-country species, it often lays its eggs on sorrel (*Rumex* sp). June is also a bumper month for moths, though they tend to be overshadowed by their exotic relatives, the day-flying butterflies. In particular it is the month of caterpillars, on which depends the successful breeding of so many woodland birds – tit, nuthatch, chaffinch, blackbird and thrush, redstart, fly-catcher, warbler, jay and magpie.

Food specialisation

An adequate food supply is basic to any animal's survival. Food provides the body with the energy it needs to maintain good condition and, in warm-blooded creatures like birds, to keep the body temperature at a constant level. This may seem to be less of a problem on warm June days, but in fact breeding pushes many birds to the limit at this time of year, demanding more food for the extra tasks of egg formation and feeding young; in addition to actually having several extra mouths to feed, the parents also have to fuel all the extra flying needed as they ply back and forth to the nest from the feeding grounds. If any more evidence that summer can be a trying time for birds is needed, we might remember that for some species, like the blackbird and great tit, as many die in the summer as in winter.

Even in summer, therefore, in fact for some birds especially in summer, the need to find food efficiently is a pressing one; moreover, many different birds and other animals are all looking at the same time to satisfy their particular demands. This has led to a high measure of food specialisation, where each species tends to concentrate on a particular spectrum of food, a diet different enough from other species around it to gain a little breathing space in the daily struggle for survival.

It is easy to think of the different specialist skills adopted by birds to earn a living. Most often we can identify the tools of their chosen trade, especially the bill, but also the feet and many features besides, including for example the owl's ability to hunt at night, when other birds of prey are obliged to roost. There is the chisel bill of woodpeckers for hammering through bark, the delicate probes of waders, the flesh-tearing bills of raptors and large gulls, the broad, flattened bills of ducks (equipped either with filters for straining off water, or a saw-edge for grasping fish) and the powerful conical bills of seed-eating finches.

Some of the more diverse bills and body forms are found among the insect eaters. The warblers have forcep-like bills for picking insects with great delicacy off leaves and buds. The flycatchers sally forth from perches to catch flying prey, and strike a compromise between a fine top and a broad base to the bill for catching and then manipulating aerial insects. If we go looking for insects ourselves, we can either pick them up one by one with fine tweezers, as warblers do, or else sweep a wide open net through the air to engulf flying ones. In principle this trawling method is the one used by swallows, swifts, martins and nightjars, the gaping mouth snapping shut on small flying insects. The long, pointed wings are built for fast and darting pursuit, the forked tail for manoeuvrability, just as the wagtail's long tail helps it to jig above streams for insects, and the magpie's and sparrowhawk's to steer at speed through dense shrubbery.

Great spotted woodpecker

Lesser spotted woodpecker

It nearly always turns out that even species which superficially look similar, like the swallows, swifts and martins, and seem to have similar requirements, differ in subtle ways, useful in reducing competition between them. They too may differ in what they eat, where they find food, when they are active, and so on.

This variation in feeding sites and habits also leads to each tit species finding slightly different food, at least most of the time. The woodpeckers likewise seek different diets. In general the lesser spotted woodpecker includes the greater proportion of small insects in its diet, including larvae of flies and gall insects. The great spotted woodpecker includes a wide range of vegetable matter in its winter food, especially hazel nuts, rowan berries, beech-mast, crab-apple pips and cherry kernels. In all respects it is able to handle bigger items, as we might expect from its greater size and longer, more robust bill.

The third common species in Britain is the green woodpecker, more often heard than seen with what Gilbert White called its 'loud and hearty laugh'. Larger than the other two species, it does not in general take proportionately bigger items, but spends much more time on the ground hunting for ants. For

Top left, *house martin*; bottom left, *swift*; top and bottom right, *swallows*

competition with common terns.

On the cliffs, June is the time to see guillemots and razorbills and, on the few cliff tops where they still survive, puffins. All are members of the auk family, 'flying' underwater to exploit fish shoals around their breeding colonies, usually located for safety on offshore islands. But while the puffin has a fairly catholic diet of small fish species, often stacking several prey in its celebrated bill for transport home, the razorbill takes fewer, often larger, fish at a time, and the guillemot only carries one. Again, the razorbill is especially partial to sand eels, while in many places the guillemot specialises on herrings and sprats.

Learning to hunt

Among birds of prey, there are a few summer visitors to this country – the osprey, which yearly gains a stronger hold on its former haunts in Scotland, Montagu's harrier, and that incomparably graceful little falcon, the hobby.

In pursuit of highly mobile birds like swallows, or mercurial insects like dragonflies, hobbies are enormously fast fliers and, as they swoop to kill, speeds in excess of 150km/h (95mph) are quite normal. If you are fortunate, you may chance to come across a whole family party of parents and fledged young. The first fledging flight is weak and tentative, and the young clearly have difficulty controlling their landing on branches. About a week later, however, they can fly confidently to a branch to meet the parent, usually the male, bringing in food. Thereafter, the young make progressively longer practice flights and instinctively begin to chase and catch for themselves large insects like chafers, and even to swoop at the odd swallow – initially with conspicuous lack of success. But with each passing day they become more discriminating and better co-ordinated.

Not all young birds of prey make the transition to independence successfully, and losses in the first year of life are great, up to 75 per cent in the peregrine falcon. Once the first hazardous months are behind them, however, their survival chances are much improved.

this it seeks out grassland, even lawns, and so likes to live in parkland, which offers a suitable mixture of trees and open ground. The lesser spotted woodpecker is also much more a species of parks, frequenting wooded suburban gardens, while the great spotted prefers more continuous stands of pine or deciduous forest. So again, habitat as well as diet is part of the specialisation of this group.

On lakesides, estuaries and seashores, different wading birds feed alongside one another, and so offer a particularly good opportunity to see how body structure has been adapted to different feeding sites and habits. The diet they seek consists largely of small crustaceans, molluscs, and worms submerged in the mud, often covered by shallow water. Birds like the curlew and black-tailed godwit can wade far out into the water on stilt-like legs, and probe deep into the mud with their long tapering bills. Success in this blind search is ensured by well-developed sense organs at the tip of the bill which tell the bird when it has made contact with something edible. The redshank and greenshank, medium-sized species with shorter legs and bills, are restricted to shallower water, while the diminutive dunlin and sanderlings feverishly and tirelessly glean pickings from the surface and water's edge, swarming up the beach if an incoming wave threatens to swamp them. The graceful avocet is something of an exception to this series: relatively slight of build but long of leg, it frequents shallow lakes, marshes and pools where it catches small creatures in the surface slime by sweeping a slender upcurved bill from side to side with a regular scything motion. In deeper water avocets immerse their heads and upend like dabbling ducks.

In the open sea, also, closely related species are adapted to slightly different lifestyles so that they are not endlessly competing with one another. This is not to say that they don't overlap at times, especially if there is a sudden glut of food that everyone can share. Just as the bird table temporarily brings the blue tit and great tit together, so common terns and Arctic terns, usually so hard to tell apart, may join in diving on a teeming shoal of fish close inshore. Normally the Arctic tern is an offshore feeder in British waters, rarely encroaching on the common tern's feeding grounds along the shoreline. There is no gentlemanly restraint here; it is simply that the Arctic tern is better adapted to offshore, pelagic life, and gives a miss to areas where it will suffer in

Hobby hunting dragonflies

July

The farmer always hopes for a warm and mainly dry July, so much so that for centuries the weather on ritual saints' days has been taken as an omen of the weather in store. It is said that if it rains on St Mary's Day, 2 July, it will rain for a month. But undoubtedly the most notorious weather day of the year in country lore is St Swithin's, 15 July:

Oh St Swithin's if thou'll be fair,
For forty days shall rain nae mair.
But if St Swithin's thou be wet,
For forty days it raineth yet.

To this day, some farmers breathe a sigh of relief if St Swithin's is dry, and regard a wet one with real anxiety. On the continent, St John's Day on 24 June was invested with a similar wealth of weather lore. It was popular belief, for example, that the sea would accept thunderstorms before St John's but not after. In nature, however, St John's is a genuine watershed, falling as it does three days after summer solstice, or midsummer. It is around then that trees and shrubs develop new buds if they have lost a lot of leaves through night frost or insect defoliation earlier on. The results of such damage are most obvious in July, often showing first as red or brown leaves, especially in hawthorn and oak. Elms often have perfect leaves at the tips of the branches whereas those at the base show signs of insect damage, which must have occurred before St John's Day.

Yellow blessing

St John has also given his name to the beautiful yellow St John's wort, which only comes into full bloom in July. If the buds are squeezed, they exude a red, oily liquid, and if the heart-shaped leaves are held up to the light they show tiny, glandular perforations, as if pierced with a needle. Both features are closely connected in folklore. The red liquid was taken as indisputable proof that the plant had grown out of the blood of the beheaded John the Baptist. A plant of such noble origin was, of course, a blessing for the people. Legend has it

Magpie or gooseberry moth

that this so angered the devil, he punctured all the leaves to destroy the plant.

Thus, St John's wort came to be regarded as a powerful talisman against the forces of evil in rural England. Cattle used to be wreathed in it to protect them from witches abroad at the solstice, while on the Isle of Man sprigs of it are worn on 5 July, Midsummer's Day on the old calendar. St John's wort also has a long-standing tradition of healing power, celebrated in old English names like 'balm of warrior's wounds' and 'touch-and-heal'. Another name, 'save', dates from the twelfth century, when it was applied to sword wounds.

Today St John's wort continues to flourish on hedge banks, scrub, moors and dunes, testifying to the triumph of good over evil. In fact yellow is a real July colour as well as a spring colour: mullein and evening primrose, sandwort and ragwort set the dunes aglow by day and night. The latter is especially true of the evening primrose, whose buds open in the last hour before sunset, sometimes even a little earlier, a process that can easily be followed with the naked eye. Keats wrote of being 'startled by the leap of buds into ripe flowers' and 'shutting again with a loud popping noise about sunrise'. Look for a swollen bud and sit by it about 8 o'clock on a July evening. At a given moment, the calyx starts to split and a little later the sepals turn downwards, quickly

Large yellow-underwing moth

followed by the unfolding petals. Next, the stamens separate and the stigma unfolds. If your patience is not yet exhausted, watch to see which insects visit and come in contact with the sticky, thread-like pollen, and return next day to see, as Keats did, what the flowers look like after sunrise.

Growth and fruiting

Ragwort often suffers from caterpillars of the cinnabar moth which can strip the foliage bare. Most animals find the caterpillars distasteful; after a first acquaintance they remember the warning coloration of black and yellow bands and usually leave them strictly alone. Their chances of survival therefore appear to be good. But anyone who has witnessed a stream of these caterpillars searching for a new food plant after gorging themselves on the last one will appreciate that starvation must be an ever present population control.

The hedge of dog roses around my garden bears its first hips in July and instantly greenfinches are on the spot to strip them of their seeds. I can hear them first thing in the morning when the one wren living in the garden wakes me up with its ranting song.

Greenfinches

The otter and the badger belong to the Mustelidae family. Both lead shy, reclusive lives

1. St John's wort
2. Dark mullein
3. Evening primrose
4. Wall rocket
5. White bryony

Peppered moth

Around this time, too, the young toads make their exodus from the ditch, often in their hundreds: how many will survive? The tadpoles of the common frog get their hind legs this month – and if they are quick their front ones too.

Inside old houses or other buildings, the death-watch beetles become active. Characteristically the adult beetles strike their heads against the wooden walls of the chambers in the beams where they once lived as pupae. This produces that eerie tapping sound, which in fact is probably a mating signal. The name 'death-watch' originates from the fact that the tapping is heard most clearly in the middle of the night, when perhaps those most likely to hear it are the sick. In the evening also, several moths approach the light of the windows: magpie moths, large yellow underwings, and the very beautiful peppered moth.

In the hedgerows, the white bryony, which emerged from its thick rhizome in April, now climbs with fantastic speed. Between the leaves of the growing tip, the spiral tendrils have been coiled like watch springs, and now they begin to stretch in search of support. When they find one, the coils contract again, drawing the stalk up behind them. Underneath each female flower is a green ball, the 'inferior ovary' and bright-red-berry-to-be. Wood pigeons like to eat the tendrils, which they pull off whole. On sunny July days, the broom pods split open with an audible crack; on some days it sounds like machine-gun fire. The seeds hurtle off, and germinate readily.

Insect activity

It is also the month when wood ants and black ants undertake their swarming nuptial flights, in which the winged queens are fertilised by the smaller winged males. Ants from nests over a wide area flight together, rising from the grass stems they have climbed for getting airborne.

In the air, swifts, swallows, martins, starlings, sparrows, and even gulls take a heavy toll of the massive swarms. After a couple of hours the queens are fertilised and descend again. In her old nest, or starting a new one, the queen sheds, or bites off, her wings: she never leaves the nest and never needs to mate again, using sperm from her mating flight to fertilise eggs as she lays them. As for the males, they have outlived their usefulness and die soon after the mating flight.

As the summer progresses, the number of biting insects seems to increase, especially in damp areas. Living in our cottage bordering the transcendent peat-bog lakes then becomes quite an ordeal, with hordes of biting mosquitoes, females of the large Aedes family, notorious in the tundras of the far north. Occasionally you get a really nasty bite as if you have been pricked with a needle, and then you see the culprit lingering on the affected spot, quite a large fly with beautifully coloured eyes, a horse-fly (*Tabanus* sp). Sometimes we are bothered by the very small biting midges or gnats (Ceratopogonidae) – called 'no-see-ums' by Americans because their diminutive size allows them to approach and bite unnoticed. These are not to be confused with their completely innocent relatives, the non-biting midges (Chironomidae).

One of the compensations for life at the water's edge is the wealth of dragonfly species (order Odonata, sub-order Anisoptera). These are now reaching their peak, as are the

July   *1. Cuckoo on elder   2. Reed   3. Yellow water lily   4. White water lily   5. Reed warbler 6. Little grebes   7. Little bittern   8. Moorhen 9. Red-crested pochards   10. Great-crested grebe 11. Black terns   12. Coot   13. Purple heron – we have the grey*

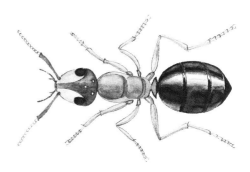

Wood ant

White bryony – male flowers

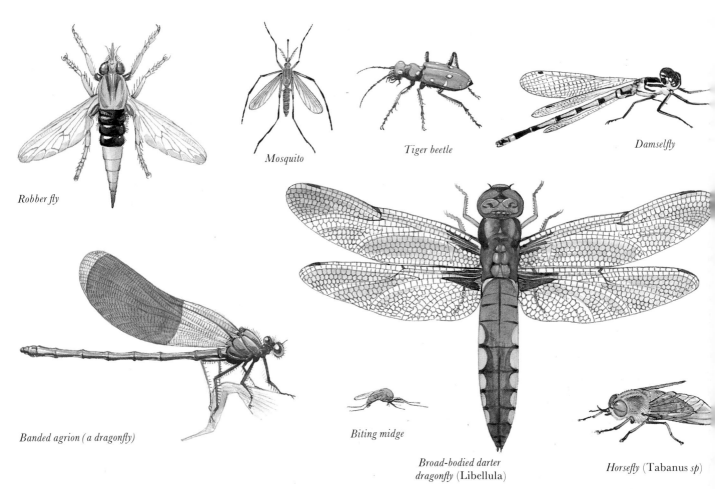

Robber fly

Mosquito

Tiger beetle

Damselfly

Banded agrion (a dragonfly)

Biting midge

Broad-bodied darter dragonfly (Libellula)

Horsefly (Tabanus *sp*)

damselflies (sub-order Zygoptera), slim, delicate species which don't fly as fast as dragonflies but are equally diverse and beautiful. Blue, green, and red, they dart over and along the water, sometimes quite a way from it. Perhaps the most breathtaking of all, the shining metallic-banded *agrions* and *demoiselle agrions* (Agriidae) are still to be found over brooks and small rivers as yet unsoiled by pollution.

Sometimes we see two dragonflies oddly connected to each other: they fly in tandem, the one in front (the male) holding the female by the neck with a clasper at the end of his abdomen. This is the first phase of mating. In the course of the flight the female will curve her body round till the tip of her abdomen touches the male's reproductive organs and collects his sperm. If you are lucky, you might see the eggs being laid soon after. These are deposited under water against the leaves or stalks of plants, underneath lily leaves for instance.

The larvae lead a predatory existence in the water, seizing prey with a diabolical-looking unfolding apparatus, the 'mask', which is the lower lip modified into a third pair of jaws. Damselfly larvae are long and slim and have a prawn-like tail through which the gill breathing surface is enlarged, for like fish they have to make do with the oxygen dissolved in

the water. Dragonfly larvae have no such tail and instead have the gills concealed in the hind-gut which is regularly flushed with fresh water. Adult dragonflies are also distinguished by keeping their four wings flatly spread out at rest, rather than over their backs as damselflies do, and by venturing further from water.

We often come upon dragonflies right in the middle of moors and along the edges of the driest coniferous forests, hawking for other flying insects, mostly flies which are by far the most numerous and offer the greatest choice. Most people think of 'flies' only as the common house fly and must believe they are followed by these creatures on hot summer days to the very heart of the countryside, where they settle so annoyingly right in the middle of our perspiring faces. But these – one of the commonest is aptly called *irritans* – are quite a different species from the house fly.

There are a lot of very attractive true flies or Diptera, not least the hoverflies. These are often mistaken for wasps because of their yellow and black stripes, which we will return to later. Then there are the slim robber-flies, giants in their family, of which the largest, the yellow and black *Asilus crabroniformis*, can grow up to 30mm ($1\frac{1}{8}$in). This formidable robber catches even bees and bumblebees; the smaller species have to be content with other flies.

In fact all the animals that are so active on warm days on the sandy moors are predators. On the ground are the iridescent green tiger beetles (Cicindelidae), beautiful animals which constantly fly up in front of us, only to descend again and carry on hunting on foot for other pedestrians. The habit of running a lot and flying little is best shown by the spider-hunting wasps (Pompilidae), a family which has specialised all over the world in this particular predatory skill. Even the large, tropical bird-catching spiders find their master here. The female spider-hunting wasps, of which the largest and best-known native species is *Anopliu viaticus* (9–14mm, conspicuous black and orange banded abdomen, dark wing edge), paralyse their spider with a stab of the sting and then dig a small shallow hole in which the victim is hidden. Before sealing up the burrow, the female lays an egg on the spider so that when the larva emerges from the egg, after about eight days, it has a ready source of food.

The lacewings

Returning to a more grassy environment, on all kinds of shrubs and bushes are the delicate, light-green lacewing flies (Chrysopidae), not flies at all, but representatives of a much more primitive Order of insects. The beautiful large wings really do have a lace-like quality. The female lays her eggs on a stalk about 1cm ($\frac{1}{3}$in) long near to aphid colonies which the oblong larvae will feed on when they hatch. They have spotted markings and are thinly covered with stiff, erect hairs, while the first and second jaws together form a pair of hollow tubes with which the aphids are impaled and then sucked dry. Some species then stick the shrivelled aphid skins on to the hooked hairs on their back, camouflaging themselves as pieces of dried debris.

When the lacewing larva is full grown it spins a silken, cigar-shaped cocoon inside which the pupa develops, lying folded double till it makes its way out later on.

In the earlier days lacewing flies are always classed along with the scorpionflies. These are also summer insects; they occur on the leaves of all kinds of plants, especially blackberries and stinging nettles. Scorpionflies are noticeably slender insects with dark spotted wings, the last three segments of the abdomen standing out reddish against the rest. The tip of the male's abdomen is swollen and turned upwards ('hence 'scorpion' fly), while the head is drawn out into a kind of beak, the tip of which bears the mouthparts. The adults and the caterpillar-like larvae live in soil, leaf litter and suchlike beneath hedgerows, where they scavenge for a diet of dead insects and other small carrion, supplemented with plant juices.

At this time of year, certain beetles are especially numerous and conspicuous. Towards evening, umbellifers, flowering shrubs and tall grasses are full of soldier beetles, red-brown beetles 8–14mm ($\frac{1}{2}$–$\frac{3}{4}$in) long, belonging to the different species of the genus *Cantharis*. They look a little bit like stagbeetles but those have much more robust antennae (feelers). During the day there are active predators, hunting in the sunshine for other insects.

Roadside verges

The roadside verges have been called the ordinary man's monuments to nature, in the sense that, in the wake of intensive agriculture and urban expansion, they represent his last surviving token gesture to open countryside. As agriculture has become progressively 'cleaner', plants like buttercups, daisies and cowslips which once carpeted meadows in summer are now restricted to verges. They have become a refuge, too, for so-called weed species like red poppies, yellow charlock and corn marigold which have virtually been eliminated from modern crops. As the chalky downs, which once supported a wealth of flowering plants, were turned from sheep pasture to cereals, their plant life has likewise taken refuge along roadsides. A few species like spring cinquefoil and perennial flax now occur nowhere else but along these narrow strips inaccessible to the plough. Verges therefore represent an invaluable reserve, though they

Soldier beetle on wild parsnip

Woolly thistle

too have come under heavy siege from spraying, mowing, exhaust emissions, salt and other traffic residues.

Ill-timed and indiscriminate mowing can be almost as destructive as sprays, often rudely interrupting a plant's annual cycle. Bird's-foot trefoil is only one of several formerly widespread plants eliminated from many

roadside verges by midsummer mowing. Particularly vulnerable are the biennials, like woolly thistle and cow parsley, which need two years to set seed and so depend on good overwintering for survival. Most biennials have already disappeared from arable and even pasture land for this reason. Too much mowing also promotes a rich humus layer if trimmings are left behind and this is harmful to many verge plants ill-adapted to rich soil. For this reason, new verges should be capped with poorer subsoil and then the herb layer will flourish at the expense of grasses. For purely economic reasons many local councils have of late curtailed spraying and mowing programmes, but ironically this may not be as beneficial as it sounds: the rank growth that results smothers delicate plants at ground level. To maintain an interesting and diverse flora, therefore, we need to manage road verges carefully, just like any other valued resource.

In recent years, County Naturalists' Trusts have increasingly sought and won the co-operation of county councils in keeping up enlightened verge-management schemes. In addition, an increasing mileage of roadside is being set aside as nature reserves where it has some special botanical or other interest. In this way a number of highly localised plants have benefited, like the Cotswold pennycress for example. In turn, to preserve a varied flora is to maintain an attractive habitat for insects, especially butterflies, grasshoppers and crickets. If we can ensure that roadside verges are a rich source of plant life and insects, then they will also be a haven for small mammals and birds. In recent years, motorway travellers in particular have enjoyed seeing kestrels hovering over the grassy embankments. These verges seem to have some special advantage as hunting-grounds, though opinions differ on what it is: perhaps small mammals and especially voles, the kestrel's main prey, find good feeding in the new grass, or perhaps it is simply that a motorway embankment is relatively undisturbd by human visitors. It has even been suggested that the vibrations generated by heavy traffic drive earthworms to the surface and so attract voles to feed on them. Perhaps also the warmth radiated from the adjacent road surface weighs in to favour the vole's tight energy budget. Yet again, prey might simply be easier for a kestrel to spot in the poor cover of the managed sward with its uniformly vertical 'pile'. No one knows the real answer and it would be a fruitful area for study.

Verges may be modest remnants, but they are worthy of our care and study. By taking notes of the range and distribution of their plants and animals, successional gains and losses, and so on, we can learn a lot of ecology and also help put it to good use.

After the breeding season

By July there are various signs that the breeding season is almost over for many birds, or at least well advanced. Adult birds, having staked out a territory and defended it the summer long, have an attachment to it; the young birds, however, are quitting parental territory and have a strong exploratory urge; they need to find a suitable future territory of their own. The parents of many species,

Newly fledged song thrush

moreover, feel little enough loyalty to fledged offspring and evict them as readily as they would other competing adults. The juveniles, lacking experience and guile, offer little resistance.

In Britain it has often been observed that in the mixed feeding flocks of adult and juvenile rooks the older birds regularly snatch tasty morsels from right under the noses of the younger ones, even from their own offspring. As dominance and status in the flock generally increase with age and experience, the juveniles are in no position to retaliate effectively and instead merely seek pickings elsewhere. Thus they often join up with others of their own age. And in summer we often find, for example, large flocks consisting almost entirely of juvenile starlings. They are distinguishable from the adults by their dowdy brown plumage.

The juveniles of many other species also differ in appearance from the adults. Young grebes, with their brown and white stripes, are strikingly different. Young robins have a sober breast of speckled brown instead of the famous red, and in this they show kinship with the rest of the thrush family – song thrush, mistle thrush, redwing, fieldfare – and blackbird, whose young also have a mottled brown breast. Juvenile gulls are dark brown and only gain the complete white adult plumage over four to five years, so the experienced bird-watcher can distinguish intermediate ages by the relative darkness of plumage.

The significance of all these plumage differences lies in the signal value of colour, which serves to distinguish age and sex when birds encounter one another. Thus, for example, there is no possibility of a young and sexually immature female being confused with a mature one by a male prospecting for a mate. In addition, the generally drab, inconspicuous colours of juveniles lend them added safety at a time when their inexperience puts them in greatest jeopardy. To the layman, these colour differences may further confuse an already bewildering variety of sorts of birds, but often

posture and behaviour help to identify species. Juvenile starlings, after all, squabble for food just as characteristically as their elders.

Once they have started to disperse, young birds can cover prodigious distances, a fact repeatedly borne out by ringing studies. Young sandwich terns, for instance, range widely up and down the British coastline after they leave their breeding colonies. This movement is much more randomly directed, and so distinct from the subsequent southerly migration to winter quarters in Africa.

Apart from the wanderings of young birds, immature adults, and adults whose breeding attempts have failed, may also abandon their breeding area prematurely and disperse. As the breeding season progresses, the urge to breed wanes, and if there are no young to rear, or no time is left to make another attempt, failed breeders often have nothing else to tie them to their territory. Sometimes in May or June we can see cases of 'premigration' in large, airborne flocks of lapwings and curlews.

Directly after the breeding season, perhaps even before it ends, most birds enter their moulting period, during which old, worn-out feathers are replaced with new ones. Usually much later, the feathers of juveniles are replaced by the adult plumage, while in some species the breeding plumage of the adults is shed and a less colourful, so less conspicuous and safer, plumage substituted. Generally these changes are gradual but occasionally we see a bird flying with a noticeable 'bite' out of its wing where a feather or two have been lost and the new ones have not yet grown in.

Ducks and geese lose all their old flight and tail feathers simultaneously, so for a few weeks they are flightless and highly vulnerable to predators. To spend this dangerous time as safely as possible, some species retire to remote areas. The shelduck even makes a special migration for this purpose, the German, Swedish, and many Dutch and British birds seeking the sanctuary of the Heligoland Bight. Other Dutch birds moult in the Schelde area, and some British ones in Bridgwater Bay in the Bristol Channel.

Ducks in our parks and ponds remain at their posts to moult, but conduct themselves more discreetly than usual, skulking in the reeds till they regain their flight feathers. Drakes which had a brightly coloured breeding dress moult into a drab, camouflaged 'eclipse' plumage.

Storm clouds and gusting winds

July is usually the warmest month of the year, with an average monthly maximum of 28.4°C (83°F) recorded at Kew Observatory over the years 1941–70. The highest air temperature ever measured in Britain was on a July day in 1868, the 22nd, when the mercury rose to 38.1° (100.5°F). It would almost certainly have been slightly lower than this had it been measured in

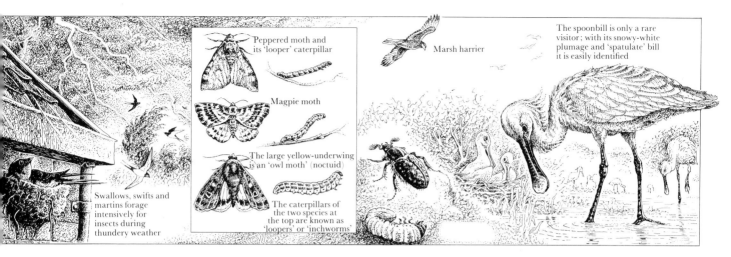

Peppered moth and its 'looper' caterpillar

Magpie moth

The large yellow-underwing is an 'owl moth' (noctuid)

The caterpillars of the two species at the top are known as 'loopers' or 'inchworms'

Swallows, swifts and martins forage intensively for insects during thundery weather

Marsh harrier

The spoonbill is only a rare visitor; with its snowy-white plumage and 'spatulate' bill it is easily identified

Stevenson screen, the meteorologist's standard equipment, and in fact it probably didn't exceed the highest temperature of 36·7°C (98°F) recorded on 27 June in the famous heatwave of 1976. On the other hand, the fickle British climate can produce quite cold weather in July. The lowest temperature ever recorded in July at Kew was 6·5°C (44°F) while the record low for July anywhere in Britain was −3·3°C (26°F) in the year 1888.

Climatically, Britain stands at the crossroads of three major atmospheric pressure systems, and it is the seasonal distribution of these that largely determines the annual pattern of weather in the country. The dominant influence in July is the area of high pressure to the south-west of Britain called the 'Azores centre'. In midsummer it is intense and widespread, extending as far north as it ever gets in the year, bringing warm, anticyclonic conditions and light, moist, Atlantic westerlies to our shores.

In such conditions there is a likelihood of thunderstorms, for only when the air is as warm as it is in July and August can it contain enough moisture to form a potential reservoir for torrential downpours. One measure of this moisture-absorbing property of the atmosphere is 'vapour pressure', which we thus find is highest in Britain in July and August. If a heatwave persists in July, therefore, we can expect thunderstorms to develop, especially in the Midlands and the south-east of England. On average, the Midlands suffer the most thunderstorms, about twenty a year, because they are the region most remote from the moderating influence of the sea, and so generally the hottest part of the country. The south-east of England is not far behind, with fifteen thunderstorms a year on average, in spite of being more coastal and so cooler. This apparent anomaly arises because thunderstorms can drift across the Channel from France and burst on the south-east coast. Records from Kew, London, for 1916–50 show that on average, with 62mm (2¼in) rainfall, July becomes the second wettest month of the year in this region, exceeded only by November. Coastal regions other than the south-east, however, experience only about four thunderstorms a year.

Thunderstorms can develop in a number of ways, but usually they are associated with Atlantic depressions, areas of low pressure. New thunderstorms tend to develop daily in the following way. As the hot July sun heats the land, the air above it is warmed by radiation and rises in 'thermals'. This alone can lead to the formation of cumulo-nimbus clouds which unleash thundery showers. If an advancing depression runs into unstable conditions of this sort, particularly violent storms can be expected, often depositing 25–100mm (1–4in) of rain within a few hours, accompanied by gusting winds, thunder, lightning and often hailstones. The highest bout of rainfall recorded in such conditions was 279mm (11in) in fifteen hours on 18 July 1955 in Dorset.

We talk of storm clouds gathering as a forewarning of trouble, and truly cumulo-nimbus clouds are a sure sign of thunder in the air. They are really cumulus clouds which have grown large enough to produce showers, but in so doing they develop a very characteristic shape, towering high into the atmosphere, often in the early hours of the morning as the sun heats the land and sets up convection currents. The puffy 'cauliflower' clouds will continue to rise if the upcurrents are strong enough, reaching heights of 15km (9miles), and even more in hot equatorial regions. At these heights the water droplets freeze into ice crystals which are teased out by the strong upper winds into the typical 'anvil' shape of the cumulo-nimbus top.

It often takes till afternoon or evening, however, for the storm to break, and often not till then is thunder heard. The storm front, visible as a dark, billowing cloud-mass arching itself around the shower complex behind, moves at considerable speed, around 50km (30 miles) an hour. Just as a vacuum cleaner sucks dirt towards itself, so fierce updraughts inside the approaching storm draw surface winds towards it. So there is a germ of truth, but no more, in the old saying that 'thunderstorms travel against the wind'.

Rolling cloud: a threatening cloud billows at the front of an active thunderstorm or shower complex

August

'What August doesn't cook, September leaves uncooked' is a saying in Europe, meaning that if August is deficient in ripening warmth no amount of good weather in September will compensate, and we can expect a shortfall in autumn. Ideally, August should be warm but not too dry if fruits are to swell, and often the month fulfils these requirements nicely. At Kew Observatory, records taken over thirty-five years show that August is on average the fourth wettest month of the year, with 569mm ($24\frac{3}{8}$in) of rainfall.

There is little reliable weather lore associated with this month, partly because it can be very variable, and not least because the word 'August' never endeared itself to rhyme-makers. In some farming communities, however, it is believed that warmth in the first week of August, including St Dominic's Day (4 August), promises a hard winter ahead. On the other hand, settled weather on St Bartholomew's Day (24 August) promises a fine autumn:

> *If St Bartholomew's Day be fair and clear,*
> *Then a prosperous autumn comes that year.*

The same day marks the end of the forty-day aftermath of a wet St Swithin's Day, as the following saying celebrates:

> *All the tears St Swithin can cry,*
> *St Bartlemy's mantle wipes them dry.*

The first half of the month is sometimes known as the dog days, and these are synonymous with hot, dry, maybe sultry weather. They are called after the Dog Star, Sirius, one of the brightest stars in the night sky and leader of the constellation Canis Major, the Great Dog. The dog days cover the period when Sirius rises and sets with the sun, generally reckoned to be 3 July to 11 August. In England, Sirius is visible as a brilliant night star low in the southern sky between about October and April. Outshining all but a few other stars, it has attracted attention since the earliest days of astronomy and was put to practical use by the Egyptians. They carefully noted when it first became visible in the dawn

The thunderstorm has all but passed, trailing a frayed cloud edge behind it

sky before sunrise, in order to predict the annual flooding of the Nile so vital to their farming economy. The rising of Sirius also heralded the first day of the Egyptian New Year.

Drought or storm

We have seen that a wet St Swithin's Day, 15 July, supposedly condemns us to a further forty days of rain. Like so many traditional predictions of the kind, this is rooted more in superstition than in fact, and meteorologists have not found any real foundation for it.

In 1975 and 1976, Britain experienced record-breaking sunny summers, and in both years August was exceptionally dry and hot. In 1975

the heatwave was much shorter and dominated the first fortnight in August. In the following winter, rainfall was below average and this trend persisted into 1976, culminating in a very dry June and August over the whole of Britain. By the end of July, reservoirs in Devon and Cornwall were less than a quarter full while the Mendip reservoirs in Somerset were losing water at a rate of 25 million litres (5·5 million gallons) every day. The Thames even dried up along 14km ($8\frac{3}{4}$ miles) of its course and, to slow the loss of river flow to the sea, water was pumped upriver over Molesey lock, the last one before the tidal reaches. Both droughts were caused by stable high-pressure systems which only occasionally withdrew to permit the approach of frontal depressions, and so rain. In

Field gentian

Spear thistle

August brings warm, silent afternoons. Bird song dies away and only insects are heard

On such days the buzzard is seen circling and soaring on warm thermals

Grasshopper warbler

Black slug

Buddleia

Where the hamster lives in the wild it is busy storing grain against food shortage later

Ling

Bell heather

Sheep

Great green bush cricket

Moorland is not a totally natural landscape, but man-made by burning, deforestation in some areas, and sheep-grazing

grasshopper warbler, the 'cricket' or 'fishing-reel' bird

August *1. Pine trees   2. Wheatear on oak branch   3. Juniper   4. Ling   5. Field gentian with large blue butterfly, wild thyme behind 6. Tormentil   7. Bell heather   8. Sundew   9. Grey hair-grass   10. Purple moor-grass   11. Broom 12. Bog cotton   13. Fox   14. Rabbit 15. Hobby   16. Tawny pipit   17. Black grouse 18. Teal   19. Sand lizard   20. Marsh frog 21. Winged ants   22. Speckled wood butterfly 23. Dragonfly   24. Meadow brown butterfly*

976, the 'blocking anticylone' diverted pressions southwards towards the editerranean which thus suffered a wet mmer, more like the ones all too familiar in ritain.

Apart from the hardship to farmers, the ought wrought some weird and wonderful anges on our wildlife. Shallow-rooted trees e beech and birch suffered sunburn and opped their leaves prematurely, while elm ees, already beleaguered by disease, received urther, blow. Certain insects reached precedented pest proportions, especially dybirds which, having dispatched local stocks aphids, resorted to plundering the nectaries plants like runner beans in order to survive. oodland and open-country butterflies also urished and gave us a glimpse of bygone ys when our countryside was a huge rbaceous border for butterflies. White mirals, wood whites and even the rare black irstreak reappeared in old haunts, while the ng spell of warm easterlies probably counted for the remarkable landfall of amberwell beauties on the east coast of gland; immigrants also numbered ousands of silvery moths. On the debit side, e dearth of earthworms, driven downwards the arid surface conditions in the soil, scomfited our moles, which spent more time an usual hunting above ground for ernative prey. Foxes and badgers, which ually take a lot of earthworms, may also have fered, for there were numerous reports of em foraging by day, presumably to mpensate for lean pickings at night.

On 29 August the drought broke amatically with heavy rain in southern gland, and as if to make up for it all, an usually wet autumn and winter were to llow. August, like July, is often a thundery onth, and never were the downpours more elcome than in 1976. Often, however, a fferent sort of transition marks the tail-end of gust. Areas of high pressure build up over Europe, a trend that strengthens in September, and with it comes the calm weather we associate with still autumn days. On the rowan trees, the appearance of red berries is another hint of autumn to come, but in the meantime one field of red poppies is enough to remind us that these are the crowning days of summer.

The cricket bird

During the course of this month, my early-morning alarm clock, the wren, begins to fail me. Once in a while it sings under its breath, but its ranting clearly decreases. At the beginning of the month, the aptly named grasshopper warbler *Locustella naevia* still sings – or rattles – in the evening, but by the second half of the month it has almost stopped. This was the bird known to Gilbert White as the grasshopper lark, and to country folk in Surrey as the 'cricket bird' or 'rattlesnake bird'. Gilbert White remarked that 'Nothing can be more amusing than the whisper of this little bird which seems to be close by, though at a hundred yards' distance; and, when close at your ear, is scarce louder than when a great way off.' This ventriloquial deception is more than accidental and must make it hard for would-be predators to pinpoint the warbler's songpost.

On warm evenings the high reeling churr of the grasshopper warbler has competition from the singing – or fiddling – of bush crickets. The great green bush cricket is the most spectacular species, nearly 5cm (2in) long. The males become active late in the afternoon and sing well into the night. Although the sound goes on for long spells without a break, it is usually outdistanced by the warbler which can sustain its song for more than two minutes.

Insects abound

In the winter and spring we can find the relatively large eggs of aphids (greenfly) on the branches of oak trees. The eggs are laid in autumn and hatch out the following spring as the oak sap begins to rise again. The new individuals are wingless females, known as 'stem-mothers' because, when mature, they reproduce without mating and every day bring forth a few young which are fully active from birth.

By August, aphid damage has turned several of the oak leaves brown. The insects have elongated sucking mouthparts which, once inserted into bark cells, can passively imbibe the sugary sap; no active sucking is necessary because the sap is under pressure in the tree and so flows freely into the insect. Aphids have an enormous rate of reproduction and this demands a high intake of protein. Though so rich in sugar, plant sap has only a small protein content, so the aphids have to drink prodigious amounts of it. In so doing they continually exceed their sugar requirements and get rid of the surplus as 'honeydew' through their abdomens.

This has led to one of the more remarkable associations between different insects. In the course of time, some ant species came to use honeydew as food, and since they do the aphids a favour by removing it, the latter co-operate by secreting honeydew whenever the ants touch them with their antennae. Some ants even keep 'herds' of aphids, milking them of their honeydew as we milk cows. When you come across an oak tree with a trail of ants moving up and down its trunk, it is an indication that this gentle symbiotic relationship between ant and aphid is operating in the canopy.

Oak trees play host to many other insects and parasites. During wet summers the leaves may be attacked by the oak mildew fungus which spreads by wind-borne spores. When a spore alights on a leaf it develops the threads known as 'hyphae' which invade the tissues and, like aphids, thrive on its juices.

August

Painted lady (top left) *and red admiral butterflies and bumblebee on buddleia flowers*

Look especially for young leaves with a flour-dusted appearance; under the magnifying glass we see a mixture of hyphae and spore-producing parts of the fungus.

On moorlands and dry grassy heaths, wild thyme is found flowering in August. It is on this plant that the rare large-blue butterfly lays its eggs. The emerging caterpillars feed on the thyme and after a while begin to secrete honey from a gland on the abdomen. Again, as with the aphids, ants (usually a small red variety of the genus *Myrmica*) are attracted to this convenient source of food. The next stage in the relationship is nothing short of astonishing. After a while, the caterpillar allows itself to be carried off by an ant, and deposited in the ants' nest. In return for supplying honey, the caterpillar is free to feed on tiny ant larvae. In spring, this strange, meat-eating caterpillar pupates, and later the adult butterfly emerges through the pathways of the nest to the open air, there to seek a mate and so start the egg-laying cycle over again.

In gardens where herbs are grown, the basil is already more than 2m (6ft 6in) tall by August, and is almost as attractive to insects as the 'butterfly shrub', buddleia. Besides masses of bumblebees, there are small tortoiseshells, red admirals, painted ladies, brimstones and whites. By now the bell heather has finished flowering but the ling has just started.

Germinative power

You can cut down a bed of plants in full flower so that no seed is formed or dispersed, and still find that new plants appear the following year. Assuming that the plot could not have been reseeded from outside, we can only conclude that the seeds were already there, in the soil, and had taken longer than average to germinate. Some, but not all, the seeds of any individual plant have this capacity for retarded germination. If the seeds of one white-clover plant are sown on an experimental plot, about 85 per cent appear to germinate within ten

days. Of the remainder, a third come up within a year of sowing, while the last 10 per cent can take up to twenty years. This widely staggered germination can help a plant species to survive a prolonged period of exceptional drought which kills all the seedlings that have sprouted simultaneously.

Cases have been known of seeds which suppressed their germination for incredibly long periods. The viable grain seeds found in the pharaohs' tombs of Egypt are remarkable enough, and even more so are the seeds discovered in peat layers in Manchuria; despite being thousands of years old, 80 per cent of them appeared to have kept their germinative power. The ability to suppress active growth varies with temperature and dampness, and from species to species. From pots of seed which the Danish botanist Dorph Peterson had buried, only 8 per cent of the plantain was found capable of sprouting after t years of interment, 87 per cent of the charlock.

Nearly one hundred years ago, the British scientist Beale buried a number of well-stoppered bottles, each containing an exactly equal collection of seeds. At first a bottle was dug up every five years, later every ten years. These experiments showed that seeds of shepherd's purse and fat hen were still able to germinate after thirty-five years, sorrel even after sixty years.

Environment and food

Looking again at the diet of woodpeckers (page 60), we see that not only does each species have a particular diet, but also the composition of the diet shows marked seasonal changes. When there is a surplus of ants and other insects in the summer, the great spotted woodpecker abandons the vegetarian side of its winter diet nuts, berries, beechmast and other seeds. Sparrows which are seed-eaters in the winter likewise switch to insects in the summer months. Often this switch indicates more than a change in what is available; to grow rapidly, nestlings need a high-protein diet and insects supply this much better than most plant foods.

Common dodder, growing on ling; enlarged on right. A parasitic plant, rooting into its host

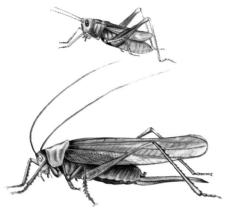

Short-horned grasshopper (top) *and long-horned grasshopper (great green bush cricket)*

For some birds, summer merely presents a wider choice of insect prey. The blackbird, for example, subsists on earthworms and insect larvae for most of the year, but includes butterflies and other adult insects in summer, and berries and fruits in the autumn. Like blackbirds, black-headed gulls take advantage of bread and other food man discards, especially in the winter. From the readiness with which they suddenly appear to scavenge at picnic sites, however, some gulls appear to profit from people all the year round. But in spring, when they start breeding, many gulls eat insects and earthworms, often gleaned by following the plough, as well as freshwater invertebrates, small fish and even frogs. Many birds are very opportunist and flexible in what they eat, adjusting to make the best of whatever the season offers and changing their haunts accordingly.

Of course birds select certain habitats for other reasons as well, such as the presence of safe nest sites; but a suitable food supply is certainly one of the most important factors. Excluding seabirds, about 589 species breed in Europe and Asia, of which about 40 per cent leave in autumn to find alternative food-rich areas for the winter. Some look for these areas outside our frontiers, southern Europe and Africa being favoured winter quarters for British migrant birds; other species find what they need closer to home, and resort to parks, villages and suburban gardens.

During August, such movements are already under way. Most of our swifts, for example, have left by mid-August, and many other birds are on the move. With the breeding season over, they are free to search more widely for food, and indeed often must do so as the summer flush of insects begins to dwindle.

Birds are not distributed evenly over the country, and if we want to assess overall bird densities we have to be careful to take into account all the habitats in the area concerned. We also have to remember that the availability and distribution of the different habitat types is constantly changing. If, for example, an orchard is felled and turned into

pasture, the bird population is likely to thin out, although certain species like lapwings, rooks and skylarks may benefit. More seriously, farm modernisation schemes in which old stone barns, perhaps clothed in ivy, are demolished, and hedgerows are grubbed up, are removing traditional nest and feeding sites for many birds. Swallows may find the new aluminium barn less attractive and barn owls certainly will find its precise walls offer no substitute nest site for the crumbling masonry of its predecessor.

In recent years, one of the most swift and dramatic changes has followed the wide-scale death of elm trees from Dutch elm disease. The fatal agent, which effectively suffocates the tree's water transport system, is a fungus, either spread from tree to tree through their shared root system, or transported by a species of bark beetle. Once the tree is dead, the hordes of beetle and other larvae in the rotting wood may temporarily benefit birds like woodpeckers and nuthatches, but the decaying trees are no longer any use to the legions of tits, warblers and other small birds that once picked insects from the foliage. Moreover, as fewer and fewer elms remain standing, rooks will lose nest sites, as will kestrels, stock doves, little owls and tawny owls. The disease must be considered a setback for our rural life.

Mixed feeding flocks

If a certain habitat offers food appreciated by birds of several species, then they may exploit it together. On mudflats in estuaries, we often come across mixed flocks of wading birds: redshanks, curlews, godwits, sanderlings, dunlin, knot and so on. The crow family is equally 'sociable', and rooks (the large, glossy-black birds with a white patch at the base of the bill in the breeding season), jackdaws (smaller, black with grey nape) and, in Scotland, occasionally hooded crows (rook-size, black with grey back and belly), may be seen feeding in the fields together in winter.

In the autumn, lapwings and starlings, though quite unrelated, may share the same field. Alongside the lapwings we may see wily

gulls waiting to harry them for a share of their earthworms. When a mixed flock is put to flight, each bird seeks safety amongst its own kind, however happy it might have been to mingle with unrelated species on the ground.

Since serious conflicts over food hardly ever develop in mixed feeding flocks, either there must be a surplus of food or the various bird species are exploiting different prey. In many cases there is good reason to believe the latter, as we saw in June. In wader flocks, for example, each species has its own food spectrum, dictated by the length of its probing bill, not to mention the length of its wading legs. The lapwing and starling co-habit the same pasture because the one probes for earthworms and the other for grubs.

In the woods we sometimes meet suddenly with a party of insectivorous birds. If we stand quietly, we may see a small flock of softly peeping tits moving past, among them blue tits and great tits, perhaps also coal tits, marsh tits and long-tailed tits, occasionally accompanied by goldcrests and the odd treecreeper, nuthatch or lesser spotted woodpecker. Such a group sometimes describes a fixed circuit through the area in the form of a circle or figure-of-eight. No one is quite sure of the advantage of these assemblages. Birds may benefit by watching where and how others feed and then copying them. The objection to this theory is that the different species usually take different foods anyway, and so cannot benefit that much from copying. Participation in flocks may also help birds to escape predators like sparrowhawks, on the principle that many eyes are better than two. Furthermore, with less time needed for surveillance, each flock member would have more freedom to concentrate on feeding. Certainly the members respond readily to each other's alarm calls which are remarkably similar between different tit species, so there is some benefit of safety in numbers. These calls, like the grasshopper warbler's song, have a strangely ventriloquial quality to the human ear, appearing to originate from somewhere other than the bird that produces it. This may

August

momentarily confuse a would-be predator and so enhance the tit's chance of escape.

Hoverflies, beetles and ants

Hoverflies, of which we have about 250 species in Britain, are on the wing from late March till November, but display their stunt-flying best in the still air of a beautiful summer's day. Its whirring wings form a blurr, but the hoverfly hangs motionless in the air for minutes, then suddenly darts forwards, sideways or even backwards a few feet, only to return a few seconds later to the same place. Now and then, one alights on a flower or leaf, and shows its black and yellow markings. Some are long and slender, clearly resembling wasps, and this deters birds from eating them. Others are short, squat and hairy like bumblebees. There may be more advantage here in deceiving the bees themselves than birds, for some bee-like hoverflies, notably *Volucella bombylans*, lay their eggs in bumblebee nests and their disguise may help them to infiltrate these undetected. One of our commonest hoverflies, the drone-fly *Eristalis tenax*, resembles a honeybee; its larva, however, lives in dung heaps and stagnant water where it feeds on organic sediment. It breathes by a 15cm (5¾in) telescopic tube at its hind end which can reach up to the surface like

a snorkel – hence its name 'rat-tailed maggot'. Other hoverfly larvae live on growing plants, including fungi or decaying wood, while some like *Volucella* scavenge in the nests of bees for debris and dead or dying bees. Many larvae are active and useful predators and consume vast numbers of aphids, a role in which they probably surpass the larvae of lacewing flies. By contrast, most adult hoverflies are harmless pollen eaters, subtly gaining everyday protection by disguising themselves as noxious stinging insects.

On the late umbellifers, as well as soldier beetles, we may come across other sorts, like longhorn beetles. These are robust, oblong, mostly brown or black insects, but their distinguishing feature is the long, jointed antennae which give them their name. They are wood-feeding insects, occasionally inflicting great damage on timber, but they can also be found resting on flowers. We may also find click beetles, so called for the sound made when the insect falls upside-down. With the 'click' the beetle also characteristically bounces up in the air. While the adults feed on pollen and nectar, the larvae, known as wireworms, feed on plant roots where they can be a serious pest for the farmer or gardener. On the ground roam the metallic, tank-like dung beetles, perhaps seeking a toadstool or other fungus

which they like to include in their diet. Dung beetles, devoted parents, lay their eggs in partly dried horse or cattle dung on which the larvae will feed. Some lay only a single egg in an elaborate burrow excavated in the dung, and then both parents tend the larva when it hatches until it leaves the burrow long afterwards. Ants, too, are hard at work foraging over the ground, hauling back food to the nest and in turn providing food themselves for birds with hungry broods.

Heather moors and heaths

August is the month of the heather bloom in the central and eastern Highlands of Scotland. The heather moor is essentially a sub-alpine heath of dwarf shrubs extending from near sea level to almost 800m (2,600ft), but mostly between 150m and 500m (500 and 1,600ft). For all its symbolic associations with the romance and history of Scotland, the moor is essentially an artificial habitat, created long ago by the clear-felling of the native pine forests and by subsequent grazing and burning. Today it is dominated by ling (*Calluna vulgaris*) together with mosses and lichens, though bell heather (*Erica cinerea*) and the red bearberry and cowberry can be locally important.

Mixed tit flock. Left to right: *marsh tit, long-tailed tit, coal tit, two goldcrests, nuthatch*

rowberries and bilberries also flourish on amper moors, while several flowering plants ccur, among them bitter vetch, bird's-foot efoil and violets.

Before the widespread introduction of sheep, e dominant grazing animal on these hillsides as the red deer. There are still large herds ven today, surviving on the herbage of owering plants, grasses and sedges, such as rple moor-grass, bog myrtle, deer's hair ass, and bog cotton. When there is a thick yer of fresh snow, however, deer come into e long heather, shake the stalks to knock off e snow, and browse the green tops.

A heather plant, by which we mostly mean ng, lives for a long time but not for ever. After out thirteen to sixteen years it reaches aturity and starts producing fewer new oots. After about thirty years it has egenerated, its shoots are woody and bare, d it is near death. To maintain good verage and encourage regeneration of nder, nutritious new shoots, the chief food of d grouse and sheep, landowners have aditionally burned heather moors. This moves the upper dry growth while the lower rts and roots survive. New shoots appear the xt year and growth is again optimum after o to three years. Sheep, and no doubt deer, so benefit from the flush of new herbs that llows burning of rank heather.

The best management policy is to burn once ery ten to fifteen years if the bulk of the eather is not to reach stagnant maturity. verburning can be as damaging as not rning often enough, since it sets back generation and allows plants like bracken d tormentil to gain a hold instead. It is stomary to 'burn off' in early spring when e moors are still inactive after winter. By ghts, burning should not be done after April if it is not to disrupt ground-nesting rds like grouse, curlew, greenshank and eadow pipit.

The heather-clad heaths characteristic of the wland, sandy soils of southern England are so at their most colourful in August. They are many of the same plants as the less posed, upland moors, especially tormentil, ilkwort, bedstraw and yarrow. However, ere are some notable additions: the rare arsh gentian may be found in damp places; warf gorse is common and, like ling, it may rbour a delicate little parasitic plant, mmon dodder, twining anticlockwise up its ems. The dodder sends sucker-like roots into e host's tissues, absorbing all it needs for its vn growth, and sometimes killing its host in e process. In dry areas we may find the tractive powder-blue flowers of the sheepsbit abious.

Gorse also provides nest sites for the Dartford arbler, one of Britain's scarcest breeding rds, which is entirely restricted to these wland heaths. The other bird characteristic this habitat is the nightjar, although again

Dung beetle, ladybird beetle and ants

it is nowhere common. In every respect it is an unusual bird. It arrives on our shores in mid-May from its winter quarters in Africa, and at first it is more likely to be heard than seen, since it feeds on the wing, mostly at night, trawling for moths with its gaping bill. Its vibrant churring or 'jarring' call, most often heard just after sunset, is unforgettable to anyone lucky enough to have heard it. When it sits on its rudimentary nest, a scantily lined, shallow cup on the ground, the nightjar effectively disappears, so perfectly does its bark-patterned plumage match its surroundings.

All six British reptiles are also found on lowland heaths, and two of them, the rare smooth snake and the sand lizard, occur nowhere else in the country. The adder or viper, our only poisonous snake, likes dry heaths, the grass snake wet ones, while the slow-worm and common lizard are tolerant of both and therefore quite widespread. Finally, heathland supports a characteristic spectrum of butterflies, including the grayling, silver-studded blue and green hairstreak, and moths such as the emperor and true lover's knot.

Grasshoppers

The grasshoppers of the summer grasslands belong largely to the short-horned grasshoppers group. These are the small green and brown insects which, like radio announcers, are known better for their voices than their looks. As a group they characteristically have short antennae and the females lack the long, curved egg-laying tube of the long-horned grasshoppers. Their song is the familiar chirping of sunny days, made by a procedure called stridulation. A ridged part of the hind leg (the 'file') is rubbed against a thick vein (the 'scraper') on the forewing, rather like drawing a comb over a piece of cardboard. Longhorns, or bush crickets, have the file on their other forewing instead. The males do most of the 'singing' with the purpose of attracting females; once they have a captive audience, they deliver a special courtship song and it is at this moment that the female may respond by chirping too. As with birds, each species has a distinctive song. The common green grasshopper, for instance, sustains a continuous chirp for 20 seconds or more, while the common field grasshopper delivers a volley of six to ten half-second chirps evenly spread over about twelve seconds.

Bilberry gin

August is the month to look for the fruits of the bilberry. In England the ripe berries are almost black and often known as whortleberries, while their Scottish counterparts, called blaeberries, are greyish-blue, rather like small grapes. They are generally found on heaths and moors on acid soils, sometimes in woods, and though fairly common they are not all that popular with berry gatherers because it is such back-breaking work collecting even a small amount. Probably this is just as well, for the plants take several years to flower and would soon get scarce if picking became excessive. Even so, they make excellent jam or pies, not to mention bilberry gin. Just as we can add autumn sloes, the berries of blackthorn, to gin to make a drink that adds welcome lustre to winter days, so we can use bilberries in the same way. All it requires is a few cupfuls of the berries, a little sugar, quite a lot of gin, and a couple of bottles with good, airtight corks. First fill the bottles three-quarters full with well-washed bilberries and then add enough sugar through a funnel just to cover the berries. Now cover the open tops of the bottles with aluminium foil and leave in a warm, sunny spot. Depending on the weather, the sugar will have dissolved in 5–7 days. Then pour in gin till each bottle is nearly full. Carefully stopper each bottle with a cork sterilised in boiling water, and store in a dark cool place. The only further requirement now is patience. Left for three months, bilberry gin is very good, but after six months it tastes even better!

September

A twilight month, still with many shades of summer, but also with the first shadows of winter. It is a time when country lore traditionally resorts to bold predictions, turning to wildlife for clues to the weather in store. In the autumn, Roman or edible snails, for example, go into hibernation in crevices, under logs, stones, and leaf litter, closing the door behind them, so to speak, by plugging the aperture of their shells with a thin lid of chalk. One observant country sage reckoned he could tell what the winter would be like from how deep the snails buried themselves, and the thickness of their lids. By the same token others believe that if mice dig their tunnels deep we can expect a long and severe winter, and if ants build their nest-mounds high even worse is to come.

Roman snail

In Europe, St Michael's Day (29 September) is one of those critical threshold days in the weather-diviner's calendar. If birds have not migrated south by St Michael's Day then winter is still a long way off, but if the acorns fall before St Michael's then the winter will 'pierce body and soul'. Indeed the timing and abundance of the harvest have always been an important, if somewhat dubious, indication of forthcoming weather; a bumper crop of berries is often quoted as a portent of a bad winter. But there is no evidence that the performance of the crops – or the snails either – is anything more than a reflection of past conditions; as Ingrid Holman succinctly put it, this is *hind* rather than fore-casting. Probably people read into the appearance of an abundant harvest some design to tide birds over hard times ahead, or else to ensure a good seed crop against anticipated losses among the plants themselves.

By halfway through the month the leaves of the lime have already turned yellow, and by the end of it many leaves have fallen, as with the poplars and birches. As the soil temperature drops, hindering the uptake of moisture through the roots, leaves of the chestnut and maple start drying at the edges; the trees are taking action to reduce transpiration. Some react much more drastically; especially after a dry summer, we may hear trees like beeches, elms, oaks and poplars shedding limbs with a mighty crack of rending timber. Such self-pruning, aimed at water economy, is not as injurious as it looks, for prior to amputation the tree has apparently already reduced the water supply to the limb and begun to seal the join.

Late flowering

Most of these phenomena, however, are associated with the tail-end of September, and the beginning of the month often has a different flavour. Many plants, like the dead-nettles, ragged robin and even marsh marigolds, seem to have a second lease of life, and may summon a last flowering effort before the autumn frosts extinguish them. By the seashore we may still find late blooms of sea rocket and sea holly, the latter providing a valuable source of food for late butterflies, notably painted ladies. Some plants continue flowering into autumn without a break, like the honeysuckle, which at the start of September may simultaneously bear buds, flowers, unripe green berries and ripe red ones.

For many of the biennials, however, September marks the end of their cycle. The evening primrose, for instance, which opened on summer evenings to be pollinated by night-flying moths, sets seed and the plant dies. So it is with members of the borage family like hound's tongue and viper's bugloss, and many others. Some of last year's seed has already

Garden spider, magnified

germinated, and the new plants have formed a rosette of leaves which manufacture and store food reserves in preparation for producing next year's flower stems. Sometimes, if conditions are difficult for them, the rosettes bolt prematurely in their first year and start to form a flower stalk, a phenomenon unwelcomely familiar to growers of cultivated plants and vegetables. Endive, for example, is very prone to bolting if seed germination is delayed beyond three days, so gardeners are recommended to sow in a hotbed if they want

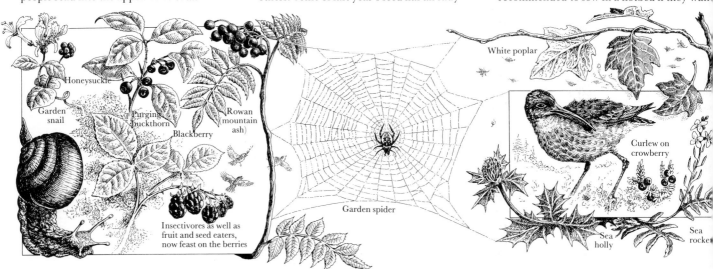

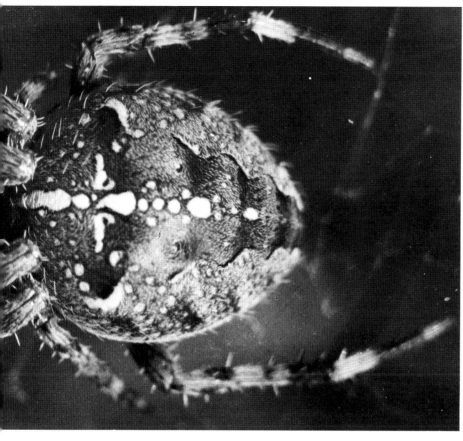

In the meantime, there is usually a surfeit – at least temporarily – of other nutritious berries: blackberries (brambles), elder, rowan, hawthorn, privet, bryony, guelder rose, spindle and buckthorn, to name some of the commonest. With the exception of blackberry and elder, all of these are almost inedible (purging buckthorn was, as its name suggests, once prescribed as a herbal purgative) or even poisonous to man, but birds relish them. A research project carried out by the Royal Society for the Protection of Birds showed that the berries most frequently taken were elder, hawthorn, yew and holly. The seeds often pass through the gut undamaged, so birds are important agents of plant dispersal. In New Zealand, once blackberries had been introduced from England it needed only the further introduction of their allies the blackbird and song thrush to make the plant spread like wildfire; the early settlers, of course, were largely unaware that the joint introduction represented a long-standing contract of mutual benefit between the species involved. The bounty of hedgerow food also attracts the first winter migrants, redwings and fieldfares from Scandinavia and Iceland, and starlings from central Europe, which greatly swell our resident population in winter.

While our attention is naturally drawn to the resplendent hedgerows, other habitats too are bearing fruit. In the Highlands, for instance, the edible, but (to us) almost tasteless crowberries have ripened and provide an important food supplement for grouse, curlews and other moorland birds.

Birds literally gorge themselves on berries at this time of year, and may quickly denude a tree of its entire crop. Eric Simms, the naturalist, once observed a party of fieldfares in Ladbroke Square, London, strip three

eir seedlings to behave as biennials should. In e little rosette, therefore, is invested the ture survival of the plant, and though ready wind-shielded by growing prone to the ound, the root now shortens itself, drawing e rosette, especially its vital heart, deeper to the soil for protection against the rigours of inter, rather as the snail does.

In the hedgerows, a few hop flowers are still be seen at the start of September, male and male flowers on different plants, both small d greenish-yellow, branched catkins in the ale, globular heads in the female, developing rough the months into the resinous cones ed to give beer its bitter flavour. Towards the d of September when most plants are on the ane, ivy breaks all the rules by bursting nfidently into small green, five-petalled wers. With insects finding it increasingly rd to balance their energy budget, the dden arrival of ivy nectar is a welcome nus, and not surprisingly the flowers become Mecca for seemingly every winged insect left ve in the garden, especially flies and bees.

ider harvest

ese insect visitors are preyed upon by iders, whose webs glisten in the early-morning sts of September. The hammock-like webs, t only in bramble thickets but also in long ass, gorse and other herbage, are the work of oney spiders'. They spin on warm mornings following a cool night and are often carried aloft in great numbers by ascending air currents, to descend later on shards of gossamer, sometimes coating fields and even ships at sea many miles from their point of levitation. This magical phenomenon is beautifully described by Gilbert White in his *Natural History of Selborne* from observations on late September days: 'On every side as the observer turned his eyes might he behold a continual succession of fresh flakes falling into his sight, and twinkling like stars as they turned their sides towards the sun.' White also noticed that it was not simply a passive process, for the spiders could apparently launch off at will, shooting out a web from their spinnerets and getting airborne at a moment's notice. When they are not aeronauts, money spiders hang beneath their webs, waiting to pounce on hapless insects which become entangled in the scaffolding of threads above the net and drop into it. The garden spider builds a different net, of the classic 'orb' type, a wheel of sticky silk which can ensnare insects as big as wasps. The spider lurks at the centre, running out unhindered along the specially dry radial threads to stab and retrieve its victims.

Fruit for birds and insects

The purplish-black ivy berries will not develop till the spring. Birds enjoy them then, eating the fruit and scattering the small, hard seeds.

hawthorns in six days. Such gluttony is no doubt facilitated by the ready digestibility of fruit – in the waxwing as little as sixteen minutes may elapse between eating a berry and excreting the indigestible seed. Apples, too, add to the birds' fare, not only now but even more usefully through the winter months. In the drought year of 1976, perhaps because the sap won from a parched soil was unusually concentrated, fermenting windfall apples seemed to have been particularly alcoholic, and there were several reports of blackbirds and thrushes reeling about half-stupefied in orchards.

Insects too make use of the sugars in fermenting September fruit. Inconspicuous earlier in the summer when they were beneficial in killing flies and other insect pests as protein food for their larvae, wasps now turn to fruit and other sources of sugar, and in so doing they may become major household and garden pests themselves. By the end of August wasp colonies, housed in those masterful architectural lanterns of papier-mâché, are at peak numbers. Males and new queens are now produced, they mate, the males die off, and the queens, like their bumblebee counterparts, go off to seek suitable hibernation sites. This signals the disintegration of the colony, and the hordes of wasps that plague aromatic kitchens – don't leave your baskets of ripe fruit near open windows! – are the redundant workers which, having gained a sweet tooth from the special saliva secreted by the larvae in the nest, now disperse in search of substitutes. Their short tongues do not allow them to get nectar from many flowers, but there are plenty of other sources. Many descend on blackberries, biting through the skin of the fruitlets to reach the flesh inside. Once pierced, the oozing juice attracts swarms of other insects – metallic greenbottles and flesh-flies (*Sarcophaga*) which dribble saliva on to the blackberry pulp, partly digesting it, and then suck up the juice.

Migratory butterflies

As the blackberries become ever more pulpy, they next attract butterflies, such as commas, speckled woods and red admirals, which can suck up the juice with long hollow tongues. The red admiral is also fond of settling on the trunks of fruit trees and of sucking over-ripe windfalls, especially pears and plums. Once called red admirables, these large handsome butterflies, with bright red and white markings against velvety black, are well known in town or country gardens in September and even later. Despite their abundance they are not native to Britain but migrate here annually in large numbers from the Mediterranean. After arriving on the south coast in April to June, they quickly spread inland, and the females start laying eggs on stinging nettles. The caterpillars, after gorging themselves, fasten two or three leaves together with silk to form a shelter or tent in which to hide, later to pupate

Wasps' nest

and metamorphose into the butterflies we see on the wing from July to August. These, in turn, may breed to yield an even more prolific second generation in September and October. Some may try to push south to reach warmer winter quarters, and a few others hibernate successfully, but in general very few survive our winter; the annual spring influx from the south is clearly vital to the continuity of the British population.

Those who notice such things will know that the red admiral population fluctuates from year to year, for a variety of reasons. Even more changeable are the fortunes of another common migrant, the painted lady, whose irregular immigration makes it abundant some years, rare in others. Nevertheless red admirals and painted ladies arrive in considerable numbers every year. Others turn up much more sporadically; they are truly 'endemic', regular in their visits, only much further south. Usually only a few vagrants of the clouded yellow and pale clouded yellow reach us, though in exceptional years, notably 1877 and 1941 for the clouded yellow, considerable numbers make a landfall in Britain. Most of our migrants undoubtedly hop the Channel

from France and Belgium, but the rare Camberwell beauty, which made its last spectacular invasion in 1976, is of Scandinavian origin, and so first appears on the east coast.

All the members of this last group have bumper years, but there are yet other butterflies which reach us only rarely and never in strength. These include the Queen of Spain fritillary, Bath white, various blues and the swallowtails *Papailio machaon*. Two cases, the American painted lady and the monarch, deserve special mention because their country of origin is North America, 4,800km (3,000 miles) west of here. The migratory feat of butterflies seem impressive enough without crediting them with powers of transatlantic travel they don't possess: probably the few individuals that reach these shores have had ship-assisted passages. The remote possibility that they fly in under their own steam has, however, yet to be disproved; some may exceptionally perform the journey unaided.

The moths also have migrant species, including one of the most dramatic insects ever found in Britain, the death's head hawkmoth, named after the skull-shaped marking on the

Death's-head hawkmoth *Hummingbird hawkmoth* *Gamma moth*

ack of its thorax. It also has the curious ability emit a squeaking sound, made by forcing air rough its short proboscis, when confronted y enemies. A night-flying moth, it migrates, metimes in great numbers, from its native frica but only rarely reaches the British Isles. Many years may elapse between landfalls here the day-flying hummingbird hawkmoth hich migrates from southern Europe, vering up to 160km (100 miles) a day. In me years this moth is widespread in Britain, elighting anyone lucky enough to see one vering over a flower just like a hummingbird ould, sucking up nectar with its long tongue nrolled. If they succeed in breeding, the new eneration of moths either migrates back to urope or stays behind to succumb to the inter. The summer population of the gamma oth, a common noctuid in Britain, is often ugmented by immigrants from Europe, whose rogeny may, like the hummingbird hawks, ake the return journey south. In no uropean species, whether butterfly or moth, owever, is it known for any single generation successfully complete a two-way orth–south, south–north) migration in its fetime, although monarchs in America do hieve just this feat, so rivalling the birds.

utumn fungi

t the close of the summer, if the weather has een dampish and not too cold for a couple of eeks, the great autumn show of fungi begins; elicate little bells appear on the lawn, fairy ngs in the fields, but the greatest variety, from inhead size to giant puffballs, on the oodland floor. In some years the fungus flora exceptionally prolific and diverse, often the sult of a combination of warm and prolonged mmer weather and a damp autumn. evertheless, and this is what intrigues us out fungi, some fail to appear for no obvious ason; for instance, *Russula* and *Lactarius* ecies were inexplicably absent from many aces in 1976 in ideal weather conditions. One panding fairy ring of *Clitocybe maxima* was udied over fifty years and only fruited once

Fly agaric

Boletus edulis

during all that time!

This makes it very difficult to predict just where and when a particular fungus will be found, but we can follow general guidelines because individual species, like any organisms, are adapted to certain habitats, like acid or alkaline soils for instance. A good place to start looking is along damp wayside verges; some will be better than others, depending on the underlying soil, but often the richest are under old avenues of oaks, birches, aspens or conifers

whose roots and litter create the right conditions for many species, among them *Boletus*. These are robust, thick-capped toadstools with the spores borne not on gills but in thousands of vertical tubes inside the cap, the openings to which are seen as pores on the underside. Several, but by no means all, of the *Boleti* make excellent eating and were much prized by the Romans (who called them 'suillus'), especially *B. edulis* which is frequently found nestling in deep grass along forest rides, notably amongst spruce, occasionally beech, where its cap diameter may reach over 25cm (10in). In some species the flesh of the cap turns blue when cut, but not in *B. edulis* which remains white. When cooked it has a sweet taste and attractive aroma. Unfortunately other animals besides humans relish it and several insects, especially flies and beetles, lay their eggs on *Boletus* for their larvae to feed on. So it is unusual to find a very big one still undamaged; the early part of the fungus season offers the best chance of getting intact specimens. As with the morels, various attempts have been made to cultivate this delicacy, but without success, and in Europe they fetch a high price in the market place.

Apart from *Boletus*, probably the best-known toadstool, impressed on our mind's eye from the illustrated tales of childhood, is the fly agaric, so-called from the insecticidal properties attributed to it in medieval times. Its vivid orange-red cap, with scattered white warts or scales, has traditionally been interpreted as a poison warning, and it does have highly disruptive effects on the nervous and digestive system, though it is fortunately rarely fatal. Related species, however, the 'white amanitas', are deadly poisonous and anyone not expert at identification should leave the whole group strictly alone. For a species so steeped in mythology and folklore, the fly agaric is not very common. It usually occurs in groups on acid soil under birch trees, less frequently under conifers, pine in particular, or sometimes under beech. This association between fly agaric, *Boletus* and other fungi and certain tree species is another example of a specially intimate relationship of mutual benefit (symbiosis); it is characteristic of all 'mycorrhizal' fungi. The underground network of fungal tissue penetrates the tree's roots, enhancing their mineral uptake from the soil. The fungus, for its part, derives nutritious sugars from the tree. So important is this association that in commercial forestry new saplings may be artificially infected with the appropriate fungus before planting.

Bird migration: why and how?

Many animals have only a limited ability to escape from their immediate surroundings when faced with hardship, and so are forced to lead a relatively sedentary life in places where they can survive throughout the year. Many early naturalists knew this and for a long time misinterpreted the seasonal comings and goings of flying creatures, especially birds like swifts, swallows, and martins, assuming that since they disappeared in the autumn and reappeared in the spring they must be hibernating nearby for the winter. It is only since man has been able to travel as widely as the birds themselves that the true nature and scale of migration has been appreciated. We now know that about half the world's birds migrate to some extent, meaning they have a seasonal movement, usually between a breeding and a non-breeding area, involving two journeys a year. And to what end?

Simply, migration is a means of seeking at a distance whatever is lacking at a given time and place. Many birds leave high latitudes in the cold, dark, barren days of winter, but return in spring when rising temperatures trigger off a superabundance of food for them – plant and animal life, especially insects, small mammals, plankton and fish. As spring passes into summer, there is the added attraction of more daylight hours for seeking and collecting food. This state of surplus is short-lived but still long enough for a vast floating population of summer visitors to raise their young and move elsewhere before winter sets in again.

The same marked seasonal contrasts prevail in both northern and southern hemispheres, and both exert a strong pull, but the northern summer is especially attractive to birds since it embraces the bulk of the world's land mass; and, moreover, a land mass of great complexity – a mosaic of tundra, coniferous and broad-leaved forest, grass and heath lands, permeated throughout with waterways of numerous kinds. So notwithstanding the extensive population of resident species which seem to be tapping the whole range of resources throughout the year, the environment is sufficiently diverse and productive to absorb each summer a huge influx of new specialists; in Europe and Asia about 40 per cent of the total tally of some 589 breeding species are summer visitors. Most of the visitors to Europe claim Africa as their winter quarters and 1,000 million birds are

Sandwich terns, now beginning to leave in small groups

estimated to commute annually between the two.

Winter arrives early in the far north, so by early September the retreat from these furthest outposts is already in full swing. Further south the migrants which make Europe their summer residence have a bit more leeway, and generally don't move till later in the month, or even October. So short is the polar summer that some birds do not have time to moult after breeding, and have to break their journey south in order to carry out this vital refurbishing of their feathers before continuing to their winter quarters. Many of the wading birds along the British shores in September belong to this category, seeking out rich feeding grounds like estuaries and shallow bays as staging posts for the energy-consuming process of moult. Some may even have come from northern Russia and made a detour west to the North Sea coast to take advantage of the late summer flush of food there.

Whimbrel

The migrant-rich September shores

A visit to the coast at this time of year is therefore an interesting and rewarding experience. First there are the waders – sandpipers, redshank, sanderling, dunlin, knot, godwits and plovers. Apart from the difference in length of bill and leg we have already discussed, they can be a frustratingly uniform group for the novice birdwatcher intent on sorting them all out, especially as many are passing out of their distinctive breeding plumage into the common denominator of mottled brown and buff that serves them through winter. Careful observation of how they behave, however, will soon expose helpful differences; some run frantically over the surface with a rapid clockwork motion, while others take measured strides, pausing to probe the mud between each. Nor is plumage really identical; flushed from the ground, some reveal bold wing flashes, hidden at rest, which are useful clues to identity, or else they may utter a call of alarm or contact, characteristic of their species. One thing you will soon notice is that all have the curious habit of roosting quite contentedly on one leg. Perhaps because legs are one of the few uninsulated parts of the body – and long ones at that in wading birds – one is tucked away whenever possible to conserve heat.

Other migrant shorebirds are the skuas, roughly similar in size to their relatives the gulls, but with darker (brown) plumage. In the summer, their breeding grounds extend from the north of Scotland into the Arctic. There they are highly predatory, killing small mammals (often lemmings), adults, eggs and

young of other birds, and pouncing on any
carrion they find. However, they are best
known for their habit of chasing and
intimidating other seabirds till they are forced
to disgorge food. All skuas are long-distance
migrants, most reaching the tropics in winter
and some travelling beyond.

It is no coincidence that their journey south
is synchronised with that of the terns, which are
prime targets in the skuas' daily quest for food.
In a prolonged pursuit, the flight skills of skua
and tern are taxed to the limit as each twists
and turns, swoops and soars. The tern may
manage to swallow its fish in flight, but just as
often it is hounded into dropping it, whereupon
the skua plummets, usually retrieving it in mid-
air. Shadowing the movements of the tern
flocks day by day, the skuas have time to pick
and choose their victims, often selecting a bird
which has just caught a particularly big meal,
such as a long sand-eel or a deep-bodied sprat.
Possession of a small fish is often unchallenged,
so a tern can usually afford to forfeit the odd
large fish to a skua and still feed itself and, if
need be, its offspring.

Migratory land birds are faced with
hazardous sea-crossings, and equally
inhospitable land crossings – the Pyrenees or
the Sahara Desert – on their journey to Africa.
Faced with such barriers, there is no stopping:
the birds must have enough energy reserves
and stamina to surmount them in a single hop.
Many warblers migrating south from Europe,
having fattened up beforehand – for fat is the
migratory fuel – resign themselves to fasting on
an unbroken flight of some 1,920km
(1,200 miles) across the Mediterranean and
Sahara. This must take a warbler at least 48
hours, and often longer, so to budget its fuel
reserves accurately in advance is a matter of life
or death.

Seabirds on migration are obviously under
much less pressure since they can replenish
themselves along the way. Even so, some must
return south in haste since ringed sandwich
terns have been recovered in their winter
quarters in Ghana, West Africa, at the
beginning of September. Perhaps these are
young unattached adults, or failed breeders.
Ringing recoveries have also shown that Arctic
terns and roseate terns may leave European
waters more rapidly than common and
sandwich terns – in the case of Arctic terns,
probably because they have so far to go. Many
of them breed north of the Arctic Circle and
migrate to Antarctic waters, a journey of at
least 12,800km (8,000 miles) each way. This
literally gives them the best of both worlds as
far as feeding conditions are concerned, since
they experience summers of twenty-four hours
of daylight at both ends of their range.

Other individuals, however, especially
common and sandwich terns, migrate in more
leisurely fashion, and because they rarely travel
in large flocks their gradual departure may go
almost unnoticed. The small flocks and family

groups may, however, assemble in larger roosts
near good feeding grounds, giving us an
opportunity to identify the different species:

1 Sandwich tern *Sterna sandvicensis*, the
biggest species, about black-headed gull size,
with a short crest to its black cap (most visible
in display), black legs and black bill with
yellow tip. It is a robust, high-diving tern,
generally whiter than the common tern in
appearance. The call is a harsh 'kirrik'.
2 Common tern *S. hirundo*, somewhat smaller
and lighter build, with a much longer, deeply
forked tail, and graceful buoyant flight. It has a
red bill with black tip, and red legs, and
haunts the shoreline, typically hovering before
diving. It is often confused with the Arctic tern
S. paradisaea, which has an all-blood-red bill,
shorter red legs and translucent wing tips, and
is less often seen close inshore: Yet a third
species, the roseate tern *S. dougallii*, may also
cause confusion, but sadly is becoming so rare
nowadays in the British Isles that it is seldom
seen.
3 Little tern *S. albifrons*, smallest of the sea
terns, about swift size, with a rapid wing-beat
and superb hovering skills, adapted for
catching prey by diving into the shallowest
pools. The forehead is white in all seasons, the
bill and legs yellow.
4 Black tern *Chlidonias niger*, one of the three
small inland 'marsh' terns of Europe. It
formerly bred in small numbers on the east
coast of England. Despite a few recent breeding
attempts it is a rarity here, but it may
occasionally be seen consorting with sea terns
on the coast in late summer, dipping lightly to

the surface for food. Sometimes it is seen on
inland reservoirs, hawking for aquatic insects,
either in the air or from the surface. The winter
plumage (5) is much whiter on the head and
underparts, which may lead to confusion with
juveniles and moulting adults of other species.
In fact from August-September onwards, all
the terns, like waders, begin changing into
duller plumage, making identification harder.
In common and Arctic terns, for example, the
bill turns black and the legs reddish-brown.

Often the family groups of terns, perhaps
only a single parent and juvenile, we see on our
coasts in September are birds which dispersed
quickly from the colony, possibly to escape the
pressure of numbers, and now take time to visit
traditionally reliable autumn feeding grounds.
For such birds there is initially no urge to go
south, and they are just as likely to go a long
way north. Juvenile sandwich terns from a
colony in Aberdeenshire have been seen well
north in the Moray Firth, and up to 65km
(40 miles) south of the colony only three days
after fledging. At this time the young are still
dependent on their parents for food and follow
them around begging with wheedling, high-
pitched calls. Food is transferred from parent
to offspring either on the water or on land,
probably more at sea as migration proper gets
under way during September. During this time
the juveniles practise plunge-diving, at first
clumsily and without success, but gradually to
more effect. It is a difficult way to obtain food,
requiring favourable weather and fine
judgement, so much so that even after several
months have elapsed in the winter quarters

young sandwich terns are often worse at catching fish than the older, more experienced birds. Apart from learning by trial and error, the amount young birds pick up from watching their parents cannot be underestimated, and in subsequent summers many return to the very same remote feeding grounds to which their parents introduced them during those apparently aimless wanderings in the first weeks after they dispersed from their natal colony.

Jam making

A beautiful September yields such an abundance of fruit and berries that we almost *have* to make jam whether we like it or not! Firstly we have to acquire, of course, the necessary equipment – jam jars and a large pan. Traditional pans were made of copper, but one of aluminium or stainless steel is just as good. Then the fruit. There is a special satisfaction in using wild berries like those of the elder, but remember to collect them not over-ripe and on a sunny day so they are dry, which will reduce the risk of contracting mould: 'Out, fruit go and gather, but not in the dew', as the old saying goes. Using them as fresh as possible, strip elderberries from their stalks with a fork, remove any bad ones, wash the rest, and mash them with a wooden spoon in the jam pan. In fact use a wooden spoon throughout the stirring, to avoid any chance of imparting a metallic taste to the brew. Bring gently to the boil and continue to boil vigorously till the pulp is reduced to about three-quarters of the original volume. After that, sugar is stirred in (1.1kg per kg of berries), as preservative and sweetener, and to help the jam set. It may be an advantage to warm the sugar before adding it as it dissolves more quickly when hot. The addition of the juice of a couple of lemons will also help the jam to set, and may improve the colour and flavour. Stir well till the sugar is dissolved, bring quickly back to the boil, and continue till a small quantity dropped on a cold plate solidifies –

Venus's looking-glass

this shows that the setting-point has been reached. Thereafter let the jam boil again for another ten minutes, stirring continuously.

Remove from the heat and pour into clean, dry, warm jars. Seal each jar with a waxed circle on the surface of the jam, and a damped cellophane cover, secured with a rubber band, over the rim. Some people turn each jar upside-down till the jam has cooled, on the principle that if there is no air gap between jam and cellophane, no mildew can form. Store the jars in a cool, dry, dark cupboard and check them every now and again for mould. If any mould should form it will be restricted to the top, so don't discard the whole jar but simply skim off the top layer and use up the rest of the jar quite quickly. The rest of the jar should taste fine and be quite harmless, but if you are in any doubt you can always re-boil. Elderberries mixed with blackberries in equal proportions make another excellent preserve; and, if you are energetic, these plus sloes, haws, crab-apples, rosehips and hazelnuts produce the deliciously blended flavour of 'hedgerow jam'.

Aphids unlimited

There is one other 'migrant' we should not overlook, and indeed sometimes cannot, even if we try. Suddenly one day in late summer you might be showered with a plague of small winged insects. They seem to descend out of the heavens, and carpet our gardens for days to come, which earned them the name 'smother-flies' in olden times. It is recorded that in 1836 and 1869, the swarms were unusually large over England, and in one place they covered an area twelve miles by five. These are aphids, though not necessarily the oak aphids we met in August, for there are about 500 different species in Britain and they infest all areas of the plant kingdom from cereals to mature timber. The ones we see aloft from roughly August to

October are winged individuals which developed on their summer host plant, and are emigrating in search of quite a different species, their winter host plant.

One of the commonest species, gardeners will ruefully agree, is the black bean aphid, found on broad beans in summer, and mostly spindle trees in winter. The winged aphids leaving after the bean crop is over are mainly females, a few males with them. Swept up to a mile or more into the atmosphere by ascending convection currents, they may be carried prodigious distances, many even reaching the British Isles from continental Europe, Scandinavia included, and aggravating the spread of viral diseases in the process. So if you garden is suddenly invaded, don't rush to blame the organic gardener next door who never uses insecticides, for the culprits may just as easily have originated a hundred miles away. Thermal activity subsides in the evening as the air cools, and the aphids, along with money spiders, mites and other members of the 'aerial plankton', drift to the ground. Many, of course, land in the sea, perhaps even the snow-covered Alps, or some other barren region, and perish, but those that land in the right sort of habitat can sense and respond to a number of cues from their host plant, in this case spindle, helping them to home in on it. Even if they do not find the target plant immediately, they are not doomed, since they can simply take off again and try elsewhere. Those winged females successful in their quest now accomplish the first of several curious feats in the life cycle – they give birth to live offspring, all wingless females, by a process called parthenogenesis, literally 'virgin birth'. These, in turn, mate with the winged males that have also made it back to the host tree, and eggs are laid which can survive the winter.

In spring, usually about March, the eggs hatch into wingless females known as 'stem-mothers' which, again parthenogenetically,

Scarlet pimpernel

give birth to live females, but no males. Some of this new generation is winged and it is these which disperse in May and June to found new colonies on broad beans, spinach or dock. Thereafter, if the gardener does nothing to prevent it, follows a rapid succession of female generations, alternating between winged and wingless aphids, all born live without the involvement of a single male or the production of a single egg. By producing a few offspring each day, a female's lifetime of two to three weeks will generate up to 50 new aphids, each of which in turn can potentially start turning out 50 of its own when it is little more than a week old. With so rapid a turnover, a seemingly minor outbreak can quickly reach epidemic proportions. It has been estimated that in one year, barring mortality, one aphid's descendants would equal the weight of 600 million men.

Obviously this potential isn't realised, not only because the aphids would soon eat, or rather suck, themselves out of existence, but because millions are destroyed by predators. As we have seen, various insects, notably ladybirds, lacewings and hoverfly larvae, can and do consume hordes of aphids, affecting their own numbers greatly in the process. Some are also preyed upon by certain bugs, beetles, spiders, and Hymenoptera. The big aphid year of 1976 led to a build-up of ladybirds which was nothing short of incredible, even to seasoned entomologists. At the peak of the outbreak, the tideline on some Norfolk beaches was carpeted for miles with a band of dead ladybirds, in many places up to a metre wide and several centimetres deep. Once the ladybirds had accounted for the aphid legions they turned, as we saw in August, to alternative sources of food, including the thrip, the 'thunder fly', itself migratory on a massive scale and occasionally a serious pest. By 1977, so many ladybirds had been parasitised and died that they ceased to play a significant role in containing aphids, and hoverfly larvae took precedence that year.

Birds also make inroads on aphids; blue tits in particular take a heavy toll in trees, both in woodland and orchards, and in some cultivated crops, but in the summer when they have broods to raise they concentrate on finding caterpillars, which offer a more lucrative return for energy expended. By the time the young tits fledge, caterpillars are on the wane and aphids may then figure more in their diet, but most of this goes on unseen in the forest canopy, and little is known about it. In general, however, tits seem unlikely to have more than a local impact on aphid numbers. On farmland, partridge chicks are very partial to cereal aphids, and in some years when little else is available their very survival depends on them. In particular these aphids have had an important part to play in the successful introduction of the red-legged partridge to this country.

Beneficial as insect and bird predators are, they cannot often do more than blunt a major outbreak of cereal aphids. The sap-sucking activities of the insects may depress yields by 10–20 per cent, but it is the risk of aphid-borne virus infections that is the greatest threat. Nor are these sorts of damage confined to farmland; even a moderate infestation of black bean aphids in a garden plot can reduce the height of the bean stem by a fifth, and the weight of beans by over four-fifths! To a large extent, the hazards in farmland are the inevitable price of modern farming methods. Fewer hedgerows, less crop rotation and more efficient insecticides have reduced the numbers and diversity of natural insect predators, while the aphids themselves find cereal food increasingly offered to them in areas of ever greater and more attractive dimensions.

Bygone harvest flowers

Modern methods of cleaning grain before sowing further reduce weeds and the insect fauna once associated with them. Mention has already been made in the July chapter of some of the traditional flowers of bygone harvests, and to these may be added the cornflower (or 'hurt-sickle' because it used to blunt reapers' sickles) and smaller plants which used to flourish in the stubble, like Venus's looking-glass and scarlet pimpernel. When the seed capsule of looking-glass is ripe, three holes at the top allow out the oblong, buff-coloured seeds which glint like tiny mirrors, hence the plant's name. Scarlet pimpernel is also known as 'poor man's weather-glass' because the flowers close before and during rain.

Even where these flower gems manage to

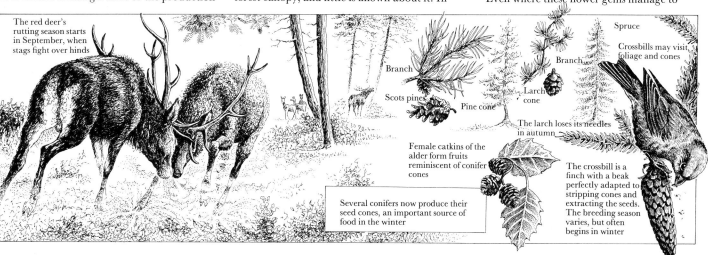

The red deer's rutting season starts in September, when stags fight over hinds

Branch

Scots pines

Pine cone

Larch cone

Branch

Spruce

Crossbills may visit foliage and cones

The larch loses its needles in autumn

Female catkins of the alder form fruits reminiscent of conifer cones

Several conifers now produce their seed cones, an important source of food in the winter

The crossbill is a finch with a beak perfectly adapted to stripping cones and extracting the seeds. The breeding season varies, but often begins in winter

September

infiltrate the cornfield and colour the stubble, their swift and final 'grim reaper' today will often be stubble-burning. This practice can also induce a dramatic change in the weather; the sun may become hazy, and rain begin to fall. This may be because moisture needs a speck of dust around which to form, and the clouds of smoke and smut billowing into the upper atmosphere induce condensation on a grand scale. Ironically, by excessive burning, farmers may thus hinder the completion of their harvests, a point wryly observed by the countryman Robin Page in his verse:

In September after burning stubble
Ponds and streams begin to bubble.

Crabs and barnacles

On the shore we often find a blackish-green to reddish crab, the shore crab, ranging everywhere from the highest pools down to below low-water mark. A hardy, versatile animal, it is mostly indifferent to substrate-type or salinity, living with equal success on sandy beaches, rocky coasts or in muddy, brackish estuaries. Shore crabs are solitary scavengers, fiercely challenging intruders, but their lives are not without hazard and they are especially vulnerable when growing-pains oblige them to moult their old shell or 'carapace' in favour of a new and larger one, which at first will be soft and penetrable.

Most crab species manufacture their own succession of armour plating, but the hermit crab has no hard exterior of its own and instead inhabits ever-larger snail shells as it grows. In fights, crabs may damage or even lose a leg, but remarkably they can grow a replacement one. Near low-water mark we find another crab, uniformly pink-brown with a characteristic 'pie-crust' edging to its shell. This is the edible crab, regrettably not a regular member of the intertidal fauna but, like the lobster, migrating offshore in winter to spawn. The eggs hatch out in shallower water, giving rise to the smaller specimens we sometimes find there. The big ones, worth eating, can measure up to 25cm ($9\frac{3}{4}$in) across the carapace, and weigh over 5kg (11lb), but are seldom seen inshore.

To think that crabs are the commonest shore crustaceans would be to overlook the myriads of tiny barnacles encrusting the rocks. Limpet-like in appearance, they may resemble molluscs, but are undeniably crustaceans, albeit strange ones. There are several species of these sessile or acorn barnacles, differing mostly in the architecture of the plates which protect their soft bodies from wave action, exposure and enemies. From a broad base cemented to the rock rise six stout, limy plates, curving inwards at the top to surround four smaller 'opercular' plates. These open like doors when the tide covers the barnacle, allowing six pairs of feathery appendages to protrude. These are the highly modified walking legs of less aberrant crustaceans like

Shore crab

Barnacles and mussel

Barnacles on metal

crabs and prawns. Looking rather like hands with the fingers half-curled, these limbs tirelessly comb the water, alternately grasping and retracting. In this fashion they enmesh tiny particles of food with their legs, literally kicking them into their mouths. When the tide is out, the hinged opercular plates close tight to prevent desiccation. The barnacle's limy fortress is, however, of no avail against the carnivorous dog whelk. This prises the plates apart, inserts its proboscis, armed at the tip with horny teeth, and rasps out the soft insides.

Ship's or stalked barnacles have the same basic plate arrangement but have long tough stalks for attaching themselves to all manner of floating objects, like buoys and driftwood. Over a time, heavy encrustations used to build up on the wooden hulls of old sailing ships, significantly hindering their rate of progress through the water. The tendency for ship's barnacles to be washed ashore attached to wood led to wild speculation in medieval times about their place of origin. One idea, more myth than theory, supposed that they grew on trees, not so illogical, but went on more fancifully to suggest that they grew into barnacle geese by sprouting feathers; to this day they are still known to some as goose barnacles.

Indian summer

By the end of September we are inclined to think that summer has outrun itself; but sometimes, late on, we are treated to a short burst of extremely fine weather, popularly known as an Indian summer. The term was introduced in the nineteenth century from North America, where such autumn days were used by the Indians for storing crops and making other winter preparations. In Britain they are caused by the North Atlantic anticyclone holding temporary sway and spreading its influence north-eastwards. If it happens it is usually in October or even early November.

At night, anticyclonic September weather is characterised by mist forming after sunset. During the day, as the sun warms the air, it increases its capacity to hold water, but after sunset the ground and the air above it immediately cool rapidly, and the surplus moisture condenses out as suspended droplets. As we have already seen, stubble burning enhances the condensation process, but all the other sorts of particles that find their way into the atmosphere likewise act as nuclei for coalescing moisture – salt from sea spray, clay dust, pollen grains and, particularly at this time of year, fungal spores. For the same reason, industrial smokes make towns and cities rather prone to misty, even foggy, autumn mornings, though compulsory use of smokeless fuels has largely eliminated the misery of the 'smogs' notorious in London in the 1950s.

Clear September nights are a good time to look for haloes – rings of rainbow-coloured light – which form around the moon when it is veiled by a thin sheet of cirrostratus, the ice-crystal cloud. Generated by the refraction of moonlight through the randomly organized crystals, we can expect the most spectacular ones on a full moon when its light is strongest. On such a night you may occasionally see more than one halo, as concentric rings. If you then take a pair of dividers, hold the hinge close to your eye, point one tip at the centre of the moon, and open the other arm till its tip reaches a halo, you will find that it subtends a known angle, commonly 22°, sometimes 46°, very rarely 8°. These fixed angles arise because the haloes are following the physical rules of optics when light passes through the faces of the prismatic ice crystals at different angles. Exactly similar haloes also form around the sun on hazy days (do not try to measure them with the naked eye), and like moon haloes they traditionally warn of approaching rain:

Last night the sun went pale to bed,
The moon in haloes hid her head.
T'will surely rain – I see with sorrow
Our jaunt must be put off tomorrow.

We have found a lot of unreliable weather lore but this is not without foundation; cirrostratus commonly precedes frontal depressions. Just as often, however, the front

A 22° halo around the sun, often a rain warning

peters out before it gets to the rain-making stage, so it is not an unfailing guide. A halo may also surround a weird and beautiful optical phenomenon popularly known as a 'broken spectre'. Sometimes, on the high tops, a mountaineer looks down to see a giant shadow of himself, encircled by a rainbow, projected on to the 'screen' of a foggy valley below. The misty atmosphere behaves like a magnifying glass to create this eerie effect, which has sped some climbers to a hasty descent, raving with tales of enchanted mountains.

Whales on our doorstep

When we read of the plight of whales, our minds tend to drift off to exotic southern oceans. If we were only more aware of the great diversity of whale and dolphin life in our own coastal waters, the news reportage might have more immediacy. Cetaceans, as zoologists call them, do mainly breed in southern latitudes, but they move into higher latitudes to feed during our summer months, and it is then that we are most likely to encounter them. The only clear exception to this is the porpoise, easily our commonest species, which is present, often close inshore, for much of the year. About five dolphin species regularly occur around

Britain, and to identify them accurately is tricky. Common, bottle-nosed and Risso's dolphins may be expected in the south, white-beaked and white-sided dolphins more often in the north and west; but in the present state of knowledge, even these crude divisions must be treated cautiously. Whales are less often seen, but three are sighted fairly regularly: the killer whale, a summer visitor to the west coast, is best known, although pilot and bottle-nosed whales are recorded just as often.

Porpoise

October

With any luck, the Indian summer embraces October; if it extends to the 18th of the month, St Luke's Day, farmers used to call it 'St Luke's little summer', for a fine spell then is often the last chance to take in a late harvest, a chance gratefully accepted. As temperatures fall, so the leaves fall with them, and not surprisingly the behaviour of the trees at this time has long been invested with predictive powers. In Europe there is a saying that 'October with green leaves means a severe winter' and, in this country, leaves failing to fall in October but withering on their branches later in the autumn asks for the same interpretation. Is there any validity in this, and if so, why? First we need to know why trees have to lose their leaves at all.

In these latitudes, all the broad-leaved trees regularly shed their foliage in the autumn – we call them deciduous – together with a few of the conifers, notably the larch, and the deciduous cypresses (*Taxodium* sp) which even shed branchlets as well. In winter, lower ground temperatures make it harder for root systems to extract water from the soil, and if the tree were to retain a vast leaf area, and all the evaporation and transpiration that entails, its tissues would soon dry out and die. So leaves are dropped for self-protection. Most of the conifers have got round the problem by evolving tiny needle-shaped leaves with thick skins which retain water with great efficiency (not surprisingly, cacti show some of the same adaptations), so they can be retained throughout the hardest winters. In fact most conifer leaves have a lifespan of three to five years or more, though those that are old and worn are more likely to be shed in the autumn than at other seasons.

The discarding of leaves is brought about by the development of a special layer of cells, the 'abscission layer', where the leaf-stalk meets wood. It forms gradually, beginning long before the leaf actually falls, so trees begin subtle advance preparations for the winter while outwardly keeping up summer appearances in the late autumn sunshine. Even if they do not, in some years, have sharply falling temperatures to trigger off these inner changes, the shortening days alone would provide a reliable cue. By accident, city trees growing near street lamps have provided an interesting piece of experimental evidence for the influence of light. The lamps effectively increase the daylength around them and may cause some trees at least to cling to their leaves longer than others left unilluminated.

In the developing abscission layer, the cells become soft and gelatinous so that they separate from one another, until finally the leaf is held on only by the 'vascular' tubes through which sap and plant products are circulated. At this stage the leaf hangs, as it were, by a thread, and eventually a gust of wind or an air frost will rupture this last connection. A good tree on which to look for the remains of these

Autumn in the woods

tube connections is the horse chestnut; the 'horseshoe-nail' scars left on the twigs after leaf fall are traces of the main veins, one for each of the five to seven leaflets.

Frosty October nights followed by sunny mornings which melt the ice around the leaf base usually result in widespread leaf falls. Sometimes, however, a night frost – especially early in the month – can retard the formation of the abscission layer, so that regardless of the subsequent weather the leaf cannot be shed on time. Notably in oaks, and some others, it is not uncommon to find some of the dead leaves over-wintering on the tree, through the failure of the vascular strands to break or of the abscission layer to develop properly. So, harking back to our original piece of country weather-lore, the association between an early frost and disrupted leaf fall was probably accurately observed, and then less accurately taken as forecasting a hard winter.

Between the abscission layer and the stem there usually forms a protective layer of waterproof corky cells; this may develop before or after the leaf falls, but either way it heals over the scar left behind, and so sets the seal on the tree's water-conservation measures for the winter.

Autumn colours

As the vitality of the leaves wanes, these profound internal changes also show themselves in the brilliant display of autumn colours. The summer green is due to chlorophyll, the pigment which manufactures the tree's sugars. Chlorophyll is destroyed by the sunlight, but in the normal course of even it is constantly being replaced; so the leaves remain green until, with the first breath of autumn, the tree begins to deprive its leaves of the necessary building blocks. Then chlorophyll is irreplaceably lost, and other pigments, yellow and red, more resistant to sunlight, come to the fore. These are not simply inert decay products; some living, healthy leaves, of the copper beech for example, have such a high concentration of red that the green of the chlorophyll is masked completely. In some trees, notably ash, walnut, sycamore, poplar and some birches, yellow is the predominant – if not the only – autumn colour. Reds tend to develop in unusually bright sunlight, so that oaks and maples in shady places don't turn red but stop at yellow. Perhaps for the same reason, bright and sunny autumns seem to bring on more vivid shows of colour than dull and cloudy ones. An abrupt change from high summer temperatures to low

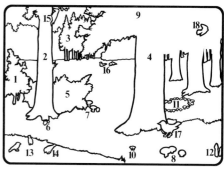

...a buckthorn berries, welcomed by winter
...igrants to Britain

...utumn ones, especially a sudden frost, also ...ems to heighten the intensity of colour, partly ...ecause there isn't time for the tree to ...ithdraw sugars from the leaves. It is known ...at leaves rich in sugar, like those of the ...aple, tend to turn the brightest red, a fact ...at all Canadians will heartily endorse. If we ...n mention again the great drought of 1976, ...at year was crowned by as dazzling a display ...autumn hues as anyone could remember; it ... likely that the sap was unusually rich, and ...ow to be resorbed from the leaves.

Fruits and birds

Many trees are bedecked in a mixture of gold and red, and some enhance their splendour with brightly coloured fruits. One of the most striking is the coral-pink, four-lobed seed capsule of the spindle tree, reminiscent of a Roman Catholic priest's hat. The seeds themselves are white, surrounded by a showy orange fleshy outgrowth, the 'aril', which is much relished by birds. For winter migrants to these shores, like fieldfares and redwings, the

conspicuous orange berries of the buckthorn, too, must be a welcome sight when they first make a landing on east-coast sand dunes. Indeed it is safe to say that vivid, shiny seedcoats evolved to attract and enlist birds and mammals as dispersal agents, just as brightly coloured flowers engage insects for pollination. Many fruits signal that their seeds are ripe and the fruit ready to eat by dramatically changing colour; often an inconspicuous green becomes bright red, as in tomatoes. At the same time they become more palatable – softer and sweeter-tasting. Many ripe fruits are black (or with mistletoe even white) and their contrast against the green foliage also helps to attract birds. Certainly mistle thrushes really do eat mistletoe berries, and they do a valuable service in dispersing yew seeds, which instead of having a complete seedcoat lure the birds with a fleshy red modified cone which cups the seed. As in spindle, the fleshy cup is an aril, which does not develop from the ovary as in a true fruit. Strawberries and apples are also 'false fruits'. That most apples are obviously too big for birds to swallow, seed and all, is largely an artefact of selective breeding by man, and originally apples too, as wild crab apples illustrate, must have been tailor-made for

When the seeds of maple and sycamore are ripe they part company, and each is then dispersed by the wind

Oak and acorns

Nuthatch

The red squirrel is one of nature's most successful profiteers from the autumn food surplus

Brambling eating Beech mast

Horse-chestnut seed (conker) and husk

Finches with their crushing bills, and more omnivorous species like crows and tits, enjoy the autumn seed crops

Garden warblers eat berries to fatten up before migrating

Many birds visit the British Isles in summer specifically to take advantage of the superabundant insect food, and have to leave in autumn when their staple diet begins to fail

Red squirrel, now, sadly, rare in Britain

avian rather than human appetites.

A walk down the hedgerows will raise flocks of birds enjoying the autumn fare, but if you need further proof of the importance of berries in their diet, look at any droppings you come across. Often they are lurid purple, the residue of elderberries or blackberries. Starlings and wood pigeons are often the birds involved. Some small seeds are specially adapted to pass through the gut undigested and some apparently even benefit, germinating more readily for the Jonah-like experience. If you know how to recognise them, don't overlook badger droppings; they may contain plum stones, a sure sign that the badger's nightly rounds are including windfalls from the local orchard, perhaps even your own garden.

Insurance against winter

Mammals and birds also seek the harder fruits; beechmast, for instance, though it does not occur in all years, is an important energy-rich supplement for tits and finches including the brambling, a winter immigrant. Nuts have the advantage of great durability, so they can be stored and become an insurance against shortfalls in winter food supply. Jays often carry large numbers of acorns some distance from the parent oak, disgorging them one by one from their crop and burying them in the ground. Inevitably they forget the location of some of their hoard, or just never get round to using them all, and the subsequent germination of abandoned acorns plays an important role in the spread of oak woods, especially uphill since such a heavy seed has no other means of moving that way. It is difficult to assess the scale and significance of the jay's clandestine activities, but in one study as many as 300,000 acorns are believed to have been taken from a wood in Germany, and in a Czechoslovakian pine forest frequented by jays a dense understory of oak is a dramatic testament to their hoarding habit. Rooks and occasionally magpies will also bury acorns, and in Europe, nutcrackers likewise cache hazelnuts, even using them in the spring to help feed their young. Squirrels store surplus food at all times of year but are particularly avid hoarders of nuts – acorns, hazelnuts and sweet chestnuts especially – in the autumn.

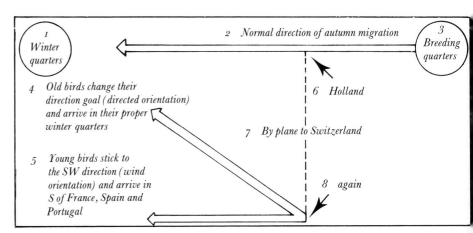

The starling displacement experiment (see page 96)

Such food stores, like all buried treasure, are fair game for anyone who stumbles on them; tits, for example, will seek out and plunder the food stores of their fellows. With so many creatures scouring the forest floor for limited pickings in the winter, some animals and birds seek security for their savings up trees. Sometimes you find nuts in the old nest of a blackbird or thrush, probably taken there by wood mice. Nuthatches embed nuts in the crevices of gnarled tree trunks, and some American woodpeckers even drill a small hole to accommodate each acorn.

Songbird migration

We have already seen how various shorebirds annually undergo a two-way migration, returning south to their winter quarters in the late summer and autumn. But for most people it is the arrival and departure of the small land birds that are noticed, since many of them embody the very essence of summer. Even knowing what we do today, their prodigious journeys remain a source of inspiration and awe, as yet still steeped in mystery. Little wonder, therefore, that our ancestors were so reluctant to acknowledge the migration theory. Writing in April 1793 about sand martins, whose tunnel-nesting habits helped to sway his judgement, Gilbert White said of their spring arrival:

> The late severe weather considered, it is not very probable that these birds should have migrated so early from a tropical region, through all these cutting winds and pinching frosts: but it is easy to suppose that they, like bats and flies, have been awakened by the influence of the sun, amidst their secret latebrae, where they have spent the uncomfortable foodless months in a torpid state, and the profoundest of slumbers.

Others, less searching than White, charmingly explained away the disappearance of cuckoos by supposing that they changed into sparrowhawks, to which they admittedly show a superficial resemblance. Much later, the advent of systematic and widescale ringing programmes – the marking of individual birds with a light metal ring or band engraved with unique number and address – confirmed that both martins and cuckoos overwinter in central and southern Africa.

Ringing has revolutionised our knowledge, but it has taken many years to build up a reasonable picture of migration, simply because relatively few of the marked birds are ever recovered. For ducks and geese wintering in Britain, with a breeding range extending north and east across Europe, the recovery rate runs at around 10–20 per cent, but this is exceptionally high, and made possible only by the fact that many are shot and reported by wildfowlers. Recovery rates for common British garden birds range from 1 to 4 per cent, many being brought to the finder's feet by the house cat; but at the other extreme of their range the chances of a small warbler foundering in the Sahara and being found and reported by a Bedouin tribesman are practically nil.

For many species, therefore, it has taken the ringing of tens of thousands of individuals to gain even a glimmer of understanding about

The large evening primrose may still show a belated bloom

(left, top to bottom) *redwing, robin, blackcap* (right, top to bottom) *redwing, swallow, chaffinch*

eir fate when they abandon these shores. Originally most of the ringed birds recovered ere those found dead and this introduced navoidable bias: thus if few recoveries were made in a remote, sparsely populated region, is usually said more about the distribution of uman beings than birds. With the growth of rnithology, however, various stations and dividuals took it upon themselves to intercept igrants en route, examine them for rings, and lease them again unharmed.

hich routes and how far?

lot, too, has been learned by direct servation of birds on passage, and more cently by tracking them on radar, a move hich has received predictable backing from viation authorities concerned with keeping jet lanes and birds apart. By piecing together all is information, we can begin to offer answers questions like: which routes do migrants llow, how far and how quickly do they travel, nd how many of them survive the journey?

One of the special difficulties of tracking nd birds is that their populations, often at oth ends of their range, cover such huge land eas, and consequently they tend to migrate ong broad fronts. We know that it is not mply a matter of making a beeline south. stead the birds use all the help geography d climate can offer, and these contribute to rging definite migration routes. Many of the ntinental birds heading for wintering ounds in Britain wait for favourable easterly inds before setting off from Scandinavia on a uth or south-south-west bearing. Chaffinches om Norway are known to fly a whole series of urses, starting south-east, changing by grees right round to north-west. This seems a undabout route but it has the merit of

avoiding a major crossing of the dangerous North Sea, a vital consideration for a small woodland bird. Broad-front migrants often converge on narrow flight corridors to avoid long and hazardous sea crossings. Most western European migrants – swallows, willow warblers, and many others – funnel down through the Straits of Gibraltar by way of France, Spain and Portugal, then pass down the west coast of Africa, hugging the less arid shoreline, rather than risk the barren interior of the Sahara. A few species like the lesser whitethroat and red-backed shrike strike south-eastwards to cross the Mediterranean at its eastern end. Again, central European birds often go by way of Italy or Greece, eastern European ones through Turkey, with the Bosphorus a famous corridor across the Black Sea, then down through the Lebanon, Israel, and across the Gulf of Suez into Africa.

That much-loved bird the European white stork has yielded up some of the secrets about how these routes come to be adopted. The particular route taken by an individual stork is dictated by where it was born. Thus birds raised in western Europe traditionally opt for the Straits of Gibraltar, while eastern birds choose the Bosphorus route, working their way down the east coast of Africa as far as the southern tip of the continent and thereby completing a journey of around 8,000km (5,000 miles).

Swallows and storks apart, however, many familiar birds undertake much less exotic migrations, often unsuspected by the layman. We tend to assume that among our garden birds the same individuals are with us all the year round but this is not necessarily so. If a species occupies a wide range of latitude, some individuals are subjected to more rigorous

winters than others and stand to gain more from evacuating their breeding grounds. In Europe, therefore, northern populations of many species, including some Scottish blackbirds and thrushes, move south or south-west for the winter, while more southerly birds stay put. These 'partial migrants' also regularly include chaffinches, robins, rooks, lapwings, grey herons, and, in some years, tits and waxwings. Britain, for all its harsh weather, is a much less inhospitable place than eastern Europe in winter, and every year our resident populations in the south are joined by a huge influx of refugees from across the Channel. Starlings, as mentioned earlier, are some of our most abundant winter visitors, and the bird feeding on your lawn in October could easily be breeding in Warsaw in the summer. Superficially, there is usually nothing to distinguish these aliens, but Eric Simms, with long experience of recording bird-song, once noticed a starling in his garden in February which mimicked perfectly the fluting song of a golden oriole, so betraying its continental origins!

In addition to these mass annual movements there are local, hard-weather movements in late autumn and winter. English lapwings, for instance, will promptly cross the Channel if the southern counties are frost-bound, and may return just as casually when conditions improve. With fruit- and seed-eaters like redwings, fieldfares, redpolls, other finches and tits also being highly mobile, plus mass roostings in flight with dispersals at dusk and dawn, a radar film of the Channel area can often look like an air-traffic-controller's nightmare.

What starts the birds off?

It has been hard enough to unravel these patterns, to understand the visible results of migration, but to discover what actually motivates the birds and guides them is even harder. Just as the shortening days stimulate trees to prepare for winter, so they may be a major cue in the timing of migration. In the few days before exodus, migratory birds show a mounting restlessness, as if suppressing a fast-mounting urge to be on the move. In many species, especially long-distance migrants among songbirds, more food is eaten to lay down the fat reserves which will fuel the flight. Some even double their weight before departure, in the sedge warbler's case from an average of 10g ($\frac{1}{2}$oz) to 20g ($\frac{3}{4}$oz) or more. Now fit and raring to go, a sudden change in temperature or a favourable wind will set them on their way.

How do they find their way?

Many young birds, hatched only weeks earlier, depart before or after their parents, so they can expect no aid to path-finding from that quarter. A number of young white storks, hand-reared and released after the rest of the wild population had already departed for Africa, nevertheless selected the correct route and successfully reached their wintering grounds. So where to fly and, just as important, when to stop flying, is often a matter of instinct. Experience, however, does also play a part, as the Dutch ornithologist A. C. Perdeck so elegantly showed in a displacement experiment with starlings. Eleven thousand birds, including adults and juveniles, were caught and ringed in Holland, transported by plane to Switzerland, and released there. Innocently, the young birds proceeded as if they were still setting off from Holland, migrating in the direction that *would* have taken them to their normal wintering quarters in northern France and England. Naturally this landed them well wide of the mark on alien soil in southern France, Spain and Portugal. The adult birds, however, were not fooled. 'Knowing' that in Switzerland they were already too far south, they made the correct adjustments to their flight path and arrived back in their rightful wintering area.

If an unerring internal instinct says 'go south-west', a bird still needs external reference points to carry out the instruction; indeed without them the experienced starlings would have been just as disorientated as the naïve ones. Somehow the map-and-compass information derived from the external world enables birds to home in on their desired destination with uncanny accuracy, like the manx shearwater taken to Boston, USA, which flew the 4,800km (3,000 miles) back to its nest burrow on Skokholm Island, Wales, in only twelve days, even beating the letter which announced its release. For a long time the basis for such navigation was a hotly debated riddle; it is only now being unravelled after much painstaking and often ingenious research.

What is becoming clear is that birds have a variety of route-finding methods at their disposal, which gives them remarkable flexibility. Different cues may be used at different times, and with such a formidable back-up system a migrant is unlikely to get lost for very long. The earliest theories sought to explain navigation in terms of the sun's position, and a lot of evidence has accumulated to uphold this idea, even if the internal clocks needed to calibrate the position of the sun are not well understood. Birds like swallows and swifts which can feed along the way and travel only by day, must rely strongly on the sun. But many others migrate exclusively at night, presumably to minimise exposure to birds of prey on such abnormally sustained flights. Moreover, land birds on non-stop flights across seas and deserts, with nowhere to halt for feeding and resting, have no option but to battle on after nightfall. Waders, ducks, most thrushes and warblers travel only under cover of darkness, and for these the night sky is the map. Mallards displaced from home and released at night take up the right roosting

(Left to right) *basidiomycetes, ascomycetes and gasteromycetales*

direction if the sky is clear, but if overcast they are totally disorientated. Their chief source of information seems to come from the so-called fixed stars, such as the Pole star, although conclusive proof of this was lacking until man learned how to simulate the night sky. Captive blackcaps, garden warblers, and lesser whitethroats were placed – at different times – in an artificial planetarium in spring when their normal direction of migration (north-east) was reflected in the movements they made inside their cage. Remarkably it was then found that their direction could be manipulated by adjusting key constellations, so that when presented with a replica of the autumn sky they altered course to head south-west, in keeping with their normal migratory path at that time of year.

More recently it has been found that some birds at least can detect the earth's magnetic field and do use it, though how they sense it remains a puzzle. Experiments with robins in a planetarium suggested that this cue may give

the birds magnetic north, the compass direction with which the bird then 'sets' its map, whether it be the night sky or landmarks.

Birds must also gain some knowledge of their whereabouts from global weather patterns, especially prevailing winds, and pigeons at least can sense variations in atmospheric pressure, whether or not they use this ability. Just as astonishingly (since it has always been assumed that most birds have a poor sense of smell) there is growing evidence that some pigeons at least can smell the wind, homing in on the odour around their loft just as surely as salmon migrating to their natal river from the sea detect the right one by the 'taste' of the water. As yet no one knows if wild birds are similarly endowed; but in the meantime we can imagine a migrant nearing its intended destination and making ever-finer adjustments to its flightline as not only the familiar landmarks – mountains, river, forests, even cities – come into sight, but also the remembered smells creep in.

Lycoperdon perlatum, a common species of small puffball

Fungal forays

With the results of summer productivity culminating in the bounty of fruits, seeds, grains and berries, fungi are lurking ready to claim their share of the harvest, for they have no means of self-maintenance other than what they can appropriate from the labours of higher plants and animals. The simplest fungi are the microscopic yeasts, plants which reproduce rapidly, mostly by budding. Theirs is a largely unseen, unspectacular existence, and yet they are arguably more important than all the mushrooms put together, for they possess the outstanding attribute of fermenting carbohydrate solutions to produce alcohol and carbon dioxide. In this way we obtain wine from grapes and berries, cider from apples, beers from malted barley and of course risen bread from dough. Although commercially available, yeasts are nonetheless alive and well in the wild, coating the surfaces of hedgerow fruits and merrily brewing the sugary pulp within. An allied group, the moulds and mildews, can be a nuisance when they invade our jam pots, bread bins, leather, paper and so on, but they too have great redeeming virtues - flavouring cheeses, and yielding vitamins, enzymes and antibodies, notably penicillin. Mould fungi (ascomycetes) are also remarkable for having united with algae, the two living in close harmony as lichens.

Some of the moulds grow parasitically on man and animals, but most of the plant parasites are larger fungi which absorb nutrients through the 'mycelium', a network of minute tubes (hyphae) usually much thinner than cobweb. In most species, the mycelium is invisibly spread within the host's tissues, but sometimes it appears on the surface as a white film. The mycelium gives rise to the fruiting bodies which are the visible and familiar fungal forms of autumn. These too are made of densely interwoven hyphae, but transformed into the immense variety of shapes we loosely term mushrooms and toadstools. Best-known of the parasitic forms are the bracket fungi which attack mature trees, some producing massive fruiting discs. Since their host is available to produce nutrients all the year round, these fungi are perennials, building bigger brackets as the years go by, and inflicting heart rot even in big trees. Many parasitic fungi, having killed their hosts, continue tapping them after death, becoming 'saprophytes' on the fallen timber. Examples are the dryad's saddle fungus which attacks and kills elm, the similar birch polypore, and the notorious honey fungus which infests a wide variety of conifers and broad-leafed trees, even attacking herbaceous plants like potatoes and strawberries.

By far the majority of fungi, however, are saprophytes all their lives, extracting food from the great deposits of dead and decaying plant debris in woodlands and open country alike. In the process these fungi help to break down organic matter, restoring fertility to the soil by

Top view of the earthstar Geastrum triplex, *a woodland puffball species. The ball itself surmounts a split fleshy collar and lets out its spores through the pore on the apex*

Anthurus muellerianus

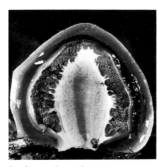

Anthurus *in section*

Young stinkhorn with slimy spore cap

Flies infesting stinkhorn cap

Old stinkhorn, stripped of slime

October

recycling nutrients and building up the humus layer. They have the same basic, long-lived mycelium as their parasitic cousins, but their fruiting bodies are usually ephemeral structures, mostly flourishing in autumn when the plant kingdom annually recharges the decomposers' crucible with windfall fruits, fallen leaves and withered herbage. Autumn is also a suitable time for reproduction because the weather, humid but not too cold, and longer nights, carry less risk of desiccation for the delicate fungi and especially their precious cargoes of spores.

Launching spores into the world

Fungi can spread locally by gradually extending their mycelium underground, hence the radial expansion of 'fairy ring' species. But for wider dispersal, fungi are dependent on spores. Equivalent to a seed, each spore deposited in a suitable environment is capable of germinating to start a new fungal colony. Unlike most plant seeds, however, spores are extremely tiny (generally 0·005–0·02mm across), consisting of one or a few cells at the most, so they contain negligible food reserves, and are highly vulnerable to adverse conditions. To compensate for this, they are produced in almost unimaginable numbers. A ripe field mushroom, for example, can produce around 1,800 million spores at an average rate of 40 million per hour, and giant puffballs have been calculated to contain seven billion spores. From looking around us, it is clear that most of these must perish, only a handful finding the exacting conditions required for germination. A few, like the club-root fungus, produce resting spores which can lie dormant in the soil till the time is ripe for active growth, but such sophistication is probably exceptional.

Most spores are wind-dispersed and, like pollen and small insects, many join the nomadic ranks of the aeroplankton circulating in the upper atmosphere; if they are lucky, they are sedimented out later by downward currents or, more likely, by rain. Fruiting bodies have evolved various methods, according to structure, to launch their spores. In larger ascomycetes (cup and flask fungi), the spores are loaded in elongated cells and often shot out with explosive force, dispersing up to 6cm ($2\frac{1}{4}$in), and sometimes appearing as puffs of smoke above the fungus. A special case are the truffles, which live underground in woodland, sometimes at considerable depth. As the fruiting body decays, the spores inside simply ooze out to be dispersed by the soil's microfauna, or else by fungus-loving mammals which then defecate the spores over a wide area. Truffles make good eating and in Europe are systematically hunted with specially trained dogs or pigs whose keen noses can track down their characteristic odour.

Most of the larger fungi belong to the basidiomycetes (typical mushrooms and toadstools). These usually bear spores on gills

Stinkhorns

or, less commonly, tubes on the underside of the cap, sometimes protected early on by a thin veil. In the gill sort, the spores are discharged under force by some mechanism, perhaps the explosion of a small bubble of gas, and if they are not trapped in the adjacent gill surface, start to fall, under gravity. Being so light, their descent is imperceptibly slow, 1mm per second from a field mushroom; spores released from a bracket fungus up a tree may take over an hour to reach the ground, providing ample opportunity for a slight gust of wind to do its work. If we want to collect spores, therefore, we must be patient and minimise disturbance. Put a piece of paper under a ripe cap (or *over* cup fungus) and leave under a saucer for a few hours. Under the microscope, spores from different species show great diversity in colour, size, shape and surface texture.

A bizarre subgroup of the basidiomycetes called the gasteromycetales (literally stomach fungi) have, like the truffles, opted to enclose their spores within the fruiting body, and have had to devise suitably elaborate ways of liberating them. Best-known are the puffballs, often huge, fleshy, white (and highly palatable) spheres when young, but brown and papery on the outside when ripe. At this stage the interior is a powdery mass of spores enmeshed in hyphal threads. Finally the outer wall ruptures and, over time, the spores are puffed out by a kind of bellows action, mostly operated by the impact of raindrops. Apart from puffball steaks, country folk formerly used them when tinder-dry and ripe for staunching blood and for starting hearth fires. Related to this group are the curious bird's nest fungi, tiny cups containing a few egg-like packets of spores. Whole eggs are splashed out by falling

raindrops and, as they arc through the air, snag on to nearby vegetation with a long sticky tail, perhaps there to be eaten and dispersed further.

Stranger still are the stinkhorns, which develop from soft, gelatinous eggs up to hen's-egg size, buried in the soil. On 'hatching' the fruiting body thrusts upwards 10–15cm (4–6in) at an astounding rate, topped with a honeycombed cap. This is coated with a viscous slime, emitting a powerful sweet-smelling odour repugnant to most humans but highly attractive to flies, which within a few hours strip the slime, spores and all. Other insects, notably carrion beetles, may be attracted, but by the time they arrive the slime cupboard is often bare; undaunted they usually demolish the rest of the fungus instead. The rare *Clathrus ruber* adopts a similar strategy to the stinkhorn but bears its slime on a beautiful coral-red latticework.

Pholiota destruens, *a parasite and saprophyte on willow and poplar; a close relative of the honey fungus*

Browsers and borers

On rocky shores, jetties and so on, we can expect to find a variety of marine snails. The common periwinkle and its three relatives are all widespread, often cohabiting on the same shore, though not on the same parts of it. To find all of them you will need to explore the whole length of the littoral zone between the tide marks. Highest up, above high spring-tide level, in the 'splash zone' where animals have to withstand prolonged exposure to the open

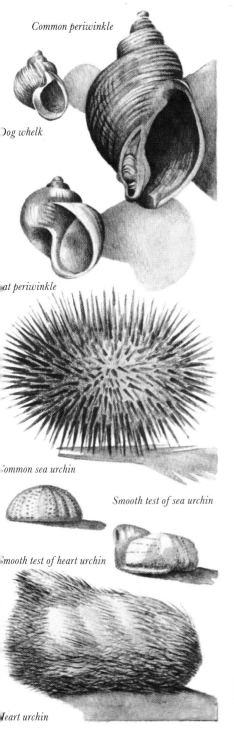

Common periwinkle

Dog whelk

Flat periwinkle

Common sea urchin

Smooth test of sea urchin

Smooth test of heart urchin

Heart urchin

air, we find the small periwinkle – about 3mm ($\frac{1}{8}$in) long – clustered in bare rock crevices. The rough periwinkle, sometimes yellow in colour, is much larger but less tolerant of desiccation, so it lives slightly lower down, again on bare rock. Flat periwinkles nestle instead amongst the clammy fronds of seaweed which satisfy their need to be constantly moist. Fourthly the common periwinkle, which is much less of a specialist than these others, and is able to survive from midshore right down to below spring-tide mark, finding sustenance even in mud and sand; this, along with its tolerance of brackish water, has enabled it to penetrate estuaries. Sometimes we find the shapely shell of a dog whelk which, apart from its often superior size and more submarine existence, differs from periwinkles in being carnivorous rather than vegetarian. The difference in lifestyle is reflected in the design of the radula, a protrusible band-like tongue studded with teeth; this is short and broad in periwinkles, for browsing tiny algae, but long and narrow in dog whelks, with fewer but more fomidable teeth, for drilling through the shells of their prey, chiefly other molluscs and barnacles.

Quite a separate group, the echinoderms, similarly contains carnivorous and vegetarian members. Best-known are the starfishes, especially the common red one *Asterias rubens*, which is often found in mussel beds, surrounded by potential victims. Its method of devouring these is nothing if not original: with the forest of sucker-like tube feet on the underside of its arms, it exerts a strong steady pull on the twin valves of the mussel, prising them apart just enough to insert its stomach which it protrudes through its mouth. In this bizarre posture it proceeds to digest its meal externally. Brittlestars are more consistent in showing the radial, five-armed symmetry and spiny-skinned features of the group, but with fewer tube feet they have abandoned the starfish's laborious hydraulic locomotion over the rocks: instead they writhe along with a sinuous motion of their slender arms.

Like brittlestars, sea urchins live near or below low-water mark, and are more often found cast up dead, the empty limy test smoothly denuded of spines. At first their kinship to the starfishes is obscure, till we discover that the series of pores, running like meridians of longitude around the body, are again the five paired rows of outlets for the tube feet. In lifestyle, the common sea urchin is closer to the periwinkles, slowly browsing on encrusting vegetation.

There is also a beach-dwelling species, a heart urchin or sea potato, whose shape and spines like swept-back hair facilitate its burrowings in the sand. There it feeds like a moving conveyor belt, shovelling a stream of sand into its mouth where the grains are delicately stripped of their meagre coating of organic matter.

Devoted motherhood

The sight of an earwig is often received with a mixture of mild alarm and disgust, and the hapless creature is all too often dispatched underfoot. It is all rather undeserved, for the superstition that the insect seeks out a human ear and bites through the eardrum is quite unfounded. Earwigs do certainly like to insinuate themselves in some dark retreat by day, classically inside old flower stems, emerging at night to seek a part-vegetarian, part-scavenging diet. Occasionally they ravage prize blooms, but in general they probably do more good than harm.

By appearance as well as reputation, earwigs invite persecution. The abdomen ends in characteristic forceps, curved in the male, almost straight in the female, which are raised forward over the back, scorpion-style, in defence. They can inflict a mild nip but not enough to break the skin. If threatened, a nasty-smelling liquid is also exuded at the rear. The wings are another hidden and almost vestigial tool, secreted well furled and rarely aired, beneath the elytra.

A jetty is often an ideal habitat for mussels

October

In the insect world earwigs excel in maternal instinct. In the autumn, when earwigs retreat to overwinter in the soil, the female lays a score or two of eggs, often in a small recess under a stone. Like a broody hen she covers them with

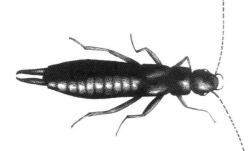

Female earwig

her body, periodically cleaning them or collecting them up if they get scattered, till they hatch in the spring. Thereafter the nymphs follow her about, receiving food and occasional brooding till they are big enough to fend for themselves and leave the nursery, which usually happens about May. By this time the female, worn out by her labours, may succumb, and if she does it is said that her corpse is gratefully devoured by her offspring in a final act of family togetherness!

Late flowering

With the summer flowering over, we tend to notice and appreciate the few autumn survivors. These are of various kinds: a few are belated blooms on plants whose flowering peak was earlier in the year. Thus the evening primrose may muster a final flower, the hogweed a new umbel, dead-nettles and stinging nettles also have a second wind, though the latter is past producing flowers. On the downs, carpets of rockrose, and the odd agrimony, may still have yellow flowers, greater knapweed its pink starry florets, while a late-blooming field gentian or felwort (autumn gentian) is a specially satisfying find.

Summer annuals usually germinate in the spring, flower in the summer and die; but a few, sometimes called ephemerals, can produce two or even three generations in the year, extending into October. They include some of our most tenacious yet not unattractive weed species, such as shepherd's purse, common chickweed and common field speedwell. Two others, groundsel and Oxford ragwort, have even been found to flower in every one of twelve consecutive months. Meanwhile the other annuals, the winter ones, are busy germinating into rosettes which will overwinter to produce flower stems the following year. Incidentally, this division into summer and winter annuals is made for our convenience, and not all plants follow the rules. Some individuals of corn gromwell and centaury, for instance, behave as summer annuals, and others as winter annuals, while centaury even harbours some biennials in its ranks.

Few plants claim autumn as their only flowering season, but one worthy of mention is the perennial autumn crocus with violet flowers scarcely distinguishable from its garden counterpart in spring. In the south, a similar-looking plant, somewhat earlier to flower, is the meadow saffron. In both species the flowers appear without leaves; these flourish in spring and die back in summer, an unusual arrangement which accounts for the quaint old name of 'naked boys' or, more popularly today, 'naked ladies'! Farmers have eliminated a lot of meadow saffron from damp pastures where it can be fatally poisonous to livestock, or at least badly contaminate cows' milk.

Even when October is fine and sunny, it becomes clear that most plants will not be coaxed into flowering again. The significant point here is that plants which do flower as late as autumn are succeeding under conditions of progressively fewer daylight hours. Experiments have shown that many plants must be exposed to just the right amount of light during the 24 hour period or they will not flower. Those restricted to blooming in autumn

(or spring) are 'short-day' plants which must have less than twelve hours daylight in order to flower at all. Without short-day plants like chrysanthemums, our gardens would be much bleaker and less colourful through the year, and many have been introduced from low latitudes (such as cosmos, from Mexico) to extend the flowering span of our herbaceous borders. Other familiar short-day plants are ragweeds, asters and sunflowers.

'Long-day' plants on the other hand need more than twelve hours' daylight, some in excess of sixteen hours, before they will flower, and these are, and have to be, the midsummer flowers. Lest we forget our vegetables, radish, lettuce and potatoes are among the long-day group. Yet others, like the ephemeral weeds, and also highly desirable plants like the tomato, are 'day-neutral' or indifferent to daylength, and have the potential to bloom all the year round.

Keeping a diary

People keep nature diaries for a variety of reasons: to invite, at some future date, the pleasure of vivid recall, or to record the changing face of nature and learn more about it. The first of these is a powerful incentive, for there is a special satisfaction in sitting down on some bleak winter night to rummage through old field notes. Written in the heat of the moment they invariably convey our impressions at the time much more pungently than any of the more polished write-ups we might make later on.

Very often it is not till long after the event that something we recorded quite casually turns out to be useful, or else something we didn't record would have been. A case in point was the drought summer of 1976, a year of rare extremes which gradually unearthed a wealth of lore about plants and animals. With the benefit of hindsight some of us wish now that we had been more scrupulous about writing down a few things which at the time seemed inconsequential.

Fieldfare

October's heavy migration traffic, best seen along the coast at dusk or dawn: many species normally active by day travel at night

Parasol mushroom

Spindle tree

Shaggy ink cap

Honey fungus

Boletus edulis

Sulphur tuft

Fly agaric

Fungi absorb ready-made nutrients from outside. Their fruiting bodies are commonest in autumn when there is plenty of rotting plant tissue to consume

Mushroom

It is probably better to write too much in a diary than too little, especially when trying to make sense of something new to us. Gilbert White's dogged attention to detail is an example to all aspiring diarists, and for it he was richly rewarded by some wonderful discoveries, not least his achievement of distinguishing the wood warbler from the willow warbler and chiffchaff, and the lesser from the common whitethroat, so adding two unsuspected species to the British list. Even with today's sophisticated field guides, these distinctions are still trophies for any keen birdwatcher. Many records which White made are still consulted, like the first dot on the graph, helping us to monitor the changing fortunes of British wildlife since the eighteenth century. Although starlings, for example, are enormously abundant today in Britain, in White's parish of Selborne in Hampshire, as elsewhere, there is good evidence that this was not always so; White faithfully recorded 200 years ago: 'No number is known to breed in these parts'.

Another invaluable yardstick of change has been the catalogue of plants growing in the vicinity of Cambridge, published in 1660 by the great natural historian John Ray; it describes localities so precisely that they, and some of their plants, can be identified to this day.

Nowadays, with Ordnance Survey maps, cameras, binoculars and tape recorders at our disposal, we can record events with a precision unavailable to these early pioneers. For many people, indeed, photography and sound recording have replaced the written word completely and become richly rewarding methods of documenting nature in their own right. To make oneself observe things carefully, however, there is still no substitute for sitting down in front of a subject with only pencil and paper. Even a crude sketch, perhaps denoting the number of stamens or petals on a flower, can be more instructive than an aesthetically pleasing photograph. If you are self-conscious about your drawing ability, there is no better way to improve than by quietly exercising whatever talent you have in the countryside or garden. Remember also that a diary can be a total self-indulgence, for your benefit alone.

For identification purposes we can learn to draw in a stylised code that instantly conveys a lot of information about particulars. But many of us will want to achieve a more faithful representation of the subject. For animals, there is no better aid than a basic understanding of anatomy. Next time you find a dead bird on the road, or have a chicken to cook, look at its shape, or better still, examine its skeleton. A goldcrest and an eagle might seem poles apart, but at the skeletal level their uniformity is more striking than their differences. Many people remain unaware of these similarities simply because they are of little value in field identification, but a little

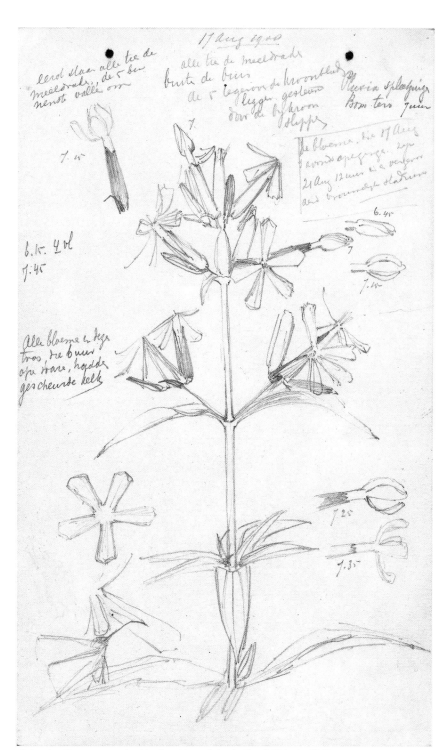

A drawing from a nature sketchbook – this one is by the Dutch biologist Thijsse

attention to them will work wonders for people aiming to make their sketches a bit more realistic, or to broaden their knowledge. Note how the lower jaw extends more than halfway along the base of the skull. The knee is high on the leg, invisible from outside the living bird; in fact we see only half the leg outside, and the only major joint showing is the heel. The wing also has more joints in it than we might have supposed, while the backbone has fewer.

Then you might want to know why the skeleton is built this way, and before you know it, your natural history has plunged you deep into zoology. In following this path you are in good company, for without exception every good zoologist and ecologist is first and foremost an explorer in natural history, the refreshing wellspring of all scholarly ideas; as Charles Elton pithily put it, 'the outlook . . . to leaven the crust of science'.

November

With the onset of November, winter begins to assert itself and tighten its grip on the land. It is a grey, gloomy month, when everything seems to be in retreat. We could be excused for wondering if even devils flee in the face of advancing November. In the village of Shebbear in North Devon a famous boulder, alleged to have been dropped by the devil on his way from Heaven to Hell, is ritually turned over by the menfolk, with the vicar in the vanguard, on 5 November: the tradition, since time immemorial, is that they ensure that Shebbear will prosper for another year.

Elsewhere, 5 November is of course Guy Fawkes Day and Bonfire Night. We all know that the flames burn, whether symbolically or in effigy, the papist conspirator confounded in the parliamentary cellars at the eleventh hour, but by staking a claim for himself in our ritual calendar in this way, Guy Fawkes in fact usurped and obscured a much older anniversary. The three days between 31 October and 2 November are Hallowe'en, a potent brew of Christian and pagan festivities. The pagan background is the festival of Samhain, which tolled the deathknell of summer and the beginning of the Celtic New Year on 1 November. The Celts then struck a note of optimism, kindling the so-called beltane fires of spring to drive away evil spirits and fan the dying embers of the wintering sun. This tradition survived longest in the ancient Celtic strongholds of Scotland and Ireland, even in some northern counties of England, but by the beginning of this century the pagan origins of November bonfires were barely remembered, any more than the religious bigotry for which Guy Fawkes became a national scapegoat on 5 November.

Winter behaviour patterns

The age-old significance of Bonfire Night at least reminds us that for early man the arrival of November heralded a critical period of survival – and for wildlife it still does. The autumn harvest is dwindling fast and plants and animals must radically change their behaviour to keep in tune with the slower tempo of approaching winter. Some of the most obvious and dramatic changes take place in freshwater ponds, which can freeze – briefly – as early as November: 'Ice in November to bear a duck, The rest of the winter'll be slush and muck!' The floating leaves of water lilies discolour and decay, but their future survival resides in the massive rootstocks anchored to the pond bottom from which new shoots will run out the following year. The roots and stems of common pondweeds, together with frog-bit, greater bladderwort and Canadian waterweed, developed winter buds (or 'turions') in the summer which now drop off as the plants die down. Sinking under their own weight, the buds find safety below the ice-prone surface, lying buried and dormant in the mud. In

Water lily pads now decay, but the roots at the pond bottom will shoot again next year

spring they draw on stored food reserves to germinate and, in so doing, become lighter, more buoyant, and float to the surface to develop into new plants.

Older frogs adopt a similar strategy, burrowing into a ready-made lair in the soft mud to hibernate under water the winter long. Immature frogs, however, like toads, usually hibernate away from water, in any convenient hole in the ground, perhaps a discarded mousehole, or even a sand-martin's nest-tunnel in a sand pit. Compost heaps, offering the warmth generated by rotting vegetable matter, are especially favoured spots. Newts also overwinter on land, but for them it is merely part of a predominantly terrestrial existence which spans the entire year outside the aquatic breeding season. The adults abandon water around the end of May and most remain on land till the following spring. In the autumn most hibernate in the ground, as described for other amphibians, but a few return to their ponds where they survive below the ice, on into the spring and a new breeding season. Newts of the spring hatch are not ready to leave the water till July, but when they do it is to spend

two or three years on land till they can return to the ponds as mature animals.

Freshwater fish also adapt their haunts to the approach of winter, seeking deeper water and generally becoming less active. In coastal regions the common three-spined stickleback may move into brackish pools on the seashore in the sure knowledge that they rarely freeze; however, they are not known to penetrate any further down the shore into the sea proper. Many invertebrates undergo particularly subtle changes in preparation for winter. Water fleas (like *Daphnia*), for example, encase their eggs in a protective capsule whose specially thickened walls can withstand freezing or – if blown off the water surface on to dry land – desiccation. Even among truly marine animals there are changes in distribution. The hardy shore crab and common shrimp can resist the worst rigours of winter without budging, but other crustaceans notably edible crabs, lobsters and prawns, migrate into deeper offshore waters where they find comparative warmth and protection.

Back on land, most birds have long since abandoned their solitary habit of summer days

Greenfinches eating rose hips

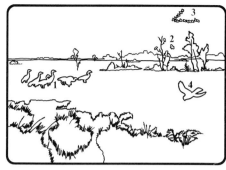

November *1. Cranes seen only rarely*
2. Carrion crows 3. Wild geese 4. Hen harrier
(male)

...and instead rove the countryside in flocks of ever-greater size in search of dwindling patches of food. Presumably the more that are looking together, the greater the chances of somebody finding a resource everyone can share. Mixed flocks of chaffinches, bramblings, greenfinches and goldfinches may number up to 5,000. One imagines that in such varied company some find the pickings of the day more appetising than others. Chaffinches enjoy many different foods but, like bramblings, are particularly partial to beech mast in years when it occurs. The more delicate bills of goldfinches are primarily adapted for handling seeds of thistle, groundsel, burdock and the like. Greenfinches are more versatile and sometimes join company with thrushes feasting on rose hips. There the two make an interesting contrast, thrushes swallowing the hips whole, while the finches chop them open to reach the seeds which they crack with their powerful bills. A visit to a birch or alder wood may be rewarded with a flock of siskins, a species which feeds on conifers in the summer and has spread along with the Forestry Commission. In years when the crop of spruce seeds fails in Scandinavia, our own siskin population may be swelled by an exodus of theirs, as well as by crossbills.

Bird roosts

Many birds which forage in flocks by day also form communal roosts at night, often much larger than any daytime gatherings.

Starling flocks, for example, may be a few hundred birds strong, but by night from August till spring they may assemble by the hundred thousand, occasionally by the million. The night roosts are focal points for numerous day-foraging flocks, often drawing on a great catchment area of surrounding countryside.

To exert such a strong pull roosts must have very great advantages for the birds involved. Just what these benefits might be have puzzled biologists for a long time. Flock-feeding, as we have seen, probably improves the chances of finding patchily distributed food, and social roosting may simply extend the opportunities for spreading the word around about good places to visit. On this 'information centre' hypothesis, birds might gain all sorts of useful guidelines, or rather flightlines, by gauging, for example, the contentedness or otherwise of their neighbours after a day's feeding, even how fat their crops look, and so on.

In winter when different species may flock together to hunt the same limited range of berries, seeds, nuts or invertebrates, they may congregate in a mixed roost, notably various finches together, or blackbirds and other members of the thrush family. Even if they don't flock together by day, different species may roost together; there are, as we shall see, other advantages to communal roosting. A small thicket, for instance, may house several hundred starlings, and lesser numbers of

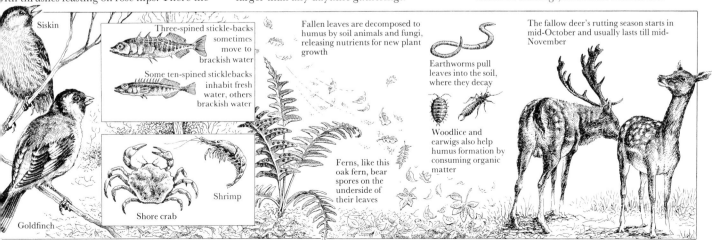

Siskin

Goldfinch

Three-spined stickle-backs sometimes move to brackish water

Some ten-spined sticklebacks inhabit fresh water, others brackish water

Shore crab

Shrimp

Fallen leaves are decomposed to humus by soil animals and fungi, releasing nutrients for new plant growth

Ferns, like this oak fern, bear spores on the underside of their leaves

Earthworms pull leaves into the soil, where they decay

Woodlice and earwigs also help humus formation by consuming organic matter

The fallow deer's rutting season starts in mid-October and usually lasts till mid-November

November

fieldfares, wood pigeons, stock doves and magpies not, admittedly, mixed freely through one another, but all attracted in the name of some common benefit. Likewise a high-water shore roost of waders may include dunlin, sanderling, ringed plover, redshank and so on.

Given that there is some strength in sheer numbers, it then becomes vital to find a suitable place to accommodate so many birds. The chosen site generally offers obvious protection against the elements. Most starling roosts, for example, are in reed beds, dense conifer thickets, thorn scrub, or the cover provided by evergreens like rhododendrons or laurels. These are relatively impenetrable to ground predators, and are also barriers against wind, the single biggest cause of heat (and energy) loss during long winter nights.

In this century, starlings have gone one better than any of these in using cities as overnight dormitories. Urban roosting has spread rapidly and nowadays city dwellers throughout the world take for granted the twilight invasion of squabbling and chattering hordes above their heads. One of the biggest assemblages is in Glasgow, where the Gothic-style buildings, bristling with handy ledges, accommodate upwards of a quarter of a million birds. Starlings commonly roost on cliff ledges, so the transition to cities was not so unlikely. Moreover, cities are generally a degree or two warmer than the surrounding countryside, not a big difference perhaps, but of crucial importance to birds in winter. Huddling on the ledges further reduces heat loss and the need to maintain a high and costly metabolic rate through the night.

The most striking use of huddling as a heat-saving device is seen in a few species which do not forage in large flocks by day, but may join forces to roost in severe weather. Wrens may gather in any suitably insulated hole in thatch, ivy, a crevice in a tree, or in an old nest. Ten were once found squeezed into a coconut shell, and forty-six in a nest box. Treecreepers do likewise, classically inserting themselves head first in the deeply grooved bark of a Wellingtonia tree. In winter, long-tailed tits consort in small parties, usually of six to ten individuals, and at night they cluster into a tight ball on a branch to roost. Observant country folk have interpreted this as a portent of hard weather; as the jingle goes: 'When the tom-tits cluster, Soon there'll be a bluster'.

In city environments, birds often single out roost sites that are much warmer than average. Starlings converge on ventilators and cooling towers, and at Schiphol Airport, near Amsterdam, used to roost with sparrows in one of the hangars, settling on the warm radiators of the prop-engined planes when they taxied in. Pied wagtails regularly resort to commercial greenhouses, often much to the detriment of the plants and the owner's good nature. At one in Middlesex, up to 500 birds roosted in autumn annually for thirty years, while

Starlings at a pre-roost assembly point

another lodged up to 1,000 birds at once. Naturally these luxurious surroundings give admirable shelter from rain and wind and in some cases offer artificial heating besides, as records of close-packed rows of wagtails perched along the hot-water pipes readily demonstrate. In addition greenhouses, like city buildings, are generally safe from predators, though this is not always true. In two separate incidents, a little owl and a cat infiltrated a greenhouse roost of pied wagtails and slaughtered virtually all the occupants. Man also may not look kindly on these trespassers. Apart from fouling tomato plants, a big roost of starlings can break down a young plantation by sheer weight of numbers and destroy the foliage in a slurry of droppings.

The roost as a larder

In the wild, predation is a constant threat, for a roost represents a vast and predictable larder, often attracting predators from miles around. Some may even take up residence in the roost,

whiling away the daylight hours till the nightly flocks of plump innocents present themselves. Foxes can play havoc, especially among birds which sleep in the open, like partridges, waders and gulls. It is hard to assess how many woodland birds fall to weasels and stoats, which can climb trees competently to great heights. Perhaps this is why adult rooks prefer to nest in the tops of trees – even though they are more exposed to the elements there – confining the young ones lower down. When hard weather sets in, however, even the old birds seek lower stations, 'pushing' the youngsters down the trees and sometimes forcing them to move altogether to other, less favourable parts of the wood.

But it is from the air that the greatest threat comes to most roosting birds. Sparrowhawks, hobbies, and less commonly peregrine falcons, kestrels and merlins, often hunt at roosts, sometimes two or three of a kind living in and terrorising them for weeks on end. They have two main opportunities to strike, firstly as the flocks are wending their way home, and then as they settle in for the night. There is a palpable tension in a large starling roost when a bird of prey is approaching. The first hint of danger is transmitted almost instantaneously to the flocks already assembled, bringing an abrupt halt to the intense social chatter, bickering and rivalry over perching sites.

As often as not, a sparrowhawk will station itself in the trees in the afternoon waiting for the flocks to arrive, regular as clockwork. Typically they come like swarms of bees, snaking and weaving in the sky, now expanding and billowing into a dispersed cloud, now contracting into a dense ribbon. At a given moment, the hawk launches vertically into the attack, beating upwards and manoeuvring itself inside the amoebic mass and causing even more violent aerial evolution than before. In the panic the flock inevitably divides, as the hawk meant it to do; a victim is singled out and struck in mid-flight, sometimes as it is diving vainly for cover. Hobbies and peregrines adopt similar tactics but usually mount the initial attack from above, stooping

Pigeons: like starlings, they roost on city ledges – as replacements for the cliffs used by their ancestors

sharply. Barn owls also regularly visit autumn roosts of passerines; over a season, regurgitated pellets of one bird included remains of sparrows, starlings, wagtails, finches, thrushes, blackbirds, robins and skylarks.

In one study at a starling roost frequented by sparrowhawks, only two out of sixty attacks were seen to be successful, suggesting that the mass aerial contortions of the flock are fairly effective against the predator. When the flock bunches it may be too risky for the hawk or falcon to swoop into it at speed; when it swirls about it may confuse and outmanoeuvre the predator, like a shooting gallery mounted on a big dipper. This would also help explain the great size of many flocks, since the chance of any one individual succumbing must be very small, buffered as it is by so many other tasty companions. To this extent the flock is really a group of selfish rather than co-operative individuals!

Signalling the way

It appears that aerial displays must serve other functions too, for as the arriving flocks coalesce, they periodically rise *en masse* with a great roar of wings, even when no predators are in sight. Within a general area, the actual roost site may vary somewhat from one night to the next, and a recent and rather ingenious idea, supported by some evidence, is that spontaneous aerobatic formations act rather like Red Indian smoke signals to inform other birds approaching at a distance where a particular night's roosting spot is to be. Some species which roost in large numbers, notably starlings and rooks, don't retire directly to their roosts from the feeding grounds; instead the flocks rendezvous at a number of assembly points on the way. Displays are often seen over these too, and may serve the same advertising purpose. Most impressive of all are the performances of rooks and jackdaws as they work their way up to the roost; their acrobatic tumblings and incessant banter have earned the names 'crows' weddings' or 'parliaments'. Lastly, it did not escape the attention of the biologist Wynne-Edwards that each roost has its own feeding grounds, mostly separate from those of other roosts, and that the nightly social gathering might be the clan's way of saying 'Let's have a head count'. If the birds could sense their own numbers and the demands on available resources (especially easy if you are starving) this might stimulate emigration when the pressure was too great, and help to keep the local population in balance with its food supply. It is very hard to assess the validity of these various explanations for aerial displays but they are all good attempts to understand some marvellous behaviour.

Some roosts are so large that it is easy to assume they absorb every bird for miles around, but this is not always so. Many adult starlings disown the gregarious life and roost solitarily near their nest sites throughout the winter, probably having a stronger claim to these come spring when the big roosts break up. It is the young, 'first-winter' birds with no previous breeding attachments, plus the immigrant starlings from the continent, that make up the bulk of the rural roosts, the winter visitors generally shunning the urban ones.

November flowers

It becomes a challenge to find flowering plants in this sombre month. On the dunes, a single lingering flower of the evening primrose may yet be found; along the roadside verges perhaps a later scarlet pimpernel, a creamy umbellifer of yarrow or, delicate in both flower and leaf, the red-stemmed herb robert. Shrubs and trees become increasingly difficult to identify as their last leaves disappear in a gust of wind, and if we wish to distinguish one from another we must now look at the nature of the wood and the overall shape, both of which are as instructive to the trained eye as the leaves themselves. Horse-chestnut is easy; as we saw in October, tell-tale 'horseshoe-nail' scars are left on the twigs after leaf fall. Dogwood is also a give-away in winter with its dark crimson twigs. The type illustrated here is *Cornus alba*, an Asian species introduced as a garden plant, but often found growing wild on waste land. Ash, one of the earliest to shed its leaves, is another easy one, with prominent velvety black buds studding the pale olive-grey wood.

In barren November, a select band of flowering shrubs are well worth cultivating – those for which late autumn and winter is the actual flowering season, not just a carry-over from an earlier peak. Best known is winter jasmine, which can easily be grown in any garden with a wall or shed. Whether it faces north or south is of no consequence to this hardy, easy-going shrub. If the temperature drops below freezing, jasmine simply closes its fragrant yellow flowers and waits for conditions to improve. Winter-flowering cherry, introduced from Japan, starts to open its bunches of pale-pink bell-shaped flowers in October and continues to blossom sporadically through to mid-April when the remaining buds all burst together.

The basement store

Today even large tracts of woodland, like the New Forest in Hampshire, are more or less 'managed', and as far as foresters are concerned, that means removing fallen and decaying timber to allow access to the living, and to get rid of a potential reservoir of injurious insects and fungi. To the naturalist, however, the modern preoccupation with tidy woods also eliminates a treasure trove; it impoverishes the forest of fauna by a factor put by Charles Elton at one-fifth. In Wytham Woods near Oxford, for instance, over 450 species of animals are known to thrive in the decaying wood which is allowed to accumulate freely on much of the forest floor, and some 500 others are known from elsewhere in Britain.

Left to its own devices, a temperate forest's capacity to build up a repository of decay products is formidable. When beech trees, for instance, are about 150 years old, they begin to shed unwieldy boughs, each of which may lie for a decade or more before being completely

Evening primrose – a few flowers may still be found

broken down, while a whole trunk may persist for a quarter of a century. The actual rate of decay depends on the local situation. If a tree falls at the forest edge, or in a clearing, where it is exposed to the sun, the wood may become heat-sterilised, effectively forming a fossil log which may lie for very many years with little invasion by decomposing agents, and consequently no decay.

In a damper situation a gradual succession of fauna and flora ensures that the tree is eventually returned to the nutrient pool from which it once drew its own strength. The following account of succession is based on Charles Elton's painstaking research in an otherwise little-charted area of ecology.

The first invaders are often specialist bark beetles, which make breeding galleries underneath the bark, a phenomenon Dutch elm disease has made all too familiar. Equipped with enzymes to break down starches and sugar, they eat away at the bark's inner tissue and cambium, gradually prising it loose from the wood. After a few months, this admits a host of secondary invaders – fungi, woodlice, millipedes, centipedes, spiders, earwigs, springtails, flies, beetles (including borers), later on snails and slugs. At this stage the food web quickly ramifies and wood-eaters, fungus-eaters, carnivores and parasites coexist for several years. Thereafter, with the tree's outer defences critically breached, fungal attack proceeds on two fronts – from without, in the former sapwood, and within, in the heartwood, the latter often starting at the roots or through some major wound. Sometimes one or more of these processes, even heart rot, may begin in the living tree (such as a beech after it has shed a big branch); when it ultimately falls it will then decay faster than, say, an otherwise healthy neighbour blown down by wind.

With the undermining of the heartwood, the spectacular bracket fungi, and their own specialised retinue of insects, may move in to exploit the nutritious tilth prepared by the earlier colonisers. At the same time, yet other insects, outsiders which contribute little or nothing to the tree's breakdown – ants, bees and wasps in particular – begin to avail themselves of the increasingly labyrinthine nature of the rotting log or stump; hole-nesting birds can also take up residence. In this complex field, many questions remain unanswered, and anyone studying the situation carefully may further our knowledge.

Sand dunes

Keith Shackleton once interpreted the special beauty of Antarctica very eloquently: 'Every form, every line, colour and texture is sculptured by elemental forces, and the growing pains of the Earth: Man's intrusive and discordant geometry is small enough to go unnoticed'. There is nowhere in the British Isles with the same sense of utter wilderness or

the sanction of millions of undisturbed years behind it, but there are still a few places moulded only by natural forces, and among these, sand-dune systems have the special merit of evolving before our very eyes. November, with its stormy weather, is a specially good time to appreciate the development of a dune system, and particularly the intimate role plants play in the process.

Often the skeleton of a major dune is a low shingle ridge but any small eminence, a piece of driftwood or even a seashell, anything that presents an obstacle to windblown sand, may start the formation of a dune. The delicately scalloped crest of sand tailing off on the leeside of such a barrier is highly unstable, likely to be demolished by a much stronger wind or an exceptionally high tide, but some survive the elements to become 'embryo dunes'. Usually the embryo dune will only be nurtured to maturity if it is colonised by the strand flora, the only agents capable of thwarting wind and water. Any plant which can gain a toehold in so shifting a world must have enormous capacities for survival, and indeed the first pioneers are among the hardiest in the plant realm.

The earliest to establish itself is usually sand couch grass, achieving this distinction by its ability to withstand saturation by sea water. Inundation by the tide is not the only hazard. Once it begins to bind the sand, couch is on a dangerous treadmill, likely to be swamped by the very sand it ensnares. It gets round this by an extensive ramification of creeping stems and rootlets which can keep pace with the mounting sand around it. Sand may also rally round sea sandwort and sea rocket but neither has couch's talent for building a substantial dune.

Couch may remain the dominant grass, stabilising a rather low, flat-topped dune, but once it has done the spadework it is often superseded by marram, which every visitor to a sandy beach knows – the spiky dune grass. Though less tolerant of tidal flooding, and so less of a frontiersman than couch, marram is the outstanding binder of sand and builder of dunes, with its indefatigable network of roots spreading both horizontally to start new clumps, and vertically downwards to tap moisture and anchor the sand. For wider dispersal it has its seeds, while its leaves, tightly rolled to reduce water loss to wind and sun, also trap and bind the sand. Marram is capable of forming higher, more domed dunes than couch; at first they are no great size, but eventually they may unite to form a ridge of 'foredunes' which will continue to grow as long as it is fed fresh windblown sand from the shore. Still quite mobile, yet increasingly stable, several other plants can flourish on them – sea holly, then ragwort, thistles, hound's-tongue, creeping fescue and sea lyme grass. Meanwhile, another row of embryo dunes may already have started seaward of the

Dogwood (Cornus alba)

foredunes, and the sequence begins afresh.

In this way, dune ridges are gradually sealed off from the immediate foreshore, and successive generations can march well inland like a series of dyke fortifications. By virtue of their plant allies and more sheltered aspect, they get higher as they become further from the sea, till the highest of all, often a near-mountainous dune crest, is reached. A transect through the system also shows an increasingly terrestrial flora, with marram, gradually starved of its lifeblood of fresh sand, thinning

Winter jasmine

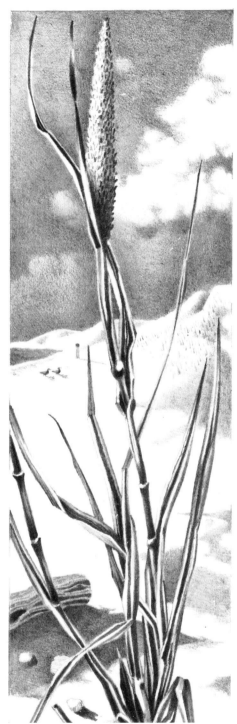

Marram grass

(unfortunately, in man's case, by far the best place for riotous picnics!). Even one small breach in the sandy wall may give the wind an edge to bite on, and gouge out pits or 'blow-outs' from which erosion may spread along either side, levelling the ridge, and thereby threatening the richer hinterland.

Ploys in ivy

Ivy continues to support seemingly half the insect kingdom in November, its succession of new flowerheads offering nectar especially accessible to insects with short tongues. It attracts a lot of flies and, if it is sunny, maybe a few late wasps which may show more interest in the flies – particularly the big blue-bottles – than in the ivy. Usually the first indication that a wasp has found a victim is a frantic buzzing, similar to that of a fly caught in a spider web. As it pounces, the wasp curls its abdomen round the fly, endeavouring to sting it, and interlocked the pair of them often topple into the grass. The fly makes desperate efforts to escape, and if it succeeds before it has been stung, it flies off, leaving its assailant flat-footed. If the wasp kills the fly, however, the victor may be joined by an accomplice and together they pull the victim apart where the thorax joins the abdomen. There rarely seems to be any competition over dividing the spoils; on the contrary, industrious co-operation is the impression given, perhaps because the wasps originate from the same colony. Once the fly is bisected, each wasp attends to its own half, sometimes airlifting it to a quiet spot, like the branch of a tree, where within five minutes the insides are devoured and the fly reduced to a husk. It is all a lot of effort for the wasp, so it never bothers with small flies, leaving them to feast on the ivy flowers unmolested.

Although they are sophisticated insects, wasps are clearly slaves to none-too-subtle behaviour patterns. If a fly struggles free, for example, the wasp may be unable to accept that the chance has been missed; losing sight of its prey it returns to the scene of battle in the grass and doggedly quarters the area around it before finally giving up. Again, watch a wasp hunting flies near a compost heap. It will examine every rusty nail-head, every small knot and blemish in the wood – indeed any small dark mark that might spell 'fly'. Even so, fly-hunting may be quite a profitable pursuit for a wasp, especially round a compost heap on an unseasonally hot autumn day. Perhaps one in ten attacks may bring reward.

Hornets are our biggest wasps, about $1\frac{1}{2}$ times the size of a common wasp, and undoubtedly one of our most spectacular insects. They too are accomplished hunters but, as befits their size, will tilt at much bigger prey, such as hoverflies and butterflies.

out. Its place on the dunes further inland is taken by familiar plants – mosses and lichens, numerous flowering species, even a few ferns and woody shrubs. Characteristically there are a number of winter annuals, small, shallow-rooted plants, easily overlooked. Common ones are early hair grass, sand cat's-tail grass, whitlow grass, chickweed and forget-me-not. All have short life cycles: the seeds germinate in autumn, the plants flower and fruit by about April, and then die, the seeds lying dormant till the following autumn. These and other plant

lifecycles mould the dune system in subtler ways than the early colonisers, building up water retention and humus, and so creating suitable conditions for soil organisms, and ultimately higher animals.

Of the latter, apart from heavily shod man with his spades and pails, only one – the rabbit – poses any real threat to the integrity of this system. Both are capable of undermining the more mobile and fragile foredunes

December

Custom and ritual throughout the ages converge and interweave, transfiguring this month into a mirror of our chequered past. Long before the Christian church left its indelible mark on December, the 25th of the month had been the focus of pagan rites celebrating the Winter Solstice, the Yule and Saturnalia, and just as the pagan fires shine strongly through Guy Fawkes night, so many of the most deep-seated pagan customs survived the new wave of Christian culture. Ironically, as so often happens, the opposition of the church probably guaranteed survival for some of the old rituals and undoubtedly gave new life to some. What the church could not expunge it absorbed and moulded, though not too much control should be read into this; rather Christmas grew, like Topsy, the sacred and profane richly entwined.

Thus Christianity made numerous concessions to the 'merry' side of Christmas enshrined in pagan belief. The Druids in their god-worship gave us yule logs and mistletoe, and perhaps there is a hint of the Norse god Odin in St Nicholas. The Roman Saturnalia bequeathed laurels, Christmas hats, charades and the traditional garb of the mummers' plays, while both Druids and Romans gave us the song, drink and laughter of Christmas. Later novelties were mince pies (popular since the Crusaders came home with exotic spices), turkeys from Mexico and Christmas trees from Germany. The ancient rites of Christmas have the redeeming merit of all pagan festivals: they illustrate a people in sensitive touch with their environment, and especially with seasonal change. With December the year was laid to rest and the certainty of spring at once celebrated and petitioned. Bonfires were lit at the Solstice to rally the sun's spirit, and evergreens hung to stir the life in dormant seeds. Holly, mistletoe, laurel and rosemary were an inspiration at this otherwise lifeless time of year, their evergreen properties symbolising eternal life. For a variety of reasons, Christianity embraced them too, with the odd exception. Ivy, for example, had a reputation tainted by associations with Bacchus, the Greek god of wine, so it was – and still is in many places – considered unsuitable to have inside the house.

Berry blessings

For wildlife, too, the berry-bearing evergreens are a blessing. In years when the rowan crop fails in the European taiga, waxwings invade Britain in large numbers, 'irrupting', as siskins, crossbills and a few other species occasionally do. Guelder-rose hips are much sought after by waxwings, as well as berries of privet, yew, holly, juniper and mistletoe. For us, waxwing winters are a great bonus, for they are exceptionally handsome birds with their long crests, and small flags of vivid scarlet and yellow setting off a soft grey-brown plumage.

Waxwing on yew

Sometimes they can be hard to pick out at a distance, showing a strong resemblance to starlings in general proportions and style of flight, but to anyone familiar with the winter birds, they jump out at close quarters – to misquote Dylan Thomas, as rare and unforgettable as a bicycle clip found in the desert.

All these fruits taken by the waxwing are well known, with the possible exception of wild privet, not to be confused with the similar garden hedge variety. Wild privet is not a full evergreen; it sheds its leaves by spring. It grows sparsely along hedgerows or on waste ground, especially on calcareous soils, in southern England. When the berries first develop they are usually shunned, presumably because they are then noxious enough to harm the intestinal lining of any animal that eats them. Later on, however, they become more palatable, perhaps – like some brassicas – improving with a touch of frost, and are readily accepted by a number of birds, including pheasants.

Indeed, birds probably cannot afford to be so choosy as winter progresses. In early autumn berries and seeds are abundant and widespread, but by December the depredations of animals have reduced them to a mosaic of localised patches with no hope of replenishment.

In December, many bulrushes still cling tenaciously to their packed seed heads; they do not shed them till about February. If we want to see the flowers that produced them, we must visit the marsh in June and July. The male flowers are then to be seen concentrated at the top of the spike, the females at the bottom. Other plants show this same arrangement and in the case of viper's bugloss, at least, an explanation for it has recently been given to me. Bugloss is pollinated mostly by bees, and observation reveals that, on arrival at a flowerhead, the insect invariably starts at the bottom, works its way up to the top and then flies off. This means that it encounters the

Gorse in bloom

on beech mast, and tit survival can even be related to the incidence of mast years. Beech, unusually among trees, is incapable of producing a rich seed crop in two successive years. But there may be more strategy here than default, for if, as it does, the winter without seeds reduces the bird (and small mammal) populations in the wood, then the pressure on the following year's seed crop is nicely relieved, and many more seeds may survive to germinate.

Rodents and rabbits also have another, less obvious, resource at their disposal, the bark of trees. For rabbits, confined as they are to the ground, bark can be a vital lifeline in hard weather when heavy snow prevents them from nibbling soft herbage. Some trees and shrubs are clearly more tasty, and so more susceptible, than others, while a few may be strictly avoided. Spindle is particularly vulnerable to rabbits which may ring-bark, and so kill, saplings over a wide area. Before myxomatosis took its dreadful toll, rabbits also made serious inroads on sycamores and beeches, and today – a quarter of a century on from the major outbreak of the disease – some trees, now much bigger, still show scars from the days when rabbits were ten a penny. Squirrels are also a serious pest in young plantations throughout the country: in Scotland, red squirrels strip bark from the upper trunk of Scots pine, less commonly larch and spruce, weakening the crowns which may then die or be 'blown out'. In the south, the introduced grey squirrel likewise attacks the sweet, sappy bark of young hardwoods in summer and may, like rabbits, fatally ring-bark some of the stems. Not surprisingly, foresters wage constant war against them.

Deer, hares and voles (see the Animal signs section later in this chapter) also strip bark, and considering these legions of mammalian teeth, it may be surprising that any trees survive to maturity. Some, however, have evolved successful defences. The spiny stems of young hawthorn are a fair match for the rabbit, as is the bark of the elder, a violent purgative to man and perhaps to rabbits too; it

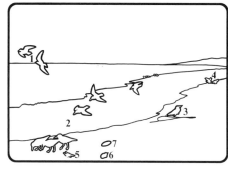

December *1. Herring gulls 2. Sanderlings 3. An oiled guillemot 4. Hooded crows 5. Mermaid's purse, the eggcase of dogfish or skate 6. Dog whelk 7. Cuttlefish bone*

can be no coincidence that hawthorn and elder are two of our commonest hedgerow shrubs. Their resistance to rabbits has done much to shape the rural landscape of England. No better proof of their immunity is their capacity to flourish quite unscathed in the heart of a large rabbit warren. Then, quite often trees that are damaged by rabbits or squirrels in winter can still transport water upwards to develop their buds, providing they are not ring-barked; that, of course, severs the supply completely. And if the downflow of sugars from the leaves through the inner bark is disrupted, the roots themselves may founder through lack of food. So a tree which may not appear to be mortally wounded in early summer may succumb later on.

Before leaving the subject of shrubs and their fates, there is one wild evergreen which earns a special place in December by flaunting its golden flowers in the bleak days – the gorse. The main bloom is from April to June but, as long as it doesn't freeze, a few flowers brave the winter, confirming the saying that 'kissing's out of season when gorse is out of bloom'. The dry, fibrous bark looks thoroughly unappetising but the new leafy shoots, spiny as they are, are relished by goats, even though they do look as if they are chewing a rather hot potato.

male flowers last, and so any pollen it collects is carried only to the female flowers at the bottom of the next *bugloss plant visited.*

Returning to seed eaters, the nimbleness of siskins is of no avail to woodpeckers and nuthatches, which need good purchase to breach the well-armoured seeds they eat. Accordingly they may wedge pine cones, hazel nuts and so on in the deep crevice of a suitable gnarled tree trunk, which serves as both anvil and vice while the bird sets to work hammering out a crude hole with its bill. Great tits are also undaunted by the tough shell of hazelnuts, immobilising them under one foot while hammering a small hole with their bill. In some winters, however, great tits, blue tits and finches, especially, are much more dependent

December

Poplars denuded of their soft leaves

Poplar catkins contribute to woodland-floor litter in spring

Tufted ducks (drake in front)

Leaf litter

In November we drew attention to the largely neglected resource of decaying wood on the forest floor, and the rich community of decomposing agents inhabiting it. But this 'furniture' in the basement sits on an equally important resource, the carpet of fruits and leaf litter, and no account of the yearly cycle in woodland would be complete without a description of it.

While the furniture is added to intermittently, and wears out only over quite long periods, the leaf litter is of course replenished every autumn, and is processed much more rapidly. The first input in many deciduous woods is from ash, then from sycamore and beech, with oak relatively late. The last major species to shed its leaves is elm, some elms still clinging to their yellowed leaves in early winter – though disease has whittled away this particular bonus to the woodland carpet to a mere shadow of its former opulence for many years to come. Weeping willows shed even later, sometimes retaining leaves in December, but as they are relatively localised this is of no great significance to the ground community at large.

Through autumn to winter, decomposers working on the forest floor have, as it were, a succession of 'courses' served to them from the trees above. At first the leaves fall in fairly distinct areas, reflecting the positions of their respective parent trees, but autumn gales soon ensure a thorough mix. Leaf falls are bigger in some years than others, sometimes by as much as a quarter, reflecting growing conditions earlier on, defoliation by insects, and so on.

Any gardener knows that some leaf moulds make much better compost than others; and what is true for soil organisms in the garden also holds for the woodland floor. One leaf looks as if made of much the same material as another, but their resistance to decay reveals fundamental differences. Some leaves, like poplar, ash, elm, hazel, sallow (pussy willow) and sycamore, are relatively soft and break down rapidly. In one study, all soft leaves had

disappeared by August of the next year with the exception of a few ash stalks and midribs. Oak proved more durable, with about a third remaining, while the beech leaves had scarcely begun to disappear at all. Indeed, the crisp, russet litter of beech is well known to survive a year after it falls, and only in the second year do the decomposers make any real impact on it.

What lies behind this remarkable resistance to decay? If we examine an oak, beech or sweet-chestnut leaf not long after it has fallen, we might describe its texture as leathery. This is due to the tannins (phenolic compounds) which accumulate in the leaf as it ages on the tree, reaching levels as high as 5 per cent of the dry weight of the leaves. Tannins are the tree's defence against defoliating insects, seriously impairing the growth and survival of caterpillars as summer progresses, and preserving the leaf tissues after death.

Flourish or flee

We mostly associate wildfowl with inland waterways of one sort or another, but the coast in winter has a fair smattering of its own. For contrast, however, the leaden grey December sea is not always the ideal background and, if you are lucky enough to own a telescope or even

a pair of binoculars, a good vantage point on a headland is often best for detecting and identifying them. In winter the coast, being milder, attracts a mixed bag of species. Some, like the tufted duck and the grebes, are to be found inland in summer but partly resort to sheltered bays in winter. Others, like the well-known eider duck and some mergansers, stay close to brackish or marine waters throughout the year. In winter the British populations of all these species are augmented by visitors, mostly indistinguishable, from northern Europe, and by numerous other species besides, notably scoters, scaup, smew, goldeneye and long-tailed duck. The so-called 'divers' are among the most exciting finds for the winter sea-watcher. Two species, the black-throated and red-throated, are resident in Britain, embracing freshwater and marine habitats in northern Scotland; the largest of all, the great northern diver, is a winter visitor from Iceland, along with three species without which the coast and its hinterland would be much the poorer in winter – greylag and pinkfoot geese, and whooper swans. Be sure to use a field guide which describes winter plumage, since grebes and divers in particular are drab and disconcertingly similar at this time of year.

Regrettably, many of these birds are becoming increasingly familiar to the public through oil spills. A relatively small one in December 1978 in Shetland claimed no fewer than 109 great northern divers, 252 long-tailed ducks and 421 eiders. Wrecks of big oil tankers

An eider, fallen victim to oil pollution, the scourge of the seas today

Eider ducks (drake in front)

Red-breasted mergansers (drake in front)

Black-throated diver in winter plumage

have become alarmingly frequent in recent years, headlined by names that linger strangely in the memory – Torrey Canyon, Amoco Cadiz, Christos Bitas, Andros Patria. These accidents take a terrible toll – at least 10,000 seabirds in the case of the Torrey Canyon. The species most commonly affected are the auks – guillemots, razorbills and puffins – which, having limited powers of flight, spend a lot of time in and on the water, diving for fish.

But serious as major oil spills are, it is not these isolated disasters but the comparatively minor yet much more frequent spillages that pose the most insidious threat to seabird populations. Many arise from vessels deliberately flushing their tanks at sea, others from leaks at the terminals. Apart from avoiding slicks altogether, birds have no defence against oil. Their protective plumage readily soaks it up, breaking down the waterproof insulation that keeps them warm. If they attempt to preen it off, the oil they ingest damages the delicate linings of their intestines and other internal organs, condemning them to a lingering death. If you find a badly oiled bird on the beach, therefore, mere cleaning may not be enough to save its life. The rehabilitation of such birds, especially feeding and cleaning, is a fairly skilled procedure, best left to the RSPCA and other qualified people, but you can help by handling any oil victim as little as possible, as it is already under extreme stress and the act of capture is another traumatic experience for it.

Birds as opportunists

Even in December a few sea duck are still straggling south into our waters. The seashore then supports the local diehards and their comrades from continental Europe, and all the summer visitors seem to have made good their escape. Or have they? We think of the seasonal migration of birds as one of the most intransigent phenomena in the animal kingdom. Poets write of compelling, irresistible urges that must be yielded to, willy nilly. It therefore comes as something of a surprise to realise that birds are opportunists and that an exceptionally mild winter will persuade some migrants to forgo the journey and tarry instead to cash in on the deserted sewage farm, where there are always rich pickings. In one such winter, 1974–5, when the month of December was the mildest for 40 years in many parts of

the country, actually warmer than October in some places, birds were quick to take advantage of the unusual situation; their travel plans were hurriedly modified or even abandoned altogether. Large numbers of belated migrants, particularly swallows and firecrests, were recorded in November and December. One swallow was seen on New Year's Eve, another overwintered in Dorset, and yet three others in Cornwall. (To give some idea of how often this happens, January swallows had been seen in only 11 of the 170 winters recorded up to that time.) Swifts are normally very hasty, in fact almost indecently so, to leave our shores, speeding south in August, but in 1974 one was seen at Ipswich in late December. Other small landbirds which stayed till January were whitethroats and garden warblers; chiffchaffs, a few of which regularly overwinter in this country, did so in unusually large numbers. Some seabirds and shorebirds also stayed put.

Such winters are indeed a bonus but we cannot afford to feel too proud of keeping these unseasonal birds from their African quarters. A sudden cold snap and they will be off, scurrying south to latitudes which guarantee food and warmth. If the snap turns out to be a major crunch, even the natives get restless, and so begin what we call 'hard-weather movements'. These are much more pragmatic than regular migrations, and may occur at any time and in almost any direction, dictated by where the hard weather is coming from and where better conditions can be found.

Depending on the severity of the weather they may range from a small trickle to a mass exodus as millions of birds flee for their lives.

In recent years there have been two major outbreaks of hard-weather movements, in the winters of 1962–63 and 1978–79. The first of these went down on record as the coldest winter in central and southern England since 1740, and possibly the snowiest for 150 years. The bitter weather started on 20 December, and blizzards from the 26th to the 28th blanketed the country in thick snow; it lay in many places till March, sealing off the food supply of countless birds for ten weeks. The situation was aggravated by recurrent freezing fog which embalmed trees in ice and made life very hard for tree-haunting insectivorous birds. Lakes and rivers froze, nonplussing water birds, and the Thames was partly frozen over in London for two to three weeks. As the sea temperature fell to between 2° and 4°C (35° and 39°F), even shorebirds were affected. Many sheltered bays and beaches froze, often to 400 metres (1,300ft) below high-tide mark, budding-off floes and small icebergs, and crowding birds into the few ice-free oases, there to exhaust the dwindling food resources. Every section of the avian community was under siege, and the outcome, inevitably, was chaos.

Hard-weather movements were mostly to the west and south in advance of the polar conditions. The first to move in force were lapwings, skylarks, redwings and fieldfares, followed by Scandinavian grebes, ducks and waders. Wood pigeons and finches were also

Left, *redwing*; right, *fieldfare*

December

prominent, and finally it was Uncle Tom Cobley and all, with almost any species possible among the diverse refugees. Although the British Isles became as inhospitable as anywhere else in Europe that winter, it was at the outset a haven compared with elsewhere, and many millions of lapwings and skylarks especially must have poured into the country in late December. Apart from visual and radar records, recoveries of ringed birds quickly reveal unusually long journeys, many of which are no doubt the last straw for birds already enfeebled by starvation. In the 1978–79 winter, recoveries of lapwings in France and Spain were well above average, and many pied wagtails also wandered exceptionally far afield. However unfortunate the circumstances, these are of course interesting findings for the ornithologist. Immigrants in such winters often include glamorous species like rough-legged buzzards, short-eared owls and hen harriers, and make bird-watching all the more exciting.

However, even harsh winters have their pay-offs. The survivors can rest assured that they have struggled and won through the worst conditions they are ever likely to meet, and may even have learned a few tricks. Some discover new food supplies they can use for ever after, like the great spotted woodpeckers that continued to visit bird tables after the severe winter of 1946–47, and the greylag geese that added swedes to their diet. In 1962–63, many birds again broke new ground; song thrushes resorted to eating periwinkles on the shore, and one heron was spotted wolfing down stale kippers. Red grouse joined domestic hens at feeding time, water rails and curlews ventured into gardens, and snipe to bird tables. Others discovered novel roosting sites, such as the wrens found in haystacks and ratholes. So we see that extreme conditions are like the eye of the needle: only the select pass through and in so doing they have not only tested to the limit the survival skills evolution has given them, but often added new ones.

Winter insects

We are not inclined to venture outdoors very much in dark December, and when we do the apparent lack of activity in the woods may persuade us that our hibernation urge is not unusual. But if we visit the woods at night we might modify our view, for a number of insects are then very active. For instance, a select group of moths – the winter moth, whose life cycle we outlined in June, the spring usher, scarce umber, dotted umber and pale brindled beauty. Their most striking feature is that the females are small, wingless, bug-like creatures which we could be excused for not recognising as moths at all. Oakwoods are a good place to find them, although – with the exception of the spring usher – none are confined to that habitat and they are just as likely to turn up among the fruit trees in your garden.

The life history of the winter moth was unravelled in Wytham Woods, Oxfordshire, by Varley and Gradwell, using elegantly simple apparatus tailored to the moths' behaviour. At dusk in November and December the flightless females emerge from the soil, walk to the oak trees, and scale them. Meanwhile the winged males, which have been taking refuge in the leaf litter, fly to the tree trunks, there to waylay and fertilise the ascending females. Traps like small lobster pots were attached to the trees to intercept females bound for the canopy. This showed that about six females were destined to occupy each metre of the oak canopy, and each would lay, on average, 150 eggs in the creviced bark and lichen high above the ground. Clearly the potential number of caterpillar births is enormous, and in some years so it is.

Thousands, though, fail to survive to pupate the following summer. Some hatch out in May to find their host tree's buds obstinately unopened, denying them their diet of tender young leaves. Rather than starve, the young caterpillars abandon ship on silken threads, in hope of being wafted to a neighbouring oak whose buds have burst. They literally cast their fate to the winds and for many the gamble must fail.

Elsewhere in the wood, the pupae of numerous other moths and butterflies lie dormant, beleaguered till the spring warmth triggers metamorphosis. But compared with the hazards of discovery by some predator, or parasitic treachery from within the pupal walls, cold is no problem for them. After a severe winter, with long periods of heavy frost, the first sunny days in May will bring forth scores of butterflies. How do they survive? It has long been known that overwintering insects become 'cold-hardy' and don't freeze, partly due to the conversion of blood sugar to glycerol, which acts as a dilute anti-freeze. Ironically a much greater threat is a mild, wet winter which lays dormant larvae and pupae open to mildew attack; again frost-free tree trunks and soil make them more vulnerable to the probing bills and snouts of birds and mammals.

Before leaving winter insects, a word must be

Mottled umber (above) *and winter moth*

said for the spartan winter gnat *Trichocera*. These small insects, close relatives of craneflies form dancing swarms throughout the year but especially in the winter months, when they will perform, jigging up and down, on any calm, sunlit day. It is hard to avoid the whimsical thought that they do this, like running on the spot, to keep warm! But really these aerial dances have a deeper purpose. If you net a swarm and examine the dancers, all of them turn out to be males. The mobile swarm is more than just a gathering; it is a conspicuous advertisement for itself, a display. Certainly it attracts the odd female which, without more ado, mates with one of the participants (apparently chosen at random) and flies off. Wynne-Edwards has emphasised the lopsided nature of these encounters: 'It is quite typical in insect leks, and bird leks also . . . that the female should appear and remain on the scene only long enough to be fertilised, whereas the males pour out their untiring energy for hours or days on end, whether there are any females present or not.'

Moult in mammals

All mammals periodically shed their old worn coat of hair and replace it with a new one. With some species this process is spread over th

Stoat in summer dress (left) *and in winter dress*

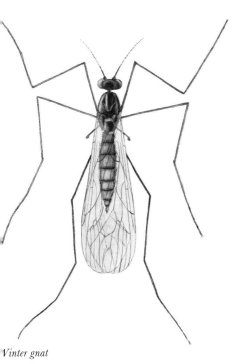

Vinter gnat

whole year, while with others it happens at set imes; but in either case it usually happens so radually that the new pelage is not onspicuous and, at a glance, is hard to detect rom its predecessor. When certain mammals noult, however, they undergo a dramatic olour change. The best known is the Eurasian nd North American stoat which moults twice year – in the autumn from reddish-brown with a white belly) to white almost all over, nd in the spring back to brown again. The utumn transformation is swift, with the hair rogressively being replaced from tail and legs o belly, round the flanks up to the back, and ast of all the head. The animal is then pure vhite except for the black tip to its tail (the ermine' condition) which is a constant feature f the colour scheme and helps distinguish toats from weasels. Reverting to brown again n the spring is often a slower affair, and roceeds in the reverse sequence, from the back o the belly. The stoat must be credited with ven more adaptive subtlety when we realise hat it dons a white coat only in the north of its ange, or else in high-altitude regions like the Alps, whereas in the south (most of England, 'rance, and Italy for instance) the coat is rown throughout the year. To complicate natters further, there are intermediate zones ke Yorkshire, the western part of the Netherlands, and a narrow belt across North America, where halfway stages occur. Here here is no set colour pattern; some have white nly on the legs, others are all white except for brown stripe down the back or a brown head.

The most obvious explanation for their eographical variation is that the stoat, a rocious hunter dependent to some extent on ealth, benefits from the camouflage a white

coat lends against a snow-clad background. It is interesting that brown weasels are found well into the snowy north, coexisting with white stoats and thriving despite their apparent disregard of camouflage. Only in the far north do weasels turn white and in the British Isles, for example, records of white ones are rare. The weasel's lesser preoccupation with camouflage is difficult to explain but, though it hunts in a manner similar to stoats, it spends a lot of time underground, pursuing voles and mice right into their burrows, something stoats don't do. Clearly body colour would be irrelevant in these dark catacombs.

But a white pelt may have another advantage other than simply camouflage. One attractive idea is that the colour white, well known for reducing radiation of energy, helps the stoat to conserve body heat in the harsh northern winter. Perhaps too, because it hunts a lot underground, the weasel has less need of a white pelt. That temperature plays an important role, at least in triggering moult, was neatly shown by taking stoats which normally stay brown in winter and exposing them to low temperatures; remarkably this induced them to turn white, or partly so. The moult process is also influenced by day length and can be speeded up by artificially shortening the day, and conversely arrested altogether by increasing day length. So it seems that temperature and day length at least affect the timing of moult.

An even more complicated moult cycle is found in the mountain or blue hare, which extends in mainland Britain from Orkney down to north Wales, with its stronghold in the Scottish Highlands. There is also an Irish race. Mountain hares perform three annual moults, from white to brown in spring, from brown to brown in autumn, and from brown to white in winter. Again the sequence varies with local conditions, and in Ireland a completely white coat is rare, some individuals never acquiring one at all. Interestingly, hares introduced from Norway into the Faroes in the 1820s turned white at first in winter, but had lost this capacity by 1860–70.

Animal signs

Winter is a time when animals save energy and – like humans – are less outgoing in their habits. For the naturalist intent on learning their ways this presents a special challenge, above all in the study of mammals, which are hard enough to observe at any time of the year, if only because so many of them are nocturnal. Careful detective work is needed. We must become as hunters, training our eyes to interpret footprints, toothmarks, food pellets, droppings and urine, and all the other clues animals leave in their wake. 'Spooring' takes a great deal of persistence to do well, and it is all too easy to stop short of real understanding. How often, for instance, did I pass a large burrow in a hedgebank, with an entrance pile of soft sand, and say to myself 'fox . . . or maybe badger'. Both may make several entrances and the two are easily confused, but whereas foxes discard surplus diggings right outside tunnel entrances, forming fan-shaped ramps, badgers usually spread it further away so the tunnel has a typically furrowed approach. Also foxes, unlike badgers, leave a strong musky odour about, reminiscent of burning rubber I always think, and once their cubs are older leave scraps of meals – bones and feathers – lying around. Badgers are more discreet but, unlike foxes, they line their setts with dry grass, leaves, and so on, and may strew bedding outside.

So badgers and foxes leave lots of tell-tale signs, and as we become more discerning, last year's subtle case becomes this year's open-and-shut one. Difficult as winter may seem for the tracker, it does offer certain advantages. To the trained eye, snow on the ground lays the animal world wide open to scrutiny. Not only may we distinguish predators from prey, herbivores from carnivores, but we can discover their favourite haunts, how far they travel, and what befalls them on the way. Also in winter, with the die-off of vegetation, soft foods give way to hard unyielding ones which each species chips, hammers, gnaws or strips in its own inimitable fashion. As we have already seen, hazelnuts are attacked in a variety of ways, and the holes made in them by

December

Oak in winter

looking at the shape of the trunk with its attendant framework of branches and twigs. Ash has a broad spreading crown, elm a tall gaunt column, beech a massive domed crown, and old horse chestnuts a skirt of limbs which spread low and then turn sharply up at the ends. If we look more closely, the growth form of the wood will be found to vary characteristically between species. Should you be in Norfolk or the north of England and further, you can still find living elms, and can delight in the fine tracery of twigs so quickly blunted by the wind on dead trees. Each elm limb grades into the next, rapidly diffusing into the domed clumps of greenery in summer that artists capture in the 'cauliflower' look. The tip are such a delicate reticulum that the eye can scarcely follow the outward ramifications of a single limb; but in other species, the beech for instance, this is a much easier task.

Note also the angles that the new wood takes to the old; in the beech, the older twigs make only a very slight angle with the main branch so that they run more or less parallel with the parent branch. The English oak, for all its fame, is often mistaken by the layman for other trees, but a careful adding together of clues should place its identity beyond doubt. The crown is usually widely and irregularly domed with a few massive, twisted boughs low down. Often, as in beech, one or two of these will have been shed in old trees, contorting the former symmetry into bizarre shapes. This, along with the bleached staghorn relics of smaller branches that bristle on the lower trunk, contributes as much as the heavily pitted bark to the oak's shaggy, gnarled appearance. In beeches the loss of side limbs can sometimes add even more grace, allowing the main trunk, smooth and rippling like muscle under skin, to soar unfettered to the crown.

Lastly, a tree that should never present any difficulty is the birch, with its brilliant white bark, sometimes peeling off, and often long pendulous 'weeping-willow' branches. It is a strange fact that, of all the trees in the wood, birches and conifers are not coated in December by an algal bloom of *Pleurococcus* which gains a new lease of life in winter when the damp, and such sunlight as there is, can freely penetrate the canopy. The acidic bark of birch and conifers gives them this immunity and guarantees their base colour throughout the year. The lowly alga has, however, its own beauty, gilding the dark trunks of the trees with a dusting of sometimes brilliant emerald green. So there are always compensations to be found in the depths of winter.

The bareness of the trees should not be a matter for regret. It is the magic of the seasons that we strangely find it almost impossible to conjure up a leafy, sun-spangled glade in December, any more than we can recall a stark beech in May. The changes would be less remarkable and the seasons poorer but for our imperfect memory.

nuthatches, woodpeckers and tits are distinguishable not only from one another but from the numerous small mammals that also eat them. Squirrels chisel a nick near the pointed end, insert their lower incisors, and use them like a crowbar to crack the shell lengthwise into boat-shaped halves, a unique approach and unmistakably squirrel. Mice and voles simply gnaw holes (slightly differently) in the side and mine out the kernel, while the common dormouse makes a typically larger hole, a clue which experienced mammalogists are presently using to map the distribution of this rare and unobtrusive animal. Reliable evidence from hazelnuts alone is filling large blanks in the dormouse map, largely without any sightings of the elusive little creature responsible.

Finally, lest we forget the estuaries and seashore, these also are bristling with animal signs; mudflats and sandy beaches offer, all the year round, the same opportunities for tracking as snow does. Moreover foxes, hedgehogs, stoats, weasels and rats frequent sand-dune colonies of gulls and terns, so we can expect more than just birds. Molluscs, like hard nuts, pose similar problems of breaking and entering for shorebirds, each of which finds its own solution, while gulls cast up pellets, as birds of prey and corvids do.

Tree shapes

Some trees have been bare of leaves for two months by now, and we may have to hunt carefully through the leaf litter to discover what they were. Often we can tell just by